Contents

**FRANCIS CLOSE HALL
LEARNING CENTRE**
Swindon Road Cheltenham
Gloucestershire GL50 4AZ
Telephone: 01242 714600

UNIVERSITY OF
GLOUCESTERSHIRE
at Cheltenham and Gloucester

NORMAL LOAN

Framing the Sign
Criticism and its Institutions

Jonathan Culler

Basil Blackwell

Copyright © Jonathan Culler 1988

First published 1988

Basil Blackwell Ltd
108 Cowley Road, Oxford, OX4 1JF, UK

British Library Cataloguing in Publication Data

Culler, Jonathan
Framing the sign: criticism and its
institutions.
1. Literature. Criticism
I. Title

ISBN 0–631–15895–2
ISBN 0–631–15896–0 Pbk

Library of Congress Cataloging in Publication Data

Culler, Jonathan D.
Framing the sign.

Bibliography: p.
Includes index.
1. Criticism. 2. Criticism—Study and teaching.
3. Semiotics. I. Title.
PN94.C86   1988b   801'.95   88–6347
ISBN 0–631–15895–2
ISBN 0–631–15896–0 (pbk.)

Typeset in 10 on 12 pt Sabon
by Opus, Oxford
Printed in Great Britain by T.J. Press Ltd, Padstow, Cornwall

Preface

Two important movements have marked literary criticism and theory in recent years. First, there has been an expansion of the domain in which critics work, attention to new sorts of objects, new kinds of texts. In the 1960s and 1970s, literary studies seemed in the business of importing theoretical models, questions and perspectives from fields such as linguistics, anthropology, philosophy, the history of ideas and psychoanalysis. In the 1980s, however, the situation seems to have changed: on the one hand, literary studies has become an exporter of theoretical discourse, as other disciplines – law, anthropology, art history, even psychoanalysis – have taken note of developments in what literary critics call 'theory' and have turned to it for stimulation. On the other hand, literary critics themselves, grown confident and sophisticated from their interdisciplinary encounters, have increasingly turned to writing about phenomena that fall outside the boundaries of traditional literary study: explicating philosophical texts – Kant, Hegel, Heidegger – analysing new historical objects or discourses – the body, the discourse of imperialism – exploring accounts of the functioning of the psyche in Freud and his successors, debating principles of interpretation in the law and studying popular culture – films and television, detective stories, Harlequin romances and science fiction. Today, if you ask a professor of literature what he or she is working on, some will say 'Shelley's Odes', or 'the late seventeenth-century lyric', 'Virginia Woolf', or 'the sources of Shakespeare's comedies', but others will give such answers as 'narcissism', 'seventeenth-century ethnographic writing', 'the construction of sexual difference', 'the politics of interpretation', 'women's bodies in the nineteenth century', 'Kant's Third Critique', or 'Hollywood sit-coms'. If there is a unity to literary studies in this new dispensation it comes not from the canon of plays, poems and novels but from an attention to mechanisms of signification which can be studied in a wide range of texts and text-like situations. As literary studies situates itself at the center of interdisciplinary exchange, some have envisaged a cultural studies that would englobe literature in a program of historical reconstruction and political critique; others, taking their cue from the writings of Kenneth Burke, Roland Barthes, Terry Eagleton, or Paul de Man, have seen literary studies as part of an expanded rhetoric, which would study the production and the play of meaning in all sorts of situations. But so far such visions have seemed attempts to rediscipline the diverse energies released by recent changes and have not secured widespread assent.

The second trend in recent literary studies springs from a desire to make criticism political. This involves, on the one hand, an interest in the political dimensions of literary works themselves, their role in promoting change, in subverting authority, or in containing social energies. Criticism has explored both literature's complicity with sexism, racism, imperialism, or state power, and its critique of ideologies of discourses of its day, charting techniques of resistance and recuperation. On the other hand, the desire to make criticism political has produced an interest in the institutional and ideological dimensions of criticism itself: in the implications of its theoretical orientations and in its relations with the institutions which empower and contain it. A favorite theme has been the way professional and pedagogical structures of universities domesticate radical theoretical discourses – as if their inherent force would be released if they could by-pass the mediation of institutional structures. The desire for an immediate emancipatory payoff, the hope of finding a method which would make the discussion of literary works an efficacious political act, is, of course, a breeding ground for facile polemic, but it is scarcely surprising that a time like ours, 'frustrated at finding itself at the same time so advanced in self-awareness and so powerless in its control over events', should seek political criticism.[1]

This book engages both of these movements, describing criticism's complex dependency on institutions, discussing the possibilities of a political criticism and moving from literary works to other objects – law, tourism, rubbish, normative social theory – which can be illuminated by types of analysis developed in literary theory. The common denominator of these investigations might be styled the problem of context: the institutional context of criticism, which serves as its condition of possibility and most immediate target for change; the wider social and historical context which is adduced by proposals for political criticism; the context of other disciplines or institutions

[1] Paul de Man, 'The Riddle of Hölderlin', *New York Review of Books*, 19 November 1970, p. 52.

Barthes broadening his outlook—
Fully self critical by Empire

which is crucial to attempts to extend literary analysis into broader
cultural or rhetorical studies. But the notion of context frequently
oversimplifies rather than enriches discussion, since the opposition
between an act and its context seems to presume that the context is
given and determines the meaning of the act. We know, of course, that
things are not so simple: context is not fundamentally different from
what it contextualizes; context is not given but produced; what cultures
belongs to a context is determined by interpretive strategies; contexts
are just as much in need of elucidation as events; and the meaning of a
context is determined by events. Yet when we use the term *context* we
slip back into the simple model it proposes. Since the phenomena
criticism deals with are signs, forms with socially-constituted
meanings, one might try to think not of context but of the framing of
signs: how are signs constituted (framed) by various discursive
practices, institutional arrangements, systems of value, semiotic
mechanisms?

The expression *framing the sign* has several advantages over
context: it reminds us that framing is something we do; it hints of the
frame-up ('falsifying evidence beforehand in order to make someone
appear guilty'), a major use of context; and it eludes the incipient
positivism of 'context' by alluding to the semiotic function of framing
in art, where the frame is determining, setting off the object or event as
art, and yet the frame itself may be nothing tangible, pure articulation.
Although analysis can seldom live up to the complexities of framing
and falls back into discussion of context, with its heuristically
simplifying presumptions, let us at least keep before us the notion of
framing – as a frame for these discussions.

Part I begins with a history of criticism of the past sixty years in its
relation to structures of the university and to other social forces, and
then seeks to explore the situation of the humanities and literary
studies in the immediate future, focusing in part on the possibilities of
political criticism. What can an activist, radical criticism do? Frank
Lentricchia defines a radical as someone who thinks 'that society
should be a function of education' (rather than vice versa).[2] But the
question is not what one believes; too much value has attached, in
recent critical debate, to public declarations of belief. The question for
a political criticism is how might one work to make society a function
of education, and so far the evidence suggests that our ability to
control this is not great. But literary critics are scarcely alone here:
when the worldly discipline of economics, which prides itself on its

[2]   Quoted by Barbara Johnson, *A World of Difference* (Baltimore: Johns Hopkins
University Press, 1987), p. 25.

practical applicability, is reduced to producing, after the fact, feeble narratives to explain the Black Monday of 1987, one must wonder whether history does not consist precisely of events that escape control and that function according to scenarios which are established in the wake of the occurrence. If history is the name of the discrepancy between intention and occurrence, then literary theory has a pertinent model to hand in its debates about the problematical relation between meaning as intentional act (of a writer or reader) and meaning as textual fact (the product of grammatical, rhetorical, textual, and contextual structures).[3] We know the difficulty of adopting either one or the other of these models – the other always forces itself upon us – and that whatever we do, there is no guarantee that the two perspectives on meaning will coincide. While criticism will cultivate political criticism as an intentional act, it must do so with the knowledge that history will work otherwise, that the meaning of one's actions will prove to be other than one wished, a function of structures one does not control and which can be described only after the fact. In short, criticism must find political strategies for intervention without allowing this attempt to foreclose other lines of exploration, which may well prove politically more efficacious in the long run than those whose immediate value seems apparent. One ought to resist the totalizing impulse that would direct all criticism towards supposed political ends, since the real value of our work may well prove to lie in the commitment to intellectual projects whose utility is presently uncertain but which may in the end do what the greatest theoretical revolutions achieve: reinvent reading so that previously unseen inscriptions may be read.

Part II takes up the work of three major critics, each of whom has ventured beyond literature to write about non-literary materials as well: William Empson and Gaston Bachelard, precursors of contemporary criticism, and Paul de Man, its most important and difficult practitioner. Empson, whose *Structure of Complex Words* is a classic exploration of the relations between language and historical or social meaning, shows that historical and contextual reference opens complexities rather than closing on a univocal meaning. Bachelard offers in his influential work in the philosophy of science an analysis of the divided character of the scientific disciplines which could illuminate problems within criticism. The long chapter on de Man, which touches on themes addressed elsewhere in the book, is a systematic exposition of his work focused on his evolving engagement with rhetoric conceived as the analysis of textual structures and discursive effects.

[3] For discussion, see William Ray, *Literary Meaning* (Oxford: Basil Blackwell, 1983).

Part III looks to the application of theory beyond the confines of literary criticism. In the field of law, where the Critical Legal Studies movement has done interesting work, we find a version of deconstruction where questions of politics take different forms and comparisons with literary deconstruction are instructive. While deconstruction takes on central doctrines that govern our thought and our lives, it has also taught us the importance of the marginal, and the next two chapters explore two massive cultural phenomena, tourism and junk, whose cultural role has been deemed marginal. A semiotic analysis of the touristic attraction shows the tourist to be a revealing model for the subject of the modern world, and rubbish turns out to play a crucial role in systems of value. Both chapters address explicitly the framing of signs – the cultural mechanisms by which signs are constituted and play their signifying roles.

Finally, Part IV turns to problems of language and to framings of the sign which are something of a frame-up: Jürgen Habermas's attempt to derive a normative social theory from the use of language itself by framing the sign in a particular way and setting aside many aspects of language use, and accounts of fiction which frame literature as imitation speech acts. Both discussions ask what is at stake in these ways of framing the sign and attempt to look beyond, as does the last chapter which looks to the framing of the sign in oral narrative and in writing, finding literature a particularly revealing framing of language.

Writing about the scientific attitude, Charles Sanders Peirce declares that 'Conservatism, in the sense of a dread of consequences, is altogether out of place in science, which has, on the contrary, always been forwarded by radicals and radicalism, in the sense of the eagerness to carry consequences to their extreme.'[4] In the humanities as well conservatives complain, 'Where will it all end?' while the radicals ask, 'Why stop there?' The radical question seems the crucial one for a serious intellectual pursuit. To explore the consequences of theoretical arguments or to push to an extreme a line of investigation cannot, however, be the only imperative for literary studies or for the humanities, but this means only that there cannot be a single imperative, and that in place of a totalized vision we must pursue projects that operate according to different calculuses, with goals both more and less immediately visible. This book takes up some of these projects and then leaves them, in the hope that others will pursue them further.

4 'The Scientific Attitude and Fallibilism', *Philosophical Writings*, ed. J. Butchler (New York: Dover, 1955), p. 58.

Acknowledgements

Most of the discussions in this book began as lectures or as contributions to journals or collective volumes – often as both. I am grateful to the organizers of these events and to listeners and readers whose comments have sparked my rethinking and revising. *Framing the Sign* itself owes its existence to Robert Con Davis, who prodded me to bring together scattered materials, and to J. Hillis Miller, Gregory Jay, and Martin Davidson who offered persuasive advice. Srinivas Aravamudan helped to work out a program of revision and Mary Ahl contributed to its execution. Over the years, many friends and colleagues have offered advice on topics discussed here. Let me thank in particular James Adams, Laura Brown, Cynthia Chase, Gerald Graff, and Neil Hertz. A fellowship from the National Endowment for the Humanities, awarded for another purpose, enabled me to complete the book, and the Center for Literary Studies at Harvard University, directed by Marjorie Garber, provided admirable conditions in which to do so.

An earlier version of chapter 1 was written for *The Organization of Knowledge in American Society*, sponsored by the American Academy of Arts and Sciences. Chapters 1–4 draw variously on material that has appeared elsewhere:

'Comparative Literature and the Pieties', *Profession* 1986 (New York: Modern Language Association of America, 1986).
'A Critic Against the Christians', *Times Literary Supplement*, 23 November 1984.
'Criticism and Institutions: The American University', in *Post-Structuralism and the Question of History*, ed. Derek Attridge and Robert Young (Cambridge: Cambridge University Press, 1987).
'The Future of Criticism', in *The Current in Criticism*, ed. Virgil Lokke and Clayton Koelb (West Lafayette, Ind.: Purdue University Press, 1987).

'The Humanities and the Public Interest', *Yale Journal of Criticism* 1:1 (1987).
'Political Criticism', in *Writing the Future*, ed. David Wood and Andrew Benjamin (London: Routledge, 1987).
'Problems in the "History" of Contemporary Criticism', *MMLA Bulletin* (Spring 1984)'.

Other chapters are based on the following essays:

Preface to William Empson, *The Structure of Complex Words* (Cambridge: Harvard University Press, 1988).
'The Reveries of Matter', *Times Literary Supplement*, 28 February 1975.
'Paul de Man', *Dictionary of Literary Biography*, vol. 67: *Modern American Critics since 1955*, ed. Gregory Jay (copyright © 1988 by Gale Research Company; by permission), Gale Research 1988.
'Semiotics of Tourism', *American Journal of Semiotics* 1:1 (1981).
'Junk and Rubbish: A Semiotic Approach', *Diacritics* 15 (1985).
'Communicative Competence and Normative Force', *New German Critique* 35 (Spring/Summer 1985).
'Problems in the Theory of Fiction', *Diacritics* 14 (Spring 1984).
'Towards a Linguistics of Writing', in *The Linguistics of Writing*, ed. D. Attridge, N. Fabb and C. MacCabe (Manchester: Manchester University Press, 1987).

I thank the publishers and editors for permission to use this material.

PART I

Institutions

1

Literary Criticism and the American University

Although literary criticism might seem less dedicated to rapid change than other domains of knowledge, the past half-century has brought major transformations. The expansion of universities and of literary studies generally has led to a vast increase in writing about literature. Bibliographies list fifty-five books and articles on Shakespeare published in 1920 and 448 in 1970; for Milton the number increases from eighteen to 136, for Mark Twain from seven to sixty-five. Such changes in scale affect the status and thus the nature of critical writing, making it a more specialized, preponderantly academic endeavor. Our century has witnessed the displacement of public criticism by academic literary criticism: not only is most criticism written by professors for other professors, but book-reviewing is increasingly a part-time activity of academics rather than an occupation of men of letters. The interpretation of literature has become part of the functioning of universities. And within universities, historical scholarship – once the main form of professorial writing about literature – has been increasingly displaced by interpretive criticism. Finally, many might argue that literary criticism has ceased to be a modest and judicious activity serving literature and its readers and become pretentious and chaotic, a domain of competing, often abstruse theories, demanding the attention that might be devoted to literature itself.

It is possible, however, that we are mistaken in thinking our own critical situation unusually confusing or confused. The accusation that critics have 'patronized Nietzsche, found something entertaining in every kind of revolutionist, and welcomed the strangest philosophies' sounds like a reaction of the 1980s, but in fact comes from the pen of Van Wyck Brooks in 1918.[1] Perhaps the sense of a confused domain is

---

[1] Van Wyck Brooks, *Letters and Leadership* (New York: B. W. Huebsch, 1918), p. 35.

only the result of making criticism an object of attention. Consciousness of criticism as a significant realm of intellectual activity seems to
date, in America, from the years following the First World War. In
1921 Brooks, author of an important work of criticism and
interpretation, *America's Coming of Age*, wrote that 'The critical
movement in America happened, as it were, overnight; and the critic
in this country is still so new a type that we cannot be surprised if he is
regarded as an undesirable alien, even a traitor.'[2] Only five years after
the appearance of this traitor, William Drake wrote in the introduction to his 1926 anthology, *American Criticism*, anticipating by fifty
years today's complaints about criticism, 'We stand today at the center
of a vast disintegration.'[3] Drake also struck another note frequently
echoed today, claiming that our creative literary spirit is enervated,
'feeble and sporadic', but 'our critical spirit is prodigiously fecund' –
this in what now seems one of the most fertile periods of American
literature (Ernest Hemingway, T.S. Eliot, Robert Frost, Ezra Pound,
Gertrude Stein, Sherwood Anderson, F. Scott Fitzgerald, Marianne
Moore and William Faulkner had recently published significant
books).

Complaints about the chaos of critical perspectives and the abusive
intrusion of criticism into literary life are not so much analytical
judgments about the domain of literary studies as symptoms of
attending to criticism: it may well be that criticism seems orderly or
controlled only when it is taken for granted, and that as soon as one
begins to study criticism one finds not an ordered activity but disputes
about norms and meanings. Writing about literature is not a science or
even a discipline but a changing collection of diverse projects. A
history of criticism then becomes an attempt to reorder what
necessarily seems disorder to the contemporary eye.

Van Wyck Brooks tells us that in 1921 the critic was a new arrival,
and the years after the First World War do indeed witness a
remarkable burgeoning of critical discourse, which can be divided into
two important bodies of writing about literature. First a body of
literary *criticism*, primarily evaluative, concerned with current literature and major authors, not associated with universities but addressed
to a general cultivated public and devoted above all to questions of
value: what was to be encouraged and discouraged, prized or
dismissed, in American writing, in American culture? On the other
hand, in the universities in this period one finds literary *scholarship* of

---

[2] Van Wyck Brooks, 'The Critical Movement in America', in *Sketches in Criticism*
(New York: Dutton, 1932), p. 11.
[3] William Drake, *American Criticism, 1926* (Freeport, N.Y.: Books for Libraries
Press, 1967), p. 25.

a historical and philological cast, more interested in establishing facts about works – their sources, their authors and their historical circumstances – than in producing critical interpretations. In 1920, John M. Manley, the president of the Modern Language Association, the professional organization for university teachers of language and literature, urged that the association be reorganized 'with a view to greater specialization and greater stimulation of research'; and in 1928 the Association changed the statement of purpose in its constitution from 'the advancement of the study of the modern languages and their literatures' to the 'advancement of research' in these fields.[4] Although in these years the articles in *PMLA*, the Association's journal, are often bibliographical accounts or studies of influence, the implicit model for literary scholarship seems to be that of classical philology, where the philologist strives to reconstruct as much as he can of classical culture. By 1900 philologists had generally established the principle that teachers of literature in universities should be professionally trained philologists, as opposed to the men of letters or lovers of literature who had often been employed for this purpose in earlier years. The result was a discourse many found stultifying. An academic critic, complained one observer, can 'spend a lifetime in compiling the data of literature and yet rarely or never commit himself to a literary judgment'.[5]

In 1928 Edmund Wilson maintained that 'what we lack, then, in the United States, is not writers or even literary parties, but simply serious literary criticism.'[6] But he listed a series of 'able leaders and powerful parties, each professing more or less explicitly a point of view and acting more or less consistently on a set of principles': H. L. Mencken, the irreverent editor of *The American Mercury*, and T. S. Eliot, an authoritative critic as well as poet, he called 'the most formidable figures on the scene' ('Mencken and Eliot between them rule the students of the Eastern Universities', he observed). He also mentions a group of social revolutionary writers and critics around the *New Masses* magazine, the 'New Humanists' Irving Babbit and Paul Elmer More, and the 'Psychological-sociological critics, Van Wyck Brooks, Lewis Mumford, Joseph Wood Krutch, and a number of others'. His complaint is that these figures and groups do not communicate with one another and thus prevent criticism from playing a vital cultural role.

In retrospect, however, the 1920s generated lively criticism and a flourishing critical debate – carried on for the most part outside universities. The major academic exception was Irving Babbitt, a

4 John Manley, 'New Bottles', *PMLA* 36 (1921), p. lx. For the constitutional change, see *PMLA* 43 (1928), p. lxv.
5 John Crowe Ransom, *The World's Body* (New York: Scribners, 1938), p. 328.
6 Edmund Wilson, *The Shores of Light* (New York: Farrar Strauss, 1952), pp.368–9.

Harvard professor and spokesman of the New Humanism, which, demanding that literature contribute to moral enlightenment, rejected romanticism and naturalism and celebrated classical values as the necessary antidote to the moral laxity of the 1920s. Mencken, a journalist, satirist and linguist, author of a major account of the American language and *The Philosophy of Friedrich Nietzsche*, served as a national iconoclast, attacking religion and puritanism, as well as genteel and sentimental literature, first in the magazine *Smart Set* and then, after 1924, in *The American Mercury*, which he edited. Championing what he called 'gusto' against middle-class values, he promoted Theodore Dreiser, Scott Fitzgerald, Sinclair Lewis, Willa Cather and Ring Lardner (though he scorned Joyce and Eliot). Meanwhile *The Dial*, a venerable American periodical, under new ownership after 1919, encouraged American artists and writers – Eliot, Pound, Sherwood Anderson, Marianne Moore – and sought to promote modernism by serious reviewing that would demand the very best from contemporary artists. At its peak in 1923 its circulation reached 18,000; it was the vehicle through which Eliot's authority was established in the United States. *Modern Quarterly: A Journal of Radical Opinion* and *New Masses*, with its slogan, 'Go left, young writers!' encouraged the Marxist critiques of American culture that led to V. F. Calverton's *The Liberation of American Literature* and Granville Hick's *The Great Tradition*, as well as the more eclectic writings of Edmund Wilson and Kenneth Burke.[7] John Crowe Ransom noted in the 1930s that 'following the excitement produced by the Humanist diversion, there is now one due to the Leftists, or Proletarians, who are also diversionists. Their diversion is likewise moral.'[8] Meanwhile there had appeared in 1920 Eliot's collection of critical essays, *The Sacred Wood*, whose account of the nature and goals of poetry would soon prove decisive for the history of American criticism.

Since the 1920s two major changes have occurred. First, the importance of public, non-academic criticism has declined. Writing about literature, like reading literature, is an activity that has come to be increasingly associated with universities. Second, within the system of American criticism, interpretive criticism rather than historical scholarship has come to be the dominant form of writing about literature. In 1951, registering this change, the MLA changed its constitution again, to add 'criticism' to its goals: 'the object of the

---

[7]   For discussion see Daniel Aaron, *Writers on the Left* (New York: Harcourt, 1961).
[8]   Ransom, *The World's Body*, p. 332.

Association shall be to promote study, *criticism*, and research in modern languages and their literatures.'

There are two distinct moments in this historical process: the rise of the 'New Criticism' from the 1930s through the 1950s, and the impact on literary criticism in recent years of various theoretical perspectives and discourses – psychoanalysis, linguistics, feminism, structuralism, deconstruction. A fuller account of literary criticism would certainly need to consider other developments than these two. For one thing, there have been several other well-known critical schools or movements, distinguished by their conceptions of literature or of the task of criticism. The 'Chicago Aristotelians' contributed substantially to the formal analysis of several literary genres.[9] The group variously known as the 'New York Intellectuals' or 'the *Partisan Review* crowd' – Lionel Trilling, Irving Howe, Philip Rahv, Alfred Kazin, Dwight MacDonald and others – sought to maintain a public, non-academic criticism fusing a radical political vision with an exploration of avant-garde writing, and exercised considerable influence from the 1940s through the 1960s, though it never developed a distinctive critical method.[10] More important, many of the most significant works of criticism are not associated with a particular school or method but with a field or period of literary study which they influenced. This is particularly true of works of scholarship, which may have established the questions that dominated Milton studies for a decade, or revolutionized our conception of the Renaissance epic, or decisively altered the course of interpretations of romantic poetry. One might contend that the history of criticism and scholarship is not susceptible of treatment in a general article because different fields or specializations follow different rhythms, and an accurate account would have to examine how certain works established the questions that preoccupied a generation of scholars, until their answers generated a new set of problems. Thus, a schematic article of this type, focusing on two major changes in criticism, might not even mention many of the most famous works of the period: literary biographies, such as Richard Ellmann's *James Joyce*, contributions to the history of ideas, such as A. O. Lovejoy's *The Great Chain of Being* and M. H. Abrams' *The Mirror and the Lamp*, or Wayne Booth's seminal study of narrative technique, *The Rhetoric of Fiction*.

Another sort of development which would merit extensive discussion in a fuller history is the rise of American Studies, which seeks a

[9] A selection of their writings is conveniently collected in R. S. Crane, *Critics and Criticism* (Chicago: University of Chicago Press, 1951).
[10] See Grant Webster's informed but hostile discussion in *The Republic of Letters* (Baltimore: Johns Hopkins University Press, 1979), pp. 209–92.

major reorganization of knowledge around what it takes to be the central question: what is American culture and how did it get to be the way it is? So far, however, American Studies has not had the influence on other disciplines that one might expect and has produced an interdisciplinary subfield rather than a reorganization of knowledge. In the early twentieth century, American literature was scarcely taken seriously as an object of study in what were quite literally 'English' departments. A first landmark was V. L. Parrington's *Main Currents in American Thought* (1927–30), which gave American thought an identity and pattern of development, but made such literary figures as Hawthorne, Poe and Melville irrelevant to central narrative. F. O. Matthiessen's *American Renaissance* of 1941 altered that story to stress Hawthorne and Melville, whose work could be shown to participate in American reflection on the problem of democracy. Charles Feidelson's *Symbolism and American Literature* raised the level of philosophical debate and placed American literature in a wider literary context, arguing that American writers were engaged in a struggle to free themselves from the mode of symbolism promoted by Puritan typology.

The American Studies movement, though it promoted and benefited from such serious study of American literature as these works encouraged, came to represent a distinct approach to literature: literary works were considered not as autonomous aesthetic objects but as products of a culture and of specific historical circumstances, which they should help one to understand. The first American Studies programs, bringing together critics, historians and other social scientists, were established in the late 1930s, but after the war their number grew rapidly. By 1970 there were some 200. The American Studies Association was founded in 1951. (Its journal, *American Quarterly*, had begun two years before.) Early statements are concerned to demonstrate that there *is* an American culture, and influential literary studies were often those that tried to identify its quintessential traits, thus providing an overall theory of American literature. Perry Miller's *The New England Mind* found the key in the reactions to the Puritan heritage. More systematically influential was Henry Nash Smith's *Virgin L. nd*, which drew upon pulp literature in describing American myths, and which soon was linked with R.W.B. Lewis's *The American Adam* and Leo Marx's *The Machine in the Garden* in what was called the 'myth–symbol' school, predicated on the notion that symbols and symbolic patterns in literary works are reflections of folk myths and thus of underlying forces in the national culture. These books provided American Studies with a subject of debate, and argument about the demonstrability of such theses encouraged a turn toward the methods of the social sciences, particularly anthropology and sociology, which were thought to give the most direct access to American culture.[11] I pass over all these matters which deserve fuller treatment in order to discuss the two shifts associated with changes in the organization of knowledge: the rise of the New Criticism and the impact on literary studies of various modes of theoretical writing.

The New Criticism originates as an argument about the nature of poetry in T.S. Eliot's *The Sacred Wood*, and as a conservative Southern resistance to values associated with science, industrialization and urbanization. From 1922 to 1925 a group of poets meeting at Vanderbilt University under the tutelage of John Crowe Ransom published a review called *The Fugitive*. Their literary discussion later took a social and political turn. Partly in response to the drama of the Scopes trial, which represented Southerners to the nation as ignorant, credulous, Bible-toting hicks, they undertook a defense of what they called the Southern way of life, in a collection of political essays, *I'll Take My Stand* (1930), whose title came from a Confederate marching song.[12] Contrasting the agrarian with the industrial, the traditional and the organic with the alienated and the mechanistic, the contributors celebrated the life of yeoman farmers in small communities and argued for a spiritual superiority of subsistence farming over cash crop farming and industrial manufacture. But their political efforts met little success, and the Agrarians soon abandoned the cause of the autonomous, self-sufficient Southern farm for that of the self-sufficient poem.

In *The Sacred Wood* (1920) Eliot had maintained that 'poetry is not the expression of personality but the escape from personality.'[13] Successful poems are disciplined artifacts that synthesize disparate

---

[11]   See Bruce Kuklick, 'Myth and Symbol in American Studies', *American Quarterly* 24 (Oct. 1972), pp. 435–50. For an interesting statement by the dean of the movement, see Robert Spiller, 'Unity and Diversity in the Study of American Culture: The American Studies Association in Perspective', *American Quarterly* 25 (1973), pp. 611–18. Gerald Graff devotes an insightful chapter of *Professing Literature* (Chicago: University of Chicago Press, 1987) to 'The Promise of American Literature Studies'.

[12]   Scopes, a high school teacher who had violated a new Tennessee law forbidding the teaching of evolution, was defended by Clarence Darrow, who skillfully made a mockery of the fundamentalists and their spokesman, William Jennings Bryan. The northern press, led by Mencken, derived much copy from the affair. For discussion of the Agrarians' reaction, see John L. Stewart, *The Burden of Time: Fugitives and Agrarians* (Princeton: Princeton University Press, 1965), pp. 107–49. For general discussion of the New Critics, see Webster, *Republic of Letters*, pp. 63–208.

[13]   T. S. Eliot, *The Sacred Wood* (London: Methuen, 1920), p. 58.

experience. Eliot's early criticism provided a theory of poetry which could be linked with the close analysis of verbal texture practiced by I. A. Richards and his pupil William Empson to produce a style of criticism dubbed 'The New Criticism' by Ransom's 1941 book of that name. Although there were disagreements among practitioners – Ransom, Allen Tate, Cleanth Brooks, Austin Warren, R. P. Blackmur, Robert Penn Warren, W. K. Wimsatt – the New Criticism that emerged from their work treated poems as aesthetic objects rather than historical documents and examined the interaction of their verbal features and the ensuing complications of meaning rather than the historical intentions and circumstances of their authors. The task of criticism was to elucidate individual works of art. Focusing on ambiguity, paradox, irony, and the complicating effects of connotation and poetic imagery, the New Criticism sought to show the contribution of each element of poetic form to a unified structure. Its concern with difficult verse and complexities of figurative language equipped it to deal authoritatively with the experiments of contemporary poetry, as in Cleanth Brooks's influential *Modern Poetry and the Tradition* of 1939.

At first, the New Criticism seemed public rather than academic criticism, for it challenged the historical scholarship of the universities. Essays in the quarterlies, eschewing footnotes and bibliographies, adopted an anti-academic stance; yet these influential journals, such as *The Southern Review* and *The Kenyon Review*, were from the outset part of the university world. *The Southern Review* (edited by Brooks and Warren from 1935 to 1942) was financed, lavishly at first, by Louisiana State University, which Governor Huey Long wished to build into a great university. *The Kenyon Review*, edited by John Crowe Ransom at Kenyon College from 1938 to 1959, was supported by the college, and after 1940 obtained a good deal of money from the Guggenheim Foundation, as did *The Sewanee Review*, sponsored by the University of the South. Most of the critics writing for these journals were professional academics.

By 1940, Janssens notes in *The American Literary Review*, 'both the *Kenyon* and the *Southern* reviews were frankly addressing an academic audience rather than the legendary "common reader"'.[14] For a symposium in 1940 on 'Literature and the Professors', published in the *Southern* and the *Kenyon*, Ransom proposed to circularize the entire membership of the MLA, which had become the audience to which the New Criticism was appealing. Ransom in fact argued, in an

---

[14]   G. A. M. Janssens, *The American Literary Review* (The Hague: Mouton, 1968), p. 225.

essay entitled 'Criticism, Inc.', that despite professors' current preference for scholarship, 'it is from the professors of literature . . . that I should hope eventually for the erection of intelligent standards of criticism. It is their business.'[15] Psychology and sociology, he contended, 'have immeasurably improved in understanding since they were taken over by universities, and the same career looks possible for criticism. Rather than occasional criticism by amateurs, I should think the whole enterprise might be seriously taken in hand by professionals.' Ransom wrote prophetically to Allen Tate in 1937, 'I have an idea that we could really found criticism if we got together on it', for 'the professors are in an awful dither trying to reform themselves and there's a big stroke possible for a small group that knows what it wants in giving them ideas and definitions and showing them the way.'[16]

As late as 1943 Cleanth Brooks claimed that 'the New Critics have next to no influence in the universities';[17] but in fact they were swiftly gaining it and becoming the professional critics Ransom had called for. Most moved to professorial positions in northern universities – Brooks and Robert Penn Warren to Yale (1947 and 1950), which became the major center from which their influence spread, Austin Warren to Iowa (1939–48) and Michigan (1948), Tate to New York University (1947–51) and Minnesota (1951), Blackmur to Princeton (1940), Ransom from Vanderbilt to Kenyon College in Ohio in 1937. In 1938 Brooks and Penn Warren published *Understanding Poetry*, a textbook which focused attention on the language of poems and showed how metaphor, tone and ambiguity should be analysed in the classroom. The pedagogical success of this volume, which taught two generations of students how to read, contributed to the hegemony of the New Criticism. After the Second World War, literary theorists undertook to transform the methodological assumptions into basic principles of aesthetics. W. K. Wimsatt and Monroe Beardsley's famous articles 'The Intentional Fallacy' (1946) and 'The Affective Fallacy' (1949) argued that questions of meaning are not to be resolved by consulting authors' intentions or readers' responses; both errors tend to make 'the poem itself, as an object of specifically critical judgment, . . . disappear.'[18] René Wellek and Austin Warren's *Theory of Literature* of 1949 drew upon wide knowledge of the history of

---

[15] Ransom, *The World's Body*, p. 329.
[16] Quoted in Thomas Young, *Gentleman in a Dustcoat: A Biography of John Crowe Ransom* (Baton Rouge: Louisiana State University Press, 1976), pp. 299–300.
[17] Cleanth Brooks, 'Mr Kazin's America', *Sewanee Review* 51 (1953), p. 59.
[18] W. K. Wimsatt, *The Verbal Icon* (Lexington: University of Kentucky Press, 1954), p. 21.

criticism and foreign work on literary theory in constructing a central distinction between 'the extrinsic approach to the study of literature' (biographical, historical, sociological, psychological) and the 'intrinsic study of literature,' concerned with the structure of the verbal artifact. *Theory of Literature*, whose judicious tone and wide learning made it the authoritative guide to principles of criticism, was a staple of graduate education for twenty years.

Nearly as important as the major graduate schools in assuring the spread of the New Criticism were its summer institutes for teachers. The Kenyon School of English was founded in 1948 with a grant from the Rockefeller Foundation and staffed by leading New Critics (Ransom, Brooks, Tate, Warren, William Empson, Yvor Winters), with a leavening of New York intellectuals associated with the *Partisan Review*. After 1950 it became the Indiana School of Letters, which offered intensive summer work in literary criticism until 1972. It was through universities – their institutions and publications – that New Criticism accomplished what Richard Forster calls 'the most extraordinarily successful of all consciously waged literary revolutions.'[19]

Finally, the institutionalization of the New Criticism may also owe something to its potential congruence with the demands of the General Education movement, whose best known models – Great Books courses at Columbia and the University of Chicago – had been established well before the Second World War but influenced many college and university programs directly after the war. Although the proponents of Great Books courses were unlikely to be defenders of modernist literature – quite the contrary – or devotees of irony and paradox, in fact teachers of the courses they established found themselves leading discussions of isolated masterpieces about which they lacked contextual knowledge (knowledge that would in any case have been tangential to the aims of the courses), and they came to practice an informal, unrigorous version of New Critical analysis, whose institutional importance was thereby reinforced. Gerald Graff suggests that 'as the introductory humanities courses at Harvard, Chicago, and Columbia became the prototypes everywhere for general education in literature, the general education program and the New Critical program gradually merged.'[20]

---

[19]   Richard Forster, *The New Romantics*, (Bloomington: Indiana University Press, 1962), p. 22.
[20]   Graff, *Professing Literature*, p. 171. Graff also points out that while the New Criticism at first promoted one sort of literature over another (roughly, metaphysical and modernist over romantic), it soon transformed itself into a way of reading poetry of every sort; 'one could now accept New Critical poetics without renouncing the poets in one's field' (p. 206).

The most widespread legacy of the New Criticism is the assumption, which still holds sway, that the test of any critical activity is whether it helps us to produce richer, more compelling interpretations of particular literary works. One effect of this assumption is to create a new type of knowledge: previously, what counted as knowledge in the field of literary studies was historical and philological information. Now, to produce interpretations of poems is to make a contribution to knowledge; and periodicals such as *The Explicator* (1942) were founded to record detailed interpretations of poems. From roughly 1930 to 1965 scholars who have reason to reflect on the state of literary studies, such as presidents of the MLA in the address with which they conclude their year in office, choose to ring the changes on the theme of 'scholarship versus criticism' – generally arguing that they should work together.[21] But if the discipline defines itself in terms of this struggle, whose harmonious resolution could always be evoked, the result seems to have been not so much a synthesis as a curious overlay. On the one hand, by the 1950s criticism seemed to have won out, in that the test of scholarly endeavors had become their contribution to critical interpretation. Yet on the other hand, the field of literary studies remained organized, for the most part, according to the historical periods identified by traditional scholarship. Introductory courses employing *Understanding Poetry* might avoid historical considerations and train students to treat poems as eternal artifacts rather than datable documents, but advanced courses divided literature according to periods, and critics, like scholars, were expected to be experts in a period. Graduate students, in particular, had to claim expertise in a historical period, since jobs were customarily defined in this way: an opening 'in the Renaissance' or 'in the eighteenth century.' These persistent institutional arrangements exert considerable pressure on criticism, encouraging teachers to engage in historical projects and substantially modifying the triumph of the New Criticism.

Indeed, though we may speak of the hegemony of the New Criticism, in fact most criticism from this period does not remain within the paradigm of explication that resolutely ignores authors, readers and history. 'Normal criticism', one might say, becomes interpretation that joins such techniques of close reading as attention to imagery with an interest in authors and in literary history. Institutional practices of teaching and writing about literature create a shifting, eclectic 'normal criticism'.

---

[21] The presidential address is published annually in *PMLA*. Two early discussions occur in the addresses of 1929 and 1930 (*PMLA*, 44 and 45). For useful discussion, see Webster, *Republic of Letters*, pp. 113–19.

Finally, though the New Criticism originated in the socially conservative politics of a Southern group, the close reading it encouraged proved adaptable to different political purposes. The flourishing General Semantics movement of the late 1930s and 1940s embodied the widespread conviction that to resist propaganda citizens must understand rhetoric, particularly connotation and figurative language, and that the analysis of language is thus crucial to education in a free society.[22] The New Criticism's attention to figurative language made it an appropriate vehicle for such political concerns. By making literary study an encounter between a student and a text it offered an approach particularly suitable to the post-war university, which took in students from increasingly diverse social and educational backgrounds, who had little knowledge in common. In addition, for the many teachers of literature who hoped that imparting the values of the Western literary tradition to the growing student population might prevent war and fascism, the New Criticism was valuable for its critical interpretive orientation, which prompted discussion of the values and conflicts of value embodied in literary works. Although in the 1970s and 1980s the New Criticism is often accused of a neglect of moral issues and an elitist concern with texture and figure, 'the pages of the New Critics', Richard Ohmann notes, 'are bound together with moral fiber, almost strident in urging a social mission for literature.'[23] Concentration on complexities of language and meaning made analysis of literature a discussion of the untenability of simplistic views or moral positions. But attention to irony, tension, ambiguity and complications of attitude suggest 'that action impedes the deeper flow of understanding and the refinement of emotion, and that wholeness of experience, paradoxically, is most available to us when we abstract ourselves from action and let consciousness reign.'[24] New Criticism is said to tame the radical force of much great literature, though against that supposed political effect must be set the benefits of training in close reading.

The other major event in our period, which may transform criticism as decisively as the New Criticism, is the impact, beginning in the late

[22]   For example, Alfred Korzybski, founder of the movement embodied in the Institute for General Semantics and the journal *General Semantics*, writes: 'Today the world at large has to consider a serious situation, unparalleled in history, when a few sick individuals, through verbal distortions, falsifications, identifications etc, have trained a whole generation in a pathological use of our neuro-semantic and neuro-linguistic mechanisms.' Foreword to Irving Lee, *Language Habits in Human Affairs: An Introduction to General Semantics* (New York: Harper, 1941), p. x.

[23]   Richard Ohmann, *English in America* (New York: Oxford University Press, 1976), p. 71.

[24]   Ibid., p. 74.

1960s, of various theoretical perspectives and discourses: linguistics, psychoanalysis, feminism, Marxism, structuralism, deconstruction. A corollary of this has been the expansion of the domain of literary studies to include many concerns previously remote from it. In most American universities today a course on Freud is more likely to be offered in the English Department or French Department than in the Psychology Department; the philosophers Nietzsche, Sartre, Gadamer, Heidegger and Derrida are more often discussed by teachers of literature than teachers of philosophy; Ferdinand de Saussure is neglected by linguists and appreciated by students and teachers of literature. The writings of authors such as these fall into a miscellaneous genre to which Richard Rorty gives an illustrious pedigree: 'Beginning in the days of Goethe and Macaulay and Carlyle and Emerson', he writes, 'a kind of writing has developed which is neither the evaluation of the relative merits of literary productions, nor intellectual history, nor moral philosophy, nor social prophecy, but all of these mingled together in a new genre.'[25]

The most convenient designation of this new genre is simply the nickname 'theory', which today has come to designate works that succeed in challenging and reorienting thinking in fields other than those to which they ostensibly belong because their analyses of language, or mind, or history, or culture offer novel and persuasive accounts of signification. Of course, there had been earlier borrowings from other disciplines in American criticism – in the Marxist criticism of the 1930s and in psychoanalytic criticism focused on authors, characters or readers – but these attempts had often seemed reductionist, ignoring complexities of literary language and making the text, in effect, a symptom, whose true meaning lay elsewhere: in the authorial neurosis or social contradiction or philosophical truth it reflected. The versions of European philosophical and psychoanalytical thought that became influential in the late 1960s and early 1970s, however, had themselves undertaken extended reflection on language and meaning and were attractive precisely because they offered richer conceptual frameworks than did the New Criticism for expounding the complexity of literary signification. Instead of reducing literature to something non-literary, of which it would be a manifestation, these various theoretical enterprises – in fields as diverse as anthropology, psychoanalysis, historiography – discovered an essential 'literariness' in non-literary phenomena.

[25] Richard Rorty, *The Consequences of Pragmatism* (Minneapolis: University of Minnesota Press, 1982), p. 66.

In psychoanalysis, Jacques Lacan's argument that 'the unconscious is structured like a language' and the rereadings of Freud by Jacques Derrida and others, stressing the constitutive role of verbal connections and word play, show the importance in the functioning of the psyche of a logic of signification that is most clearly observed in literary discourse. Philosophical inquiry also demonstrates the inescapable centrality of figurative language: the very attempt to separate literal from figurative depends on concepts which themselves are scarcely free of rhetorical or metaphorical qualities.[26] In anthropology, Claude Lévi-Strauss identified a 'logic of the concrete' at work not only in myths but also in forms of social organization: the totems of totemic systems are selected not because of their economic importance but because they are 'good to think with,' lending themselves to the construction of the powerful thematic polarities through which literary works characteristically organize the world (blond heroes and heroines versus dark ones, sun versus moon, terrestrial versus celestial, and so on).[27] In historiography discussions of the character of historical understanding have found it profitable to focus on what is involved in following a story, thus taking as the model of historical intelligibility literary narrative. Hayden White argues, for example, that to describe historical narratives we must consider them as verbal fictions, whose explanatory effects depend on operations of emplotment. 'By "emplotment" I mean simply the encodation of facts contained in chronicle as components of specific kinds of plot structures, in precisely the way [Northrop] Frye has suggested is the case with fictions in general.'[28]

These discourses roughly assembled under the nickname 'theory' identify the literary not as a marginal phenomenon but as a logic of signification that generates meanings of many sorts. Their engagement with irreducible complexities of language provides a link with the New Criticism that has facilitated the American reception of these interdisciplinary theoretical discourses, even though they challenge the specificity of the aesthetic and eschew the New Critical project of demonstrating the organic unity of individual works.

Though many critics, starting with Northrop Frye in the introduction to *The Anatomy of Criticism*, have denounced the use by critics of theoretical frameworks and categories from other disciplines, the result has not been, as they feared, a take-over of criticism by

---

[26] Jacques Derrida, 'White Mythology', in *Margins of Philosophy* (Chicago: University of Chicago Press, 1983).

[27] For discussion see my *Structuralist Poetics* (Ithaca: Cornell University Press, 1975).

[28] Hayden White, *Tropics of Discourse* (Baltimore: Johns Hopkins University Press, 1978), p. 83.

linguistics, or philosophy, or psychoanalysis, but rather a certain loose, doubtless confusing interdisciplinarity, which might be conceived as a new, expanded rhetoric: a study of textual structures and strategies, in their relations to systems of signification and to human subjects. This is a study in which literature does indeed play a central role, but where its contact with varieties of human experience and problems of signification is important. 'Literary criticism', wrote Leslie Fiedler in 1950, 'is always becoming 'something else', for the simple reason that literature is always "something else"'.[29]

These developments in American criticism began, through the agency of French departments, in the 1960s, though the greatest impact is not felt until the 1970s. With the rise of structuralism in France, the work of its leading practitioners – Claude Lévi-Strauss, Roland Barthes, Jacques Lacan, Michel Foucault – attracted attention, and universities found money to invest in conferences, visiting professors from abroad and new journals, providing forums for these new ideas. Notable early events are the appearance of the issue of *Yale French Studies* devoted to structuralism in 1966 and a conference at Johns Hopkins the same year, which brought together Lévi-Strauss, Barthes, Lacan, Derrida, Poulet and others, and whose proceedings were later published as *The Languages of Criticism and the Sciences of Man.*

We can distinguish several strains of this new theoretical criticism. First there is the attempt to develop a poetics, a body of theory and description that would stand to literature as linguistics stands to language: that is, as a description of the norms and conventions that make possible the production of literary effects.[30] Northrop Frye's *Anatomy of Criticism* of 1957, with its accounts of basic plot structures and generic modes had started American criticism in this direction, but French structuralism, and the work of the Russian formalists on literary conventions which the French promoted, gave poetics a more technical and linguistic orientation. The structuralist enterprise extends the methodological models developed by linguistics to all aspects of culture and studies signification as the product of underlying systems of rules and norms, like the grammar of a language. The most highly developed branch of structuralist poetics has been *narratology*, the study of the basic components of narrative and their possibilities of combination. In the United States, structuralist and Russian formalist analyses of the relations between plot

---

[29] Leslie Fiedler, 'Towards an Amateur Criticism', *Kenyon Review* 12 (1950), p. 564.

[30] For discussion see Culler, *Structuralist Poetics.*

structure and narrative discourse in both literary and non-literary narratives were integrated with the native tradition of analyzing point of view in fiction.[31]

Second, interest in the conditions of meaning in literature led to critical and theoretical work focused on the reader. Wolfgang Iser's *The Implied Reader* and *The Act of Reading*, translated from the German in 1978 and 1979, made available a practical criticism of the novel based on a phenomenological theory of the text. Stanley Fish's early study of 'the reader in *Paradise Lost*', *Surprised by Sin* (1967), was followed by a series of accounts exploring how readers and communities of readers create meaning. Many of Roland Barthes's works, particularly *S/Z* and *The Pleasure of the Text*, contributed to a criticism focused on the reading process and how works generate meaning by complying with or disrupting the codes with which readers approach them. Despite the difficulty of dealing with readers and disputes about the relevance of ideal readers, implied readers, informed readers and real readers, American criticism increasingly maintains that any account of literary meaning must focus on the act of reading. This presumption makes an interpretation a story of reading: a narrative of what happens as a reader encounters a text.[32]

Third, the combination of French feminist theory and the more pragmatic thinking of American feminist movements has produced an active, heterogeneous feminist criticism concerned both with the tradition of women's writing, which needs to be rescued from neglect and studied for what it can teach, and also with the dubious assumptions of male literature and male criticism. The latter branch of feminist criticism is interested, as Elaine Showalter puts it, in 'the way in which the hypothesis of a female reader changes our apprehension of a given text, awakening us to the significance of its sexual codes'.[33] Feminist criticism has also questioned the nature and status of sexual difference, as well as the extent to which fundamental notions such as rationality are complicitous with male privilege; one form this takes is

---

[31]   See Wallace Martin, *Recent Theories of Narrative* (Ithaca: Cornell University Press, 1986), Mary Louise Pratt, *Towards a Speech Act Theory of Literary Discourse* (Bloomington: Indiana University Press, 1977) and Susan Lanser, *The Narrative Act: Point of View in Fiction* (Princeton: Princeton University Press, 1982).

[32]   For discussion see Jane P. Tompkins (ed.), *Reader Response Criticism* (Baltimore: Johns Hopkins University Press, 1980); Steven Mailloux: *Interpretive Conventions: The Reader in the Study of American Fiction* (Ithaca: Cornell University Press, 1982); and Jonathan Culler, *On Deconstruction* (Ithaca: Cornell University Press, 1982), pp. 31–83.

[33]   Elaine Showalter, 'Towards a Feminist Poetics', in *Women Writing and Writing about Women*, ed. Mary Jacobus (London: Croom Helm, 1979), p. 25. For further discussion of the hypothesis of the female reader, see my *On Deconstruction*, pp. 43–64.

the analysis of how texts that rely upon hierarchical distinctions work to put them in question, exposing them as ideological impositions. Feminist readings of Freud, applying techniques of literary criticism to discourses of great cultural power, have shown how the moves by which psychoanalysis establishes a hierarchical opposition between male and female rely on premises that dispute that hierarchy.

However, one should also count psychoanalytically inspired criticism as a fourth strain. Indebted to Derrida's and Lacan's rereadings of Freud, which argue that the force of Freud's insights can be detected in the way his writings are themselves structured by the processes of repression, displacement, and transference that he describes, psychoanalytic criticism has become not a psychoanalysis of authors, characters or readers, but an analysis of processes of signification as illuminated by Freud's writings. Particularly important for new psychoanalytic criticism is the role of transference and counter-transference: significance emerges not so much from the application of the analyst's scientific metalanguage to the patient's discourse as from the way in which analyst and analysand get caught up in a transferential repetition of a central scenario. The new understanding of transference has transformed psychoanalytic criticism, making it a rich mode of speculative interpretation often combining with what are here listed as other modes.[34]

There has also developed a Marxist criticism informed by theoretical work in structuralism and psychoanalysis. The problem for Marxist criticism has long been the extreme reductionism of a model which treats literature as part of a superstructure determined by the economic base; but Louis Althusser's critique of mechanical and expressive causality in Marxian models and his articulation of 'structural causality', which assigns the economic mode of production a place within the system of relations comprising the social totality but grants each level a relative autonomy, has opened the way to to a more varied and pertinent engagement with literature, as in Fredric Jameson's influential *The Political Unconscious*. Literary works are read as symbolic acts through which men live their relations to their real conditions of existence, and they reveal something of the cultural repression of history. In an account that englobes most of the possibilities of a sophisticated Marxist criticism, interested in bringing other theoretical models within a Marxist horizon, Jameson

[34] See Shoshana Felman (ed.), *Literature and Psychoanalysis, Yale French Studies* 55/6 (1977). Other notable recent works are Jane Gallop, *The Daughter's Seduction: Feminism and Psychoanalysis* (Ithaca: Cornell University Press, 1982); and Samuel Weber, *The Legend of Freud* (Minneapolis: University of Minnesota Press, 1982).

distingushes three levels of interpretation: works may be read as symbolic resolutions of social contradiction, or as fragments of a discourse of the class struggle or, at the level of what he calls the ideology of style, as variously bearing traces of modes of production.[35]

Most prominent in quarrels about criticism in recent years, though, is deconstruction. The term comes from the philosophical project of Jacques Derrida. To deconstruct the hierarchical oppositions of Western metaphysics is to reveal them as constructions — ideological impositions — by showing through a close reading of philosophical texts how they are undermined by the discourses that affirm or rely on them. Deconstruction affects literary criticism in two ways. By disrupting the hierarchical oppositions on which criticism depends — literal/metaphorical, inside/outside, original/imitation, form/meaning — deconstruction raises theoretical issues that critics must pursue and prevents methodological concepts from being treated simply as tools to be employed. It encourages critics, rather, to see how these concepts are affected by the works they are being used to interpret: what the works have to say about the categories one uses in discussing them. Second, deconstruction encourages a style of reading which Barbara Johnson calls 'a careful teasing out of warring forces of signification within the text itself'.[36] Alert to value-laden hierarchies, to moments when a key term attempts to hold together conflicting implications, to apparently marginal phenomena which reveal what is centrally at stake, the analyst also explores how conflicts within the text are transferentially reproduced as critical conflicts about the text. Deconstruction has been the greatest source of energy in criticism in the 1970s and early 1980s – the source not only of such major works as Paul de Man's *Allegories of Reading* and *The Rhetoric of Romanticism* but also of controversy about signification and about the American institutionalization of philosophical and ideological analysis as a form of literary criticism.

Associated with deconstruction is what might be styled simply the reinterpretation of romanticism, an enterprise that has also drawn upon psychoanalysis but is less accurately identified with either than with a certain 'Yale School' – de Man, Geoffrey Hartman, Harold Bloom and their students. The New Criticism's celebration of the wit and irony of metaphysical and modern poetry had led to a historical scheme where modernism arrives as a sophisticated demystification of

---

[35] Two fine discussions are William C. Dowling, *Jameson, Althusser, Marx: An Introduction to 'The Political Unconscious'* (Ithaca: Cornell University Press, 1984) and John Frow, *Marxism and Literary History* (Cambridge: Harvard University Press, 1986).

[36] Barbara Johnson, *The Critical Difference* (Baltimore: Johns Hopkins Press, 1980), p. 5. For discussion see my *On Deconstruction*.

the delusions of romanticism; this is what recent work has refuted. Hartman's *Wordsworth's Poetry: 1787-1814* began a fundamental revaluation. Readings of Wordsworth and Rousseau by de Man and his students have demonstrated the workings within these texts of ironic deconstructions, whose force leads them constantly to be misread. Finally, Harold Bloom's series of studies since *The Anxiety of Influence* of 1973 have recast the history of English poetry as a scenario in which strong poets (of which the romantics are the classic exemplars) must struggle to overcome their precursors, particularly Milton, by combating and distorting the prior work so as to clear a space for their own poetry. Poems are therefore to be interpreted as misreadings of the works of a great precursor – a principle that has generated sensitive and spectacular critical readings. These critical writings make romanticism the acme of literary insight and achievement and in the process have established a flourishing area of critical investigation.

Finally, a 'New Historicism' focused especially on the writing of the English Renaissance and profiting from the lessons of recent theory, seeks to avoid the totalizing determinisms of an older historicism, which presumed to read in every text the beliefs deemed characteristic of its era, and instead juxtaposes literary with non-literary works, exploring their interaction and producing illuminating effects of montage. Originating in works such as Stephen Greenblatt's *Renaissance Self-Fashioning* of 1980, with its interest in the discursive construction of the self, the New Historicism has evolved in Foucauldian ways to focus on new historical objects, such as the body, and on the effects of discursive practices in their relation to power.[37] While calling for criticism to become historical and political, it has so far failed to develop a convincing program for a politically emancipatory criticism, but it has produced a new awareness of interest and complexity of non-literary texts, which cannot be treated simply as documents but must be *read*, in the same way as literary works.

The preeminence of 'theory' and theoretical debates for over a decade has understandably produced a reaction, particularly a so-called pragmatist argument that, lacking any privileged standpoint, theory has no purchase on practice and thus no real work to do.[38] Nevertheless, there is no sign of a waning of theory, whose domain has been augmented by the theoretical writings of pragmatists themselves,

[37] For a fine example see the special issue of the new-historicist journal *Representations* (Spring 1986) devoted to 'Sexuality and the Social Body in the Nineteenth Century'.
[38] See W. J. T Mitchell (ed.), *Against Theory: Literary Studies and the New Pragmatism* (Chicago: University of Chicago Press, 1985).

and which is increasingly the focus of critical debates, as critics argue about the relations among different sorts of discourses and their role in history and culture. Indeed, theory should be understood not as a prescription of methods of interpretation but as the discourse that results when conceptions of the nature and meaning of texts and their relations to other discourses, social practices and human subjects become the object of general reflection. Theory does not give one an interpretive method which one then applies to a literary work so as to infer from it meanings of some other order. On the contrary, what literary works have to tell us often bears crucially on theoretical questions. Theory is literary, in fact, insofar as it presumes that literary works have particularly important things to teach us here.

The recent activity of criticism leads one to imagine that the focus of criticism in the immediate future will be on theoretical questions produced by the intersection of feminist, psychoanalytic, Marxist, deconstructive and new historicist discourses, to which can be added black criticism, whose debates about the nature of a literary tradition and its relation to signifying practices and social institutions have a bearing on problems that have been differently posed in the predominantly white world of theory. In fact, the key issue for many of these theoretical perspectives is the relation between the literary and the non-literary, on which much of the most powerful work of the recent past turns out to have focused. A list might begin with Paul de Man's studies of Rousseau in *Allegories of Reading* which, studying literary and non-literary texts, focus on relations between tropological structures and rhetorical force, and thus the political impact of the relations between performative and constative dimensions language in these texts. Jacques Derrida's readings of Plato, Mallarmé, Kant and Blanchot, and especially the juxtaposition of Hegel and Genet in *Glas*, explore the bearing of literary and non-literary texts on issues raised by each. In *The Sense of an Ending* Frank Kermode urges the development of a general theory of fictions which would elucidate how fictions generate meaning in discourse of all sorts. Hayden White has advanced this project in studying narrative structures produced by Kenneth Burke's four 'master tropes': metaphor, metonymy, synecdoche, and irony. Mary Louise Pratt's *Towards a Speech Act Theory of Literary Discourse* undertakes to demonstrate that 'ordinary language' possesses many of the features of literary discourse and that both literary and non-literary narratives can be treated by the same models. René Girard's account of mimetic desire began, in *Deceit, Desire, and the Novel*, as the study of a fundamental structure of novels – triangular desire, in which what is desired is the image produced by another desire – but from this discovery he went on to argue that such structures are the basis of culture itself. Or again, Edward Said's *Orientalism* draws on the literary and the non-literary in analysing the invention of the Orient and Orientals. Jacqueline Rose's *Sexuality in the Field of Vision* moves over film and popular culture as well as literature in its grappling with the textual determination and instantiation of the structures of desire.

It would be no exaggeration to say that critical theory has in recent years reached its greatest intensity when focused on theoretically defined problems that take in both literary and non-literary texts.[39] Those who think of contemporary criticism as a battlefield of conflicting methods miss this shared interest in connecting the literary and the non-literary.

The question is, how did institutions make this sort of critical development possible and influence the directions it took? One obvious but crucial condition of critical change seems to have been the availability of financial resources in the late 1960s and early 1970s for activities that helped make accessible European influences and American work stimulated by them. Symposia, visiting professorships, and especially new journals permitted the exploration of these new critical possibilities. The growth of theoretically oriented criticism is facilitated by the foundation of new journals: *New Literary History*, created in 1969 when the centenary of the University of Virginia made available money to give the university and its strong but traditional English department greater visibility, quickly became a major forum for the translation of foreign work. Although its announced program envisioned the revitalization of literary history (in opposition to the New Criticism), in fact the result was different and more radical than envisaged: the journal became increasingly devoted to articles concerned with the way continental theory of various sorts would lead to a rethinking of literary studies. *Diacritics*, founded in 1970 to enhance the 'visibility' of the Cornell department of Romance Studies and conceived as a forum for analytical reviews of contemporary theory and theoretically oriented criticism, swiftly discovered that its most successful issues were those explicitly concerned with recent French theory. Other journals that provided an outlet for and thus decisive encouragement of new theoretical work included *Sub-stance* at Wisconsin (1971), *boundary 2* at SUNY–Binghamton (1973), *Semiotexte* at Columbia (1974) and *Critical Inquiry* at Chicago (1974), in addition to reviews devoted to feminist work: *Women's*

---

[39] In fact a surprising number of thinkers have called for criticism to become a generalized rhetoric, studying the production, structure and reception of texts of all sorts.

Studies (1972), *Women and Literature* (1972), *Feminist Studies* (1973), and *Signs* (1975).

It is striking how far in the United States, unlike Britain, this assimilation of foreign, often avant-garde thinking was entirely a university activity. In the 1960s *Partisan Review* showed an active interest, publishing articles by de Man and Hartman, several translations of Barthes and Lévi-Strauss, and some discussions of structuralism, but eventually joined the opposition to structuralist and post-structuralist thinking. With the notable exceptions of Susan Sontag and Richard Howard, the New York literati took no part in these developments. *The New York Review of Books*, which a 1972 survey by Hover and Kadushin identified as much the most influential intellectual forum,[40] was first cool and then hostile, eliminating critics who became involved from its list of contributors, rejecting sympathetic reviews of theoretical criticism, avoiding participation even in feminist theory and criticism. Surprisingly, its attacks had little effect. When the *New York Review* joined *Time* and *Newsweek* in middle-brow opposition, it seemed to succeed only in depriving itself of influence in the domain of contemporary criticism and revealing to what extent criticism had become a university enterprise, part of the functioning of what had arguably become the most important American institution.

This relation to the academy gives contemporary theoretical criticism a problematical character. Interdisciplinarity, in the academic world, involves competition for funds, positions, and students, but above all, arguments about disciplines that would not necessarily occur in the sphere of public criticism. When a professor of French or English teaches or writes about Freud or Heidegger, this is anomalous in the university world, which is organized into departments that supposedly represent distinct intellectual fields. 'Theory', as we call it, thus occupies a strange position: studied and practiced within universities, disseminated by the academic media, 'theory' is an academic activity, yet within the university it is anti-disciplinary, challenging not only the boundaries of disciplines, on whose legitimacy the university structure seems to depend, but also these disciplines' claims to judge writing that touches their concerns. In practice, 'theory' contests the right of psychology departments to control Freud's texts, of philosophy departments to control Kant,

    [40] Julie Hover and Charles Kadushin, 'The Influential Intellectual Journals', *Change Magazine* 4:2 (March 1972), pp. 38–47.

Hegel, and Heidegger.[41] Yet since this subversion of the university's articulation of knowledge takes place within the university structure, there is considerable scope for disagreement about what is happening – occasion for both radical claims and charges of inescapable conservatism. Neither the practitioners nor the opponents of recent criticism find it easy to situate changes which repeatedly transgress university boundaries.

These developments are associated with changes in the scale and structure of universities. The extension of university education to a higher percentage of the population and the enormous growth in student numbers – from half a million in 1920 to eight and a half million in 1970 – has important consequences. First, expansion can favor critical innovation and the proliferation of critical possibilities by permitting universities to add new courses and programs, without having to choose between one or another way of teaching and studying literature. A survey of college catalogues shows that most institutions have added new courses without eliminating the old.[42] The 1960s, for example, witnessed the addition of thematic courses, such as Literature and the City, The Literature of Adolescence, The Novel of Protest, The Hero in Literature. Since then, in many universities a further layer of courses consonant with recent critical concerns has been added, with titles such as Literature and Psychoanalysis, Introduction to Narratology, Deconstruction and Literary Criticism, Theories of Language and Literature, French Feminist Theory, The Semiotics of Literature, Meaning in Culture. In retrospect, it seems possible to argue that student protest movements, which energized and disrupted universities in the 1960s, had the effect of disturbing a stable order and weakening the presumption of departmental control, so that when new critical and methodological possibilities emerged, as they very shortly did, they could be more easily introduced into teaching, at a time when other sorts of institutional innovation were made difficult by financial restrictions.

In a period of expansion, universities could add entire programs and departments – comparative literature departments, for example, even

---

[41] A remarkable case in point is the tiny Literary Studies Programme at the University of Toronto. The success of its undergraduate teaching and the professional distinction of its few faculty members did not prevent the foreign literature departments, many of them the largest in the world, from seeking in 1985 the elimination of the program, on the grounds that the works of Dante, Chekhov and so on belonged to them and no one else should be allowed to teach them.

[42] For discussion of curricula, see Elizabeth Cowan (ed.), *Options for the Teaching of English: The Undergraduate Curriculum* (New York: MLA, 1975) and Thomas W. Wilcox, *The Anatomy of College English* (San Francisco: Jossey-Bass, 1973).

though comparative literature represents not a supplement to national literature departments but a claim that the study of literature ought not to be organized along national lines. Programs in women's studies and black studies, which organize the humanities and social sciences quite differently from traditional disciplines, have grown up alongside them. Laurence Veysey has shown how the growth of the modern university depends upon the substitution of bureaucratic administration for a traditional ideology; 'quarrelsome debate, including that based upon conflicts among academic ideals', is minimized as 'individuals, cliques, and factions who do not think in the same terms' are linked by a bureaucratic structure rather than common educational goals.[43] The counterpart of this in literary studies is a pluralism that admits the right of alternative approaches or conceptions of literary studies to be represented in the university, so long as one's own particular turf is not threatened. Except in times of budget cuts, this principle permits the institutionalization of new approaches.

Courses and programs that articulate literary study in a particular way generate critical writing within this new subfield, which gains respectability as publications multiply and journals are founded. Publishers have been interested in identifying growing fields, especially where textbook markets may emerge, and so have become particularly receptive, for example, to books on literary theory or in women's studies, thus encouraging critics to orient their work in these directions. A crucial factor in the development of criticism may have been which programs emerged as possibilities at moments when money for expansion was available. American Studies programs and Comparative Literature programs succeeded in obtaining funding before the end of university expansion in the 1970s; Women's Studies programs, despite their strong enrollments, have generally been constructed without much additional funding. Proposals for programs in semiotics, critical theory, or literature and psychoanalysis, have generally not been successful because they became plausible at an unpropitious time, although in the late 1980s, with university finances in a healthier condition, this appears to be changing. Programs that were established earlier, such as the undergraduate semiotics program at Brown University and the graduate Semiotics center at Indiana, the undergraduate Literature Major at Yale or the Center for the Psychological Study of the Arts at SUNY–Buffalo, are being joined in the late 1980s by a series of humanities centers devoted to the principle of interdisciplinary work and by special degree programs,

[43] Laurence Veysey, *The Emergence of the American University* (Chicago: University of Chicago Press, 1965), pp. 308 and 315.

such as the Program in Literature at Duke University. The availability of foundation grants for educational projects does encourage universities to devise new programs, but in recent years grants have been directed more toward writing programs than to innovations in literary education.

The expansion of universities has had a second consequence: the need for more teachers of literature has led to the development of numerous sizeable graduate programs. Between 1920 and 1924 188 PhDs in English were awarded; between 1970 and 1974 there were 6,668, a thirty-five-fold increase.[44] Part of this is attributable to the government support for graduate study, which became available even in the humanities: in 1960–1 over 400 graduate fellowships were awarded in the humanities under the National Defense Education Act (NDEA) (though literary studies were given lower priority than the study of 'essential languages'). This over-expansion – in 1964 Harvard admitted 152 new graduate students in English – led to the job crisis of the 1970s and 1980s, whose effect was to stimulate the production of critical writing, since, as current wisdom has it, more publications are needed to get a job interview today than were required twenty years ago for tenure. The expansion of graduate programs has a more general impact on criticism, since graduate study in literature in the United States, more than elsewhere, involves methodological instruction, and the larger the graduate program, the more critics are led to consider theoretical and methodological questions. Expanded programs not only generate a great deal more writing about literature – all these seminar papers, theses, and the books and articles derived therefrom – but foreground issues of critical and scholarly method, as students are instructed in the writing of criticism.

The growth of graduate programs is linked to the development of distinctive intellectual styles or critical approaches; and though graduate programs have seldom been as monolithic as rumor suggests, the association of the New Criticism with Yale, or neo-Aristotelian criticism with Chicago, of intellectual history with Johns Hopkins, and later of deconstruction and literary theory with Yale is an important feature of the development of criticism. This specialization seems not to have been as marked as in philosophy departments, which often seem impelled to develop a distinctive type of philosophy (based on a view of what counts as a serious philosophical question) and have sometimes chosen to neglect large areas of what other departments regard as philosophy. The most eminent literature departments, for example,

[44] Lindsay Harmon (ed.), *A Century of Doctorates* (Washington DC: National Academy of Sciences, 1978).

have usually maintained their eminence despite changes of orientation: Yale is generally thought to have had the leading departments of English, French, and Comparative Literature from 1945 until 1985, though what they have been thought to stand for has changed. Johns Hopkins has remained an important graduate literature program, despite swift and dramatic variations in the commitments of its best known critics of the moment: from the intellectual history of Lovejoy to the stylistics of Leo Spitzer, the phenomenological criticism of Georges Poulet and J. Hillis Miller, the vivid, Catholic eclecticism of Hugh Kenner, the psychoanalytic criticism of Jeffrey Mehlman and Samuel Weber, the reader-response criticism of Stanley Fish, and today the deconstructive work of Neil Hertz and Werner Hamacher. Berkeley has remained a major English department, even as attention shifted from a historically oriented American studies to a New Historicism anchored in the English Renaissance. The doldrums of literary studies at Harvard seem to have been due not to its commitment to any particular approach but rather to disengagement from most of the developments in criticism since the War. New programs such as the University of California at Irvine's and SUNY-Buffalo's that have made a commitment to theoretically oriented criticism have not succeeded in commanding the attention and respect one might expect, even though they have trained excellent young scholars. Duke, which in 1985–7 repeated on a grander scale Buffalo's experiment of the 1960s, hiring a number of distinguished senior literary theorists, will provide an interesting test of the possibility of creating a new theoretically-oriented program that will have a decisive impact on literary studies. So far, however, the overall reputations of graduate programs in literature remain somewhat independent of their commitment to particular critical approaches, even though the young teachers emerging from them vary enormously in what they have learned to do.

With the growth of the academic profession, writing and publication became the best way to establish a reputation. The impetus to establish a reputation is part of the ethos of professionalism and thus of the attempt by workers in a capitalist system to control their own conditions of employment and to separate the factors that determine their identity from market forces in the economy. The role of criticism in this attempt is decisive: professors speak of teaching and administrative tasks preventing them from 'getting on with their work', identifying the production of criticism as their essential role. Ironically, it was precisely the expansion of universities in the 1960s and the market demand for more teachers of literature that permitted teachers to define themselves as writers of criticism. In 1968 a

well-informed observer described the situation in terms that a
shrinking job market would soon make risible:

A growing college population, the shortage of qualified college teachers of
English, and federal funds for curriculum research and teacher education
have enabled the college English teacher to broaden the range of his activities
significantly. With higher salaries, research grants from foundations and the
government, and freedom from the need to moonlight, he can undertake
research in libraries around the world . . . Salaries at the upper end of the
schedule have risen even more than beginning salaries . . . Some colleges still
maintain an aura of genteel poverty for faculty, but the limited supply of
college English teachers . . . is gradually forcing them, too, to acknowledge a
changing academic world . . . Hundreds of excellent college departments
spread across the country, however, find it increasingly difficult to attract
faculty members from the small pool of approximately 500 new Ph.D'.s in
English produced in 120 institutions in America each year . . . The need to
recruit and keep qualified teachers of English leads, inevitably, to higher
salaries, better working conditions, and a richer professional life for the
college teacher of English, with or without the Ph.D.[45]

The reduction of the teaching load at research universities and elite
colleges that has been achieved since the war (from six or eight
courses per year to four, on average) encourages the notion that the
primary task of professional professorial critics is research and
publication. One can argue that the system of publication exists not
just to accredit professionals (a system of degrees would do that) but
to distinguish those accredited from providers of services (such as
nurses and school teachers), to accredit them as participants in an
autonomous enterprise – a quest for knowledge – where in principle
projects are not imposed by outside forces but flow from the critic's
own curiosity or from the so-called 'needs' of the field itself.
Professionalism, Jencks and Riesman note, is 'colleague-oriented
rather than client-oriented'.[46] In the academy, professionalism ties
one's identity to an expertise and hence to a field in which one might
be judged expert by one's peers. This induces a proliferation of
subfields: writers of letters of recommendation find that they have a
stake in defining some area – say, psychoanalytic interpretations of
Shakespeare – such that their candidate may be deemed one of its
most accomplished experts. The connection between criticism and

[45]   Michael Shugrue, *English in a Decade of Change* (New York: Pegasus, 1968),
pp. 86–7.
[46]   Christopher Jencks and David Riesman, *The Academic Revolution* (New York:
Doubleday, 1968), p. 201. See also Ohmann, *English in America*, pp. 234–51.

the continuing professional evaluation on which promotions, grants, and prestige depend may thus generate a more specialized yet more innovative criticism than would some other arrangement. The need to make 'an important new contribution' is built into the American academic system, in ways that it is not in Britain, for example, where teachers of literature spend much less time evaluating one another. In the American system the fact that publication is the grounds for judgments we take seriously (such as tenure decisions) strengthens the assumption that publications should be serious: works of criticism or scholarship, not newspaper articles, nor works of popularization, nor, especially, commentary that does not take itself seriously.[47] Professionalism makes a critic's career depend upon the judgments of experts in his or her field: deans, departments, publishers and foundations have, in the interests of professionalism, increasingly relied on peer reviews in decisions to hire and promote, to publish books and articles, and to award grants. While reducing capriciousness and favoritism in important decisions, this progress of professionalism shifts power from the vertical hierarchy of the institution that employs a critic to a horizontal system of evaluation. Critical writing, which is the medium of exchange of this system, thus becomes central to the professional situation and identity of teachers of literature.

Criticism has been affected by the role of departments – -that distinctively American contribution to the system of higher education. The structure which makes the university a consortium of departments competing for students and money may encourage visible, innovative enterprises. As resources for expansion disappear, competition for money and positions often takes the form of competition for students and thus encourages incursions into new areas – film studies, women's studies, psychoanalysis, intellectual history, neglected philosophical writings – which are not claimed by other departments and offer possibilities of stimulating courses and research. The combination of the professionalization of faculty (which makes one's peers the principal audience for one's work) and the organization of the university into competing departments creates a situation in which departments are expected to vie with departments at other universities for eminence, both by attempting to hire their most distinguished critics and by encouraging their members to seek greater professional

[47] The fact that Kenneth Burke, despite the manifest brilliance of his writings and his ability to relate literature in its most formal aspects to philosophy, psychoanalysis and politics, did not have more influence on American criticism is quite possibly due to an apparent lack of seriousness: his writings about particular works often seemed something other than serious acts of interpretation, as witness his celebrated rewriting of 'Beauty is Truth, Truth Beauty', as 'Body is Turd, Turd Body'.

standing. Parsons and Platt note that institutions have not been content to excel in some fields while letting other departments remain less eminent.[48] Provosts and deans apply pressure that makes even conservative chairpersons willing to encourage publication that will attract attention. For deans in the American system, 'visibility' may have become more important than what is called 'soundness'.

Criticism has also been affected by changes in the membership of university faculties. Commentators suggest that in the early part of our period literary scholarship was a marginally-acceptable genteel vocation for white Anglo-Saxon protestant males of a certain social standing and economic status. The New Critics who challenged the Old Scholars were of the same sex and class, but they were followed, Leslie Fiedler writes, by a second generation of modernist critics,

not renegade WASP bearers of infectious aesthetic doctrines, but many of us the offspring of non-English-speaking stock, with a veneer of Anglo-Saxon polite culture no more than a generation thick. . . . By the last years of the fifties, we former outsiders had established ourselves as insiders. The end of World War II had seen the influx into colleges and universities of vast hordes of government subsidized students, ex-G.I.'s, many the first of their families ever to have been exposed to higher education. To teach the succeeding waves of the continuing invasion, new faculty had to be recruited out of the first waves: sons and daughters of working class or even petty-bourgeois parents, not even predominantly North European, much less *echt* Anglo-Saxon, after a while overwhelmingly East European Jewish (and to make matters worse, graduates of land-grant universities or city colleges).[49]

This is something of an overstatement, since as late as 1969 only 7 per cent of English department faculty were Jewish (13 per cent in what one survey identifies as the 'better' universities').[50] Lipsit and Ludd note that the humanities were the last disciplines to accept Jews.[51] However, this situation did change and the increasingly prominent role of Jewish critics has had an impact on criticism, as Jewish teachers

[48]   Talcott Parsons and Gerald Platt, *The American University* (Cambridge, Mass.: Harvard University Press, 1973), p. 146.

[49]   Leslie Fiedler, *What Was Literature?* (New York: Simon and Schuster, 1982), p. 60.

[50]   Stephen Steinberg, *The Academic Melting Pot: Catholics and Jews in American Higher Education* (New Brunswick, NJ.: Transaction Books, 1977), pp. 119–22. These figures agree with those of Seymour Lipset and Everett Ludd, 'Jewish Academics in the United States', *American Jewish Yearbook* (1971).

[51]   Lipset and Ludd, ibid., p. 96. Lionel Trilling recalls, 'my appointment to an instructorship in Columbia College (in 1930) was pretty openly regarded as an experiment, and for some time my career in the College was complicated by my being Jewish' ('Young in the Thirties', *Commentary* (May 1966), p. 47).

of literature in the generation that followed Trilling, after making their reputations by writing on canonical literary works (Harold Bloom on romanticism, Geoffrey Hartman on Wordsworth, and Robert Alter on Stendhal), have frequently begun explictly to take up elements of the Jewish tradition in their contributions to literary studies (Bloom on Kabbalah, Hartman on sacred interpretation, Alter on the Hebrew Bible).

Even more obvious has been the impact of the slowly increasing number of women faculty members and of black teachers of literature. The presence of more women faculty, energized by feminist thinking and feminist social movements, has produced an expansion of the traditional literary canon (each new edition of the *Norton Anthology of English Literature* contains more women authors than its predecessor), an increasing number of popular and successful courses on women's writing, and a lively, polemical feminist criticism which treats traditional male authors and general issues relating to gender and sex, as well as women's writing. A new area of critical debate has emerged; and while these developments in criticism are in part a consequence of wider social movements, criticism has also been an instrument of social change. Pioneering works of feminism, such as Simone de Beauvoir's *The Second Sex* and Kate Millett's *Sexual Politics*, played an important role in the growth of feminist movements, and they are in large part works of literary criticism: readings of literary works. The combination of social and political goals with new ways of reading creates vigorous teaching and writing about literature.

The introduction of Afro-American writing to literature courses owes much to the civil rights movement of the 1960s, when James Baldwin, Ralph Ellison and Richard Wright became canonical authors, but at the same time the Black Power movement energized the Black Arts movement, with its quest to identify a Black Aesthetic, 'so as to break the interpretive monopoly on Afro-American expressive culture that had been held from time immemorial by a white liberal critical establishment'.[52] In the 1980s, however, two factors combined to change the situation: on the one hand, the remarkable efflorescence of black women's writing (Toni Morrison, Alice Walker, Maya Angelou and the rediscovery of Zora Neale Hurston), which had been neglected by the men promoting the Black Aesthetic, reopened the question of the nature of the black tradition; on the other hand, the efforts of critics such as Houston Baker and Henry Louis Gates, Jr. to

[52] Houston Baker, 'Generational Shifts and the Recent Criticism of Afro-American Literature', *Black American Literature Forum* 15 (Spring 1981), p. 9.

bring contemporary theoretical concerns to the reading of black literature effected an intervention of black writing in contemporary theoretical debates.[53] Even though large numbers of blacks and members of other minority groups have not been hired by literature faculties, the role of Afro-American and Third-World writing in literary studies has been transformed.

One cannot, though, discuss these issues fruitfully without considering the models by which universities operate and how they may affect critical writing. One can distinguish two general models at work in this period. The first makes the university the transmitter of a cultural heritage, gives it the ideological function of reproducing culture and the social order. The second model makes the university a site for the production of knowledge, and teaching is related to that function: in early years students are taught what they need to know in order to progress to more advanced work; in later years they follow or even assist their teachers' work at the frontiers of a discipline.

The first model – social and cultural reproduction – is linked with the experiments in general education that were so prominent in the years between the wars, from the first Contemporary Civilization proposals at Columbia in 1917, through programs at Amherst College, and the Hutchins College at the University of Chicago, and culminating after the war in Harvard's 'Redbook', as it was known, *General Education in a Free Society* (1945), which Alain Touraine calls 'the supreme expression of the ideology of general education at the very moment when it begins to decline'.[54] By this model the university should be integrated: agreed upon and focused on the heritage it is seeking to transmit. The New Criticism succeeded as well as it did, one could argue, because it could function as a way of making the literary heritage accessible to a growing and more diversified student body entering universities. This model would lead one to expect literature departments to devote considerable energy to controlling the content of offerings and debating what ought to be required of an undergraduate major or a graduate student. It gives criticism the role of interpreting the canon, elucidating the 'core' of knowledge to be conveyed. This model was promoted by the National Endowment for the Humanities under the Reagan administration, which has actively supported and solicited proposals for summer seminars devoted to canonical authors and withdrew

[53] See Henry Louis Gates, Jr, 'Criticism in the Jungle', *Black Literature and Literary Theory* (London; Methuen, 1984).

[54] Alain Touraine, *The Academic System in American Society* (New York: McGraw-Hill, 1974), p. 29.

support from apparently successful programs that did not promote a traditional canon.[55] The *reductio ad absurdum* of this model is the list of constituents of the core in E.D. Hirsch's *Cultural Literacy*.[56]

The other model casts the university as producer of knowledge. Its success is related to the growth of the sciences and of funded scientific research. A university is not an integrated unit commanded by a concept of education so much as an administrative apparatus for managing a series of loosely-integrated activities, each of which follows a particular logic, determined by developments in the discipline, priorities set by funding agencies, or pressing social issues. Aside from elementary courses, what gets taught and what research is conducted will depend more on professors' sense of the important problems in their specialities, or the availability of grants and their success in obtaining them, than on departmental decisions about what should be transmitted to the young. This structure can be conducive to the production of knowledge, because it encourages individual faculty members to pursue, in their teaching and writing, whatever sort of enterprise seems most likely to bring them recognition.

The increasing availability of research grants, a major feature of this model of the university, is a decisive change for literary studies in the post-war period. Before the Second World War, critical scholarship was pursued on one's own time or supported by private means, and very substantial projects, for which today's investigators would expect massive, multi-year grants, were carried out with no subventions. The Guggenheim Foundation's fellowship program, begun in 1925, offered few awards in literary studies (27 in 1925–8 and only 16 in 1937–40) but after the war the numbers increased dramatically: to 176 in 1961–4 and 149 in 1977–80.[57] Fulbright, Rockefeller, and Amercan Council of Learned Societies fellowships increased the number of awards available, and in 1967 the National Endowment for the Humanities began its grant program, with 275 grants totalling $1.8 million, which rose in 1980 to 831 grants totalling $16 million. While Guggenheim and Rockefeller panels have been generally conservative, ACLS and NEH fellowships have supported work in contemporary theory (though since 1985 NEH has resisted funding theoretically-oriented projects by younger scholars). Particularly

---

[55] Cases in point would be the continuing support for many years of a summer institute on Dante and active solicitation of proposals for institutes on classic eighteenth-century texts, on the one hand, and cancellation after the first year of a successful institute on the avant-garde, conducted at Harvard.

[56] E.D. Hirsch, *Cultural Literacy* (New York: Houghton Mifflin, 1987).

[57] John Simon Guggenheim Memorial Foundation, *Reports of the President and Treasurer* (New York, 1979), p. xxxii.

useful have been Mellon Fellowships which enable universities to take in for a year or two young theorists they might be loath to hire permanently.

The availability of grants affects criticism first by producing a new goal: to devise research projects that will obtain awards, and thus to imagine what will impress granting bodies, who draw upon the expertise of other professors. One is encouraged to cast one's project in terms that suggest novelty and breadth of perspective. In addition to encouraging the *appearance* of innovation (which sometimes does generate innovation) the grant system reduces the power of departments and universities over their members, making critics think of a professional peer group as their most important audience. And since this group judges writing, critical writing becomes the chief activity by which one's standing is determined. The increasing availability of grants encourages critics to reflect on their critical activity: in seeking to justify what they propose to do to an audience they take to be representative of the profession, critics help enunciate the rationality of a discipline, generating a *lingua franca* in which new approaches or projects are justified in familiar terms and traditional research is given some new, attractive twist.

Though this model of the university may seem designed for the sciences and is frequently resisted by teachers of literature, it does have certain benefits for the humanities. The emphasis of the first model on shared values and integration of the university can manifest itself as intolerance of dissidence and difference. Analysts have had difficulty in explaining why the percentage of women faculty members *declined* between the 1920s and the Second World War, but this model of the university as reproducer of culture may well bear some responsibility. If so, this would be a further reason to resist the attempt to reimpose this model of the university as transmitter of mainstream culture. The university as loosely-knit producer of knowledge can be more tolerant, allowing people to go their own way as long as they attract students, or research money, or the esteem of their professional peers.

The first model gives criticism the function of elucidating the masterpieces of the cultural heritage that is taught. The second model gives criticism no specific educational function but makes critical progress or innovation the goal of teachers of literature. Critical investigation, in this second model, is simply what professors do: to write criticism is to generate knowledge, and though a canonical body of texts may serve as a starting point, the only prescribed goal is to advance one's understanding of cultural phenomena. This, incidentally, is one reason why the situation of criticism seems confusing today. The now dominant model of the university as a site for the production of knowledge has altered the function of criticism and the role of critical invention.

Universities are structured by the conflict between the model of the production of knowledge and the model of the reproduction of culture. There is tension between them, with local variations that may be quite difficult to interpret. Though the vast expansion of funded scientific research led the second model to become dominant after the War, the play of the two models continues, especially in educational rhetoric. The resistance to literary theory and speculative criticism often takes the form of appeals to the importance of reproducing or transmitting the cultural heritage. Harvard, which has been one of the world's most successful entrepreneurial universities or research consortia, has devoted considerable energy to proclaiming the other model of the university: in the Redbook and then in its Core Curriculum. The relation between these much touted projects and the fortunes of literary criticism at Harvard might repay investigation. One can say in general, though, that despite the importance for recent developments in criticism of the pluralism and interdisciplinarity fostered by the model of the university as producer of knowledge, American criticism is distinguished by the links, produced by universities, between criticism and pedagogy: specifically, between criticism and a pedagogy attempting to cope with America's unparalleled experiment in mass higher education.

Consider the case of American 'reader-response criticism'. European criticism has frequently encouraged consideration of readers and reading. In *Qu'est-ce que la littérature?* Jean-Paul Sartre provides a splendid capsule history based on the social destination and function of French literature. Roman Ingarden's account of *Unbestimmtheitsstellen* or places of indeterminacy shows that an adequate description of literature must treat the text as a formal structure that solicits the activity of an implied reader. Hans-Robert Jauss's aesthetics of reception describes works as responses to questions posed by the 'horizon of expectations' against which they are received. In the United States, however, reader-oriented criticism has received a pedagogical and democratic inflection. I. A. Richards, who first brought the study of readers' responses to criticism and saw poems as devices for creating psychic equilibrium, worked on Basic English and language reforms designed to facilitate reading for the largest possible public. In the 1970s, however, a different step was taken. Stanley Fish was only the first to equate the meaning of a literary work with the reader's experience of it. Hesitations, erroneous conjectures, moments of puzzlement, and so on, are part of a reader's experience and hence inseparable from the work's meaning.[58] The growth in the United States of criticism focused on the experience of readers may stem from its relevance to the common American pedagogical situation in which a teacher confronts a class of inexperienced, puzzled, somewhat recalcitrant readers. Teachers have found it productive to maintain that a student's puzzlement is not a reason for silence but part of the meaning of the text, and thus material for discussion.

The pedagogical context in which criticism is produced has encouraged theories and methods that help generate interpretations, for, ever since the New Criticism, discussion of the meaning of a work is the form that literary instruction most commonly takes. The fate of theoretical movements and discourses in America is tied to the readiness with which they lend themselves to interpretive projects: Marxism and structuralism, which are not fundamentally methods of interpretation but which urge analysis of elaborate mediating systems, have been relatively unsuccessful here (despite the broad appeal in the 1980s of Marxism as means to a political criticism), while the attention to problematical textual details fostered by deconstruction (and its productive framework for thinking about such matters) has more readily found a place in interpretive critical practice.

Finally, the pedagogical link has helped to advance feminist criticism. Since the study of women's literature and women in literature is frequently thematic – concerned with women's experience as a literary theme – it can be pursued in elementary classes and generates considerable excitement for students and teachers. The success of these courses has stimulated work in feminist criticism and given teachers leverage with their departments – freedom to teach those courses that correspond to their critical interests. In our entrepreneurial university, good enrollment in courses may be what permits a faculty member to pursue projects his or her seniors find dubious.

But criticism's link with pedagogy can work in other ways. For the most part, appeal to teaching is a conservative, even reactionary gesture: the suggestion that thinking and writing about literature ought to be controlled by the possibilities of classroom presentation is usually an attempt to dismiss new lines of investigation or abstruse critical writings without confronting them directly. The traditional link between literary studies and the reproduction of culture gives such appeals a plausibility that they would not have in other fields. Few would seriously suggest that physicists or historians should restrict

[58] See Stanley Fish, *Is There a Text in This Class?* (Cambridge, Mass.: Harvard University Press, 1980).

their work to what can be communicated to 19-year-olds. A further complication for literary criticism is that critics teach in departments that devote considerable time to the teaching of foreign languages or of English composition. These tasks fall most heavily on the young and badly paid; and in this situation someone is always prepared to argue that instead of writing another book or teaching a graduate seminar, critics should devote more of their energy to basic education. Those whose critical orientation is out of favor may be especially vociferous in calling their colleagues to abandon difficult speculative or interpretive projects for freshman writing.[59] The American peda-gogic context may have a fundamentally conservative impact, insuring that theoretical reflection cannot go very far by forcing it to justify itself – as it is not so forced to do in France or Germany, for example. Moreover, the teaching of composition can encourage a functional attitude to language, as critics find themselves adopting an ideology of lucidity; and despair at the awkwardness of student prose can encourage a sentimental reverence for anything well-written. The activities of the departments in which it is produced give criticism a situation unlike that of any other form of writing and research. The professional pressure to publish is always countered by forces working against advanced or innovative critical speculation.

In addition to universities, the institutions that have been most important for criticism have been those controlled by universities: university presses and academic journals, and summer institutes run by universities. What the Kenyon School of English and the Indiana School of Letters did for the New Criticism, the School of Criticism and Theory, held first at the University of California at Irvine and then at Northwestern University and at Dartmouth College, has done for recent critical theory. The summer seminars for college teachers organized by the National Endowment for the Humanities, aimed at teachers in colleges that lack graduate programs and library resources, have helped to disseminate the work of advanced criticism to smaller colleges. All such activities increase the emphasis on theoretically informed criticism, affecting the intellectual climate of teachers who are not involved as well as those who are.

Finally, one distinctive feature of current criticism is its lack of connection to a recognized literary avant-garde. The New Criticism succeeded in part because it made it easier for critics discuss modernist

---

[59] For example, E.D. Hirsch, who urged critics to discover authors' intentions in *Validity in Interpretation,* (New Haven: Yale University Press, 1967), and Frederick Crews, champion of the psychoanalysis of characters in fiction in *The Sins of the Fathers* (New York: Oxford University Press, 1966), turned to freshman composition and exhorted others to follow them.

poetry such as Eliot's, while situating it in the tradition of English literature. Cleanth Brooks' *Modern Poetry and the Tradition* helped make the New Criticism indispensable. Moreover, the authority of New Critics such as Ransom, Tate and Penn Warren came in part from their accomplishments as poets. The success of certain aspects of structuralism seemed linked to its ability to make intelligible the literary practices of post-modernism, particularly the French *nouveau roman.* More recent modes of criticism meet special resistance because they cannot be seen as explicating or promoting some new literary practice.

One might conjecture, though, that the power of innovation and defamiliarization, which previously lay with a literary avant-garde, behind which academic criticism lagged, has now passed to criticism. One result of the current organization of criticism in the universities has been the discovery of the capacity to innovate by exposing and questioning the assumptions on which prior critical, literary and cultural practices have depended. If, as Gramsci says, intellectuals in the capitalist state function as 'experts in legitimation', then theoretical criticism might be deemed the place where critiques of legitimacy are continually being carried out – in a quarter where they may seem to pose the least direct threat to social and political institutions. Whatever the political potential of these critiques, which is by no means clear, this possibility seems to have arisen through the transposition of a certain power of literature. The quality of the 'modern', the sense of crisis that literature provokes, now inheres in the critical process of exposing the assumptions of prior discourses. Criticism has built into critical reflection, as a means of innovation, the defamiliarizing analysis of the conditions of possibility of prior interpretations; so that the study of criticism becomes, among other things, the practice of generating questions about discursive knowledge, of reflecting on interpretation itself and pursuing the contestatory movement that used to be associated with avant-garde literature.

I am suggesting that institutional pressures and the interested activities of departments and individuals within professional, disciplinary systems have contributed to criticism's taking on a defamiliarizing, critical role. This is an ironic result, of course, responsible for much of the confusion about the politics of criticism that surrounds us, for these institutional influences cannot but vitiate the innovating, critical effects which they have helped to produce.

We can, then, identify several salient changes in the organization of knowledge in the field of literary studies since the beginning of the century. In 1920 one might have distinguished a realm of taste and a realm of knowledge: the first the domain of public critics, the second the domain of scholars in the university and consisting of historical information. With the success of the New Criticism, an awareness of interpretive possibilities – familiarity with prior interpretations and the possession of one's own interpretations of literary works – became a major form of knowledge. Today, understanding of a range of difficult theoretical discourses has come to count as knowledge in the domain of criticism (universities increasingly expect such knowledge of new PhDs they hire). Finally, as I have just observed, the practice of reflecting on interpretation itself and pursuing the kind of contestatory, self-transcending movement associated with avant-garde literature has now become an activity of literary criticism.

Another way to put this would be to say that formerly the history of criticism was part of the history of literature (the story of changing conceptions of literature advanced by great writers), but that now the history of literature is part of the history of criticism. Specifically, the history of literature in our day depends on what happens in the critical communities in universities: what is canonized, what is explicated, what is articulated as a major problem for literature. One might, of course, suggest that today the literary avant-garde simply *is* literary theory and criticism; but William Drake's remarks of 1926 about the fecundity of the critical spirit and the barrenness of literary production induce caution here. What one can say with confidence is that criticism today, because of its reorganization around an interdisciplinary investigation of signification and its entanglement with the entrepreneurial structure of universities and the processes of professional advancement, bears a new relation to literature. Any attempt to move beyond criticism as it is presently constituted will itself be part of the system of questioning that criticism and its institutions have developed.

2

The Humanities Tomorrow

In *Hedda Gabler* Eilert Lövborg, the reformed rake, has published 'a big book, dealing with the march of civilization', which has made quite a stir; but he confides that 'the real book – the book I have put my true self into' – is the continuation, a book not yet published. 'This one', he says, 'deals with the future'.

'With the future', exclaims George Tesman, a historian. 'But good heavens, we know nothing of the future!'

'No', admits Lövborg, 'but there is a thing or two to be said about it all the same'.

This is very much the situation of those who speak of the future of the humanities or of literary criticism. We know nothing of the future but we invariably find that there is a good deal to be said about it all the same, prophesying, perhaps, that if criticism proceeds on its current course it will bring about the destruction of literary studies, the emptying of the American mind, perhaps the decline of civilization or at least the end of humanistic education as we know it. Talk of the future tempts speakers to produce apocalyptic visions, crisis narratives, in which their fears or dissatisfactions about aspects of present practice can be imaginatively dramatized as tales of disaster, but it nevertheless has its uses. It compels us to imagine the consequences of our actions and in particular to postulate how our thinking, teaching and writing might work itself out in institutions.

Since what we traditionally mean by the humanities – literature, philosophy, history, history of art – are subjects studied in schools and universities and articulated by university teachers, questions about the future of the humanities are increasingly questions about how the concerns and activities of those who teach and write about these materials will function in institutional contexts and what effects they may have. How, for example, will university structures adapt to changing social and political circumstances, such as a cultural situation in which film and television form the common background of members of a culture or a political situation where the threat of right-wing dogmatism looms increasingly large? To reflect on the future of the humanities is in part to imagine, as I have already suggested in chapter 1, how the organization and orientation of disciplines within universities can respond to these situations and to ask how university structures are affecting and are affected by intellectual activity.

In 1984 and 1985 a series of reports on higher education in the United States, sponsored by independent foundations and educational organizations, as well as by the federal government, concurred in identifying 'a crisis of the humanities' in education and emphasizing the need to restore the humanities to their former central role in colleges and universities.[1] Within literary studies themselves, spokesmen for traditional approaches have joined the chorus, mourning the loss of a common culture which they believe has occurred as teachers focus on recondite theoretical issues or else on black literature, women's literature, or writings by other minorities.[2] There are a number of different crisis narratives, but they tell much the same story: once upon a time there was a canon of great cultural monuments, a consensus about what should be taught, and a group of teachers dedicated to the transmission of this material and certain moral values it was thought to entail. Then, for whatever reason – a general questioning of authority, a host of fashionable theories, self-interested professionalism which directed teachers' interests toward increasingly narrow and specialized concerns – everything changed, and if we do not arrest the slide, reverse the tide, stop the rot, or take such action as the chosen metaphor for decline demands, the result will be recondite specialization of a fragmented faculty, chaos in the university, and ignorance and moral imbecility of the students.

The attraction of crisis narratives is their ability to resolve the complex predicament in which teachers and observers find themselves, providing a focused thrill in these situations of proliferation and indeterminacy. Today an interest in theoretical issues and interdisciplinary connections, as well as in the burgeoning literature of any

---

[1] The reports are: *The Conditions of Excellence in American Higher Education* (Washington: National Institute of Education, 1984); William J. Bennett, *To Reclaim a Legacy: A Report on the Humanities in Higher Education* (Washington: National Endowment for the Humanities, 1984); *Integrity in the College Curriculum* (Washington: Association of American Colleges, 1985) and Ernest L. Boyer, *College: The Undergraduate Experience in America*, Carnegie Foundation for the Advancement of Teaching (New York: Harper and Row, 1986)

[2] See W.J. Bate, 'The Crisis in English Studies', *Harvard Magazine* 85:1 (1982), and René Wellek, 'Destroying Literary Studies', *The New Criterion*, December 1983.

particular field, leaves us faced with too many things to read, too much to grasp, too many possibilities. Confronted with the range of materials and problems that threaten a dispersal of effort and loss of direction, the most cheerful thing we can do is to conceive of this situation as one of crisis, hoping thereby to situate ourselves at a decisive moment or turning point. When the problem is precisely that we don't know where we are, find it difficult to collect ourselves among all the possible writings and projects, it is flattering to claim that where we are is precisely a crucial point, perhaps *the* crucial point for the future of an institution, a discipline, or the humanities in general. The lurid rhetoric of crisis seeks to transform our situation from a hapless, even ridiculous diffusion to a decisive, focused condition of choice.

Those who speak of a crisis incline to blame professors and administrators for a failure to defend the old rationale for the humanities – in their view a simple failure of nerve in the face of professional or vocational demands of students on the one hand and the professional demands of academic disciplines on the other. Teachers of literature and the humanities are invited to dismiss the recent tendencies of their disciplines as unfortunate aberrations and to join administrators in promoting a return to old values and requirements.

Attempts to reinstate prior values seldom succeed in any event, but here one can question whether there ever was a consensus about the teaching of literature and the relation of literary criticism or of the study of the humanities generally to ethical and cultural purposes. There is no lack of evidence to suggest that we are mistaken in perceiving a unique crisis and in thinking our own critical situation unusually confusing or confused. As we saw in chapter 1, accusations that critics have 'patronized Nietzsche, found something entertaining in every kind of revolutionist, and welcomed the strangest philosophies' and that 'We stand today at the center of a vast disintegration' can be heard already in the 1920s, at the very beginnings of literary criticism in the United States.[3] Gerald Graff, who attacked contemporary criticism in *Literature Against Itself* for its failure to attend to the social and ethical import of works of literature, has gone on to demonstrate, in a study of the teaching of literature, that recent controversies 'echo old ones as far back as the beginning of the profession'.

When I first began this inquiry I vaguely assumed that the founders of academic literary studies must originally have had a shared idea of their rationale that had somehow got lost along the way. I imagined that this shared rationale had

[3] See pp. 3–4 above. These quotations are from Van Wyck Brooks, *Letters and Leadership* (New York: Huebsch, 1918), p. 35, and William Drake, *American Criticism* (1926) (Freeport NY: Books for Libraries Press, 1967), p. 25.

something to do with concepts like 'humanism' and 'cultural tradition', more or less in the sense associated with the name of Matthew Arnold. What I discovered, however, was that although the transmission of humanism and cultural tradition in the Matthew Arnold sense was indeed the official goal of the literature department, there were from the outset fundamental disagreements about how that goal should be pursued. Early educators who identified themselves with the Matthew Arnold view of literature and culture strenuously objected to the philological and historical scholarship that had qualified literary studies for departmental status in the new research university.[4]

The same complaints about specialization, professionalization and lack of concern for ethical questions animate discussions of literary studies throughout the past century, though the targets of these accusations change. 'It is worth pondering', Graff notes, 'that the kind of scholarship that we now think of as traditionally humanistic was regarded as a subversive innovation by traditionalists of an earlier era'. 'Whatever the sins of recent theory', he concludes,

those who blame the problems of the humanities on them – and on other post-1960 developments – only illustrate their own pet maxim that those who forget the past are condemned to repeat it. The solutions they propose – a return to the great tradition with no investigation of why that tradition has come to be questioned – figure only to send us yet one more time around what we will see has been an oft-repeated cycle.[5]

Teachers who do not wish to promote these solutions – and, indeed, doubt that they could ever be solutions – are none the less placed by the present educational climate in circumstances that invite them to produce a new rationale for the humanities, since the old cannot altogether suffice. What is evoked as the old rationale is universalist and foundationalist. It proposes, roughly, that the humanities, by studying the greatest products of the human spirit, the best that has been thought and written, masterpieces of literature, art, philosophy and history, will provide an understanding of 'man', as we used to say: insights about the human condition but above all basic principles – methodological, epistemological and ethical. Knowledge of literature, history and philosophy would train the moral intelligence, working to produce a community with shared values, and would provide foundations for thought and action.

   [4] Gerald Graff, *Professing Literature: An Institutional History* (Chicago: University of Chicago Press, 1987), pp.2–3.
   [5] Ibid., p. 4

A new rationale is needed not only because the old one seems not to have worked, but also because much of the most interesting recent work in the fields of the humanities has involved critiques of foundationalist and universalist claims. In philosophy, the analytic project turns out not to have brought us closer to firm foundations but to have rendered problematic this conception of the philosophical enterprise: are its investigations truly of a different status from those of other disciplines, so as to empower it to adjudicate other discourses' truth claims, for example?[6] In other realms, the critique of foundationalism emerges particularly in demonstrations that meta-languages are worked by the forces they purport to describe or analyze. The simplest example is the way in which an account of the political forces in a state is itself affected by those forces and thus belongs to the political domain rather than outside it. Notable examples of this ubiquitous structure have been analyzed in psychoanalysis, in literary theory, in philosophy: readings of Freud's case studies show them to be structured by the mechanisms of the very psychic forces which they analyze – operations of condensation, displacement, and repression, for example;[7] literary critics have been astute in identifying in other critical analyzes the transferential replaying of scenarios from the works being interpreted;[8] philosophical discussions have shown, for instance, that a philosophical discourse on metaphor does not escape or get outside metaphor.[9] The difficulties of the foundationalist project are nowhere better illustrated than in its most ambitious modern version, Jürgen Habermas's attempt to ground rationality in norms presupposed by the exercise of language, or communicative action. Even this shrewdly limited modern version of foundationalism has been found wanting in numerous ways, as we shall see in chapter 11.

Universalist assumptions have fared no better. We have become alert to what is left out when 'the best that has been thought and written' is selected or when discussion focuses on 'man'. We have

[6] See Richard Rorty, *Philosophy and the Mirror of Nature* (Princeton: Princeton University Press, 1979).

[7] On Freud, see Samuel Weber, *The Legend of Freud* (Minneapolis: University of Minnesota Press, 1982); Jeffrey Mehlman, 'Trimethylamin', *Diacritics* 6:1 (1976); and Cynthia Chase, 'Oedipal Textuality: Reading Freud's Reading of Oedipus', in *Decomposing Figures* (Baltimore: Johns Hopkins University Press, 1986).

[8] See Barbara Johnson, *The Critical Difference* (Baltimore: Johns Hopkins University Press, 1980), ch 1; Shoshana Felman, 'Turning the Screw of Interpretation', in *Literature and Psychoanalysis* (Baltimore: Johns Hopkins University Press, 1982).

[9] See Jacques Derrida, 'La mythologie blanche', *Marges de la philosophie* (Paris: Minuit, 1972); Paul de Man, 'The Epistemology of Metaphor', *Critical Inquiry* 5:1 (1978).

learned to ask whether universalist claims do not in fact promote as a norm the concerns of a particular group and set aside as partial or limited those of other groups. Characteristically in literary studies, for instance, a boy's experience of growing up has been deemed universal and the girl's marginal. The critique here takes two forms: on the one hand, the demonstration of what has been excluded by a particular humanistic canon and on the other hand, the questioning of the centralizing and universalizing project itself, which is necessarily exclusionary and ideological, whatever the intentions of its agents. The idea of a humanistic core entails the designation of peripheries, and one must reflect on the effects of relegation to the periphery.

Of course, advocates of a core are not in the least disturbed at the prospect of making decisions about what is central and what is marginal. On the contrary, they relish the power to declare, for instance, that '*Benedict Arnold* is part of national cultural literacy; *eggs Benedict* isn't'.[10] However, E.D. Hirsch, from whose best-selling *Cultural Literacy* this example comes, is clearly sensitive to the charge that his list of what every American needs to know describes the culture of a particular group, which he seeks to impose upon an entire nation, and he devotes a good deal of energy to arguing that a national culture, like a national language, belongs to no group (groups have their own particular culture) but is a construct, even an arbitrary construction, like a language. 'History has decided' what the elements of national culture are, and there is no more point to arguing about this than to arguing about spelling (p. 107). He claims that his list is purely descriptive, containing 'words that appear in newspapers, magazines, and books without explanation' (p. 146). But of course the point of his project is to promote a norm and, interestingly, when he comes to science he immediately, without qualms, abandons his descriptive claim, choosing to list not the scientific terms that literate Americans in fact know but those 'truly essential to a broad grasp of a major science' (p. 148). The list, that is, no longer identifies references culturally literate Americans share but what they ought to know, and thus it is both revealing and a cause for concern that his list seems to give more weight, for instance, to Australia than to Africa: Brisbane appears, but not Ghana, Addis Ababa, Accra, Lagos or Tangiers; Canberra but not Cameroon, Kenya, Chad or Ivory Coast; Tasmania but not Somalia, Uganda or Zaire.

Hirsch's *Cultural Literacy* proposes, however, not a core or a canon – the books on his list are works 'that culturally literary people have

[10]   E. D. Hirsch, *Cultural Literacy: What Every American Needs To Know* (Boston: Houghton Mifflin, 1987), p. 26.

read about but haven't read' (p. xiv) – and at one level his project challenges universalist and foundationalist presumptions. To rebut the charge of imposing a particular group's culture, he insists that the contents of the common national culture are arbitrary and that what matters is not what everyone knows but that they all know the same things (since all communication is founded on shared information). Americans must know about Shakespeare, not because Shakespeare is superior to Dante, Racine or Goethe, but because other Americans know about Shakespeare. 'It is cultural chauvinism and provincialism to believe that the content of our vocabulary is something either to recommend or to deplore by virtue of its inherent merit' (p. 107). This rationale undercuts the foundationalist project, which claims precisely to select the best for its inherent merit, or at least the best of the Western cultural tradition, whose superiority is not thought to require demonstration.

To give a clearer focus to this issue one might consider the case of St John's College, Annapolis, a college whose Great Books curriculum is often hailed as exemplary by those arguing for a traditional canon of masterpieces to be read by everyone, and which actually promotes serious reading and discussion rather than simply acquaintance with a body of past material. As I was preparing an earlier version of this discussion, I received a letter from the Dean of St John's inviting me to deliver a lecture. 'I do not know how much you know about St John's', he wrote, 'so let me describe it briefly. St John's is a small, non-church-related liberal arts college. We have an all-required four-year curriculum based on reading and discussion of the best works in the Western tradition we can find'. (This evokes an image of the St John's faculty earnestly combing the shelves of the library to see what great works they can unearth.) 'Our curriculum', the Dean continues, 'does not get much more modern than the 1920s, and we do not study such things as literary criticism as such. . . . A Great Books curriculum, by its nature, does not include many books written by women, and it has become a matter of some concern here to think about how to address that problem'.

A good deal could be said about the conception of 'greatness' that, even in the 1980s, yields a corpus of works written by white males prior to 1920. The Dean's letter suggests, and a visit to the college confirms, that the St John's faculty is at once uncomfortable at what their universalist principles exclude and devoted to the principle of a canon of 'the best'. They can therefore be engaged in debate on two quite different fronts: on the one hand, by the argument that certain excluded works (written by women, by blacks, or since 1920) would serve the declared purposes of the canon better than some of those that are included and thus that the application of the principle of greatness has not been as disinterested as they believe; and on the other hand by the demonstration of the specific ideological character of the operative conception of greatness and of the very idea of a canon. One thing the humanities ought to teach is diversity. If this goal is to remain effectively in view, one must be prepared both to marshall arguments to rectify the exclusions of a particular canon and to harass the canonizing impulse. In an important sense humanity is one, but perhaps more important, given the traditional rationales for the humanities, humanity is plural: *humanities*, we ought perhaps to remind ourselves occasionally, is *humanity* in the plural. 'The central function of imaginative literature', writes William Empson, 'is to make you realize that other people act on moral convictions different from your own'.[11] A particular virtue of literature, of history, of anthropology, is instruction in otherness: vivid, compelling evidence of differences in cultures, mores, assumptions, values. At their best, these subjects make otherness palpable and make it comprehensible without reducing it to an inferior version of the same, as a universalizing humanism threatens to do. The dramatization of graspable plurality is one of its major duties.

There are difficult theoretical issues here that require continuing debate: should one, in the interests of the representation of otherness, seek to include a 'representative' sampling of works from non-Western traditions and from minority traditions within Western culture? Are we, in fact, aiming at a multi-racial international canon – a comprehensive Whitman's sampler or Cooks tour? Should we not insist, rather, on the necessity of reading works in relation to other works of their traditions and thus resist the idea of a more comprehensive canon, countering it with a series of deeper, more locally-accurate studies? The debate about ends must be pursued, but it suggests, as a practical political strategy, the appropriateness of action on both fronts at once: transformation of the canon and resistance to canons. When dealing with American materials, for instance, the humanities can advance awareness of cultural difference by promoting both the conception of more comprehensive canons and the notion of American culture as an arena of competing, marginalized, suppressed interests, situations, traditions, rather than as a common possession.

A perspicuous program for the humanities tomorrow thus ought not, it seems to me, to conform to a principle of unity but may be a series of divided, not entirely compatible imperatives. Such

---

[11]   William Empson, *Milton's God* (London: Chatto, 1965), p. 261.

imperatives, like the doubled injunction to transform canons and resist canons, structure a space of action and debate with a division that may be a condition of intellectual vigilance and vitality.

A crucial problem for the future of the humanities is the relation of the humanistic education to a 'common culture'. Since 'the humanities' means both non-scientific culture and a group of departments in universities, rationales for the humanities tend to presume that teachers in these departments should transmit culture, introduce the students to the materials that will constitute a common culture. William Bennett, as the US Secretary of Education, championed the view that to return to 'standards' in education would be to return to a canon of the Greeks, the Renaissance, Shakespeare, and those moments of American history calculated to flatter patriotism. Cultural proliferation and specialization are always potential subjects for complaint, especially for those who see education as the transmission of a common heritage (familiarity with a series of cultural monuments) rather than training in habits of critical thinking. But when one thinks about the future of our multi-lingual, multi-racial society, one finds it hard seriously to imagine the establishment of a common culture based on the Greeks or other classics. Such common culture as we have will inevitably be based on the mass media – especially films and television. The point to stress is that students are already in a culture when they reach universities, and they remain to some extent in the same culture whatever books we decide to assign or require. We may occasionally think of at least some of our students as *tabulae rasae*, but if that were true our tasks might be easier – certainly different. The humanities in universities cannot simply constitute culture but necessarily undertake cultural critique.

Complaints about failures of the humanities seem to me frequently to misunderstand this situation. The humanities are said to neglect the shaping of the moral intelligence, leaving a vacuum, but there is no vacuum here. The problem is rather a dubious plenitude: what television programs most imperiously do, for example, is to form a mainstream moral intelligence. The main constraints on plot structures and generally on what can be represented involve conceptions of good and evil, of innocence and guilt, and of the limited scenarios in which they should figure. Political commentators have expressed surprise that Americans watching the Iran–Contra affair hearings on television should have responded so favorably to Colonel Oliver North, but in fact the code of a relevant television genre establishes a perfect vehicle for North's posturings. The basic plot of the action and police serials that flood the evening airways pits a results-oriented officer or activist against a bureaucracy that finds his methods inappropriate and refuses to recognize that he is the most effective servant of its genuine interests. Whether the agent is a tough policeman willing to cut corners to catch criminals (Hunter), or an independent detective or adventurer who works outside the government system but for the interests it is supposed to protect (the Equalizer), viewers have learned to trust that his commitment to justice will excuse his deceptions and illegalities, preventing them from going wrong. Viewers expect the authorities ultimately to overlook the irregular procedures that helped achieve desired results. North's scenario, which cast him as the man of action working around a bureaucracy to advance a cause he believed in and to which his government was committed, came from a generic formula of the medium in which he appeared, and viewers could scarcely help but accept him in the familiar role. Reflection on the moral intelligence established by television might have predicted this result but would also predict that viewers would swiftly lose interest in North, as they turned back to other familiar action dramas, whose heroes actually achieve desirable results. It is ironic for conservatives to complain that television has produced a generation without values, when television in fact promotes precisely the values to which they often subscribe.

The problem, in short, is scarcely that the media do not promote values. Advertising too is concerned to represent to Americans what it sees as the major dilemmas that should concern a contemporary consciousness and the values on which decisions should be based. In this situation, the humanities have above all a critical, adversarial relation to a culture already firmly in place. To speak as if culture were produced by required courses is hopelessly to mistake the situation. E.D. Hirsch initially speaks of cultural literacy as a knowledge of the referents of words that national journals do not explain, but such literacy must be completed by the inculcation of what he calls 'a civil religion that underlies our civil ethos', which includes 'the belief that the conduct of the nation is guided by a vaguely defined God', as well as beliefs in American 'practicality, ingenuity, inventiveness, independent-mindedness, its connection with the frontier and its beneficence in the world' (pp. 98–9).

Hirsch maintains that 'There is no point in arguing about our civil religion or our vocabulary. They are our national givens, our starting points. Our civil religion defines our broadly-shared values as a society' (p. 103). But precisely such notions of the United States's special beneficence and divine mission have contributed to blind self-righteousness in the application of American power, and a goal of education in the United States ought to be the critique of such nationalistic pieties and myths. There are many strategies that can be adopted but most involve using our texts – literary, historical, philosophical, artistic – including the 'sacred texts' that are supposed to support this secular religion, for critical leverage against elements of this common culture. Once again this requires compelling representations of other values, other dilemmas, other choices, and the encouragement of critiques of whatever is taken for granted.

Here disciplines such as comparative literature can be particularly important, for, notoriously, comparative literature is defined as literary study that does not take a national literature as the natural and inevitable unit of study and thus is not linked to the pieties of nationalisms and their secular religions. Every comparatist will have favorite examples of how knowledge of other literatures deflates the partisan pretensions of nationalistic critics: how Spanish conceptions of the originality of Cervantes are qualified when he is read in relation to Boccaccio and the tradition of the novella or how the conception of Coleridge as the fountainhead of modern criticism is modified by the demonstration that he got most of his ideas from unacknowledged Germans. Comparative literature, with its broader vision, exercises a critical demystificatory force on the cultural pieties of a nation.

Hirsch's book, with its presumption that a national culture is the one that matters and his unabashed promotion of American secular religion, makes clear the pertinence of such critiques today – not only in literary studies but in other disciplines as well. Equally important is the critique of other cultural pieties of the Western tradition, where once again literary studies leads the way, exposing Eurocentric notions about the nature of 'man'. The study of women's writing reveals the contingency and partiality of dominant male traditions. The inclusion of Black literature – Black women's writing, for example – in discussions of the novel complicates our association of the novel with the rise of the European bourgeoisie and the assumption that the European novel's ways of posing questions about the insertion of subjects in social experience are the necessary and crucial ones. Third World writing helps to situate European writings in a larger spectrum of possibilities and impels more perspicacious readings of their ideologies, identifying forms of cultural racism at work in our readings of other cultures and our definition of a Western tradition. 'The Orient in 18th century English or French literature' is a classic literary subject, but now literary studies involves analysis of the production of 'the Orient' and the role of that production in the construction of Western culture.

Indeed, the developments effected by 'theory' in the field of literary studies which I sketched in chapter 1 give universities the potential to respond to this cultural situation. The capaciousness of current theory

authorizes unorthodox juxtapositions of literary, historical, sociological, anthropological and psychoanalytic materials; and the institutionalization of the drive to find new questions and new objects of study makes possible wide-ranging studies of the production of signification which ignore traditional disciplinary boundaries. Through this combination of expansion of boundaries and critique of
✗ the principles at work in the construction of objects of analysis, the humanities becomes an active, contentious domain.

To the authors of the reports which argue that the duty of the humanities is above all to reflect and transmit culture and to instill
✗ values rather than critiques of value that may leave students not knowing what to believe, one can reply that examples from the past show that there is little danger of our writing and teaching not reflecting our age, not transmitting our culture. We will do so willy-nilly, most powerfully in ways that we do not recognize; hence we can engage our energies in the critical enterprise, using always the best works we can find for this purpose, which will not always be
✗ canonical. Black literature, Third-World writing, not to say women's writing can have powerful critical effects – but so, of course, can works of the canon, which provide critical leverage against a cultural tradition that may pay them lip service but does not in fact know what they might teach.

This is a point that deserves emphasis, for there should be no question of avoiding canonical texts. They are often, as deconstructive readings of the great works of English and German romanticism have
✗ shown, the most powerful demystifiers of the ideologies they have been said to promote. They may exercise even greater critical force than exotic texts from other traditions, whose very strangeness tends to make the reading of them a process of naturalization, a matter of fitting them to our own categories.

The humanities, in sum, should teach reading. This is not a unified imperative because reading comes in many forms. There is no reason to believe that these should be standardized, that any comprehensive theory of interpretation could or should provide the rationale for the humanities. The plural form, *the humanities*, brings together different ways of treating the texts that surround and support us: ways of exploring overt, covert, or even absent messages – messages striking in their absence. Strong forms of reading are often attacked as subverting the bases of the humanities, but it is that postulation of a repressive basis that we have to resist, challenging other reading strategies instead by critical examination of their premises and results, remembering above all that universities and especially the humanities are the home for the most extreme pursuits and investigations of the intelligence. Accepted forms of thought can take care of themselves; the task of 'rationales' is to protect and encourage the innovative and unconventional.

Indeed, it seems increasingly apparent that proposals for a return to the canon are not committed to the serious investigation of any particular materials or important issues. William Bennett's embrace of Hirsch's list of items to be identified confirms what one might already have suspected: that what is at stake is the repression of critical reading, the deflection of the sorts of critical analysis – deconstructive, Foucauldian, psychoanalytic, Marxist, feminist – that have come to recent prominence. If one inquires further what is at stake in these proposals, one is struck by the fact that in literary studies, at least, a return to the traditional canon would eliminate above all courses in women's writing, which are often among the most successful and energetic regions of our literary curricula, courses where literary works are having palpable effects on students' lives. The call for a return to the traditional canon, and especially the classics, which would proscribe all such courses, looks like another attempt in the field of social policy to reassert patriarchal authority.

These repressive inclinations, disguised as plausible proposals to improve an educational system in dire need, make it the more imperative that we work to protect what is frequently called the chaos of contemporary theory – at the very least that we not allow the term *chaos* to frighten us into futures less capacious than we might desire. A 'normal criticism', elucidating masterpieces within given parameters, is not something we need be nostalgic for. Criticism goes with crisis, itself generates a rhetoric of crisis, insofar as it calls one to rethink the canon and to reflect on the order of a culture's discourses and the relations among them.

If the first imperative for the humanities tomorrow doubles a call for the expansion of humanistic canons with a critique of the project and mechanisms of canon-formation, and if the second couples a critique of cultural values with a enlistment of canonical texts in that critique, the third imperative divides between the professional and amateur orientations of the humanities. One danger associated with calls for a new rationale for the humanities is that the importance of the humanities for general education will lead to rationales based on a role in undergraduate education, as though the principal justification for work in the humanities must be the contribution they make to the formation of what we used to call, in the days before diets and fitness, the 'well-rounded' student. Deans and administrators frequently incline to associate the humanities with general education, and this assumption underlies the reports on higher education mentioned earlier. It often serves those of us who work within the humanities themselves as an ideologically acceptable way of dismissing approaches or concerns that we find recondite. We should therefore not only bear in mind but publicly affirm that thought in the humanities, as elsewhere, becomes truly valuable and interesting only as it becomes extreme: the goal is the most advanced, most self-reflective, most rigorous, most subtle work possible. Even if we cannot live by or live up to the extremities of thought but must retreat to compromises tending to cliches, we must not advance a rationale for the humanities that turns from its frontiers, from the furthest reaches of lines of thought. Since recent reports on education make the specialization or professionalization of humanistic disciplines the scapegoats for a general cultural situation, we must assert the value not just of specialization but of professionalization also, explaining how professionalization makes thought possible by developing sets of questions, imposing norms which have then to be questioned and thereby promoting debate on key problems. Thought *can* flourish under utilitarian pressures, but it also needs discursive spaces where it can pursue questions as far as possible without knowing what general use or relevance the answers might prove to have. To say, as we should, that philosophy or literary criticism must be free to set its own agendas is to take steps towards establishing a critical or self-critical space within which discoveries and critiques can take place.

But this defense of specialization must be accompanied by the recognition that texts do not belong to particular disciplines or departments. There should be no monopolies in the humanities. The objects that interest us are in general accessible to a non-specialized public, which is frequently also ourselves, as we move from one field to another: literary critics look at paintings or read history or philosophy, and philosophers or art critics do readings of literary works. The rights of the amateur should be asserted, for the amateur's perspective has special value. Encouraging the application of one discourse to another, it provides critical corrections of the assumptions of disciplines and generates new insights, as well as errors that can lead specialists to rethink what needs to be said to prevent them.

This imperative, then, calls for unconstrained specialization on the one hand, and cross-disciplinary amateurism on the other. What it does not call for and thus implicitly combats is the middle ground of a discipline governed by a gentlemanly ideal: anti-professionalism, an idea of specialization associated with collecting, and hence the presumption of connections between expertise and disciplinary ownership of texts. One of the familiar crisis narratives blames our present difficulties and future plight on increasing professional specialization, but as I suggested in chapter 1, this has its compensating strengths – an encouragement of innovation, for example – and one must remind oneself of the alternatives which the opponents of professionalism promote: a vision of the humanities as repository of known truths and received values, which a dedicated non-professional corps of workers present to the young. This middle ground the divided imperative seeks to avoid. A call for professionalism and amateurism treats the humanities as fields of exploration and critique rather than materials for transmission. A professional/amateur imperative promotes a divided and contentious future but, I think, an engaging and productive one.

In pursuing these imperatives, the humanities must make their way between, on the one hand, a traditional, foundationalist conception of their task and, on the other, the so-called 'new pragmatism' to which some critics of foundationalism have retreated. If philosophy is not a foundationalist discipline, argues Richard Rorty, then it is simply engaged in a conversation; it tells stories, which succeed simply by their success.[12] Since there is no standard or reference point outside the system of one's beliefs to appeal to, critical arguments and theoretical reflections can have no purchase on these beliefs or the practices informed by them.[13] Ironically, then, the claim that philosophers and theoreticians tell stories, which originates as a critique of ideology – what presents itself as objective reason is in fact a narrative promoting some interests and obscuring others – becomes a way of protecting a dominant ideology and its professionally successful practitioners from the scrutiny of argument, by deeming that critique can have no leverage against everyday beliefs and that theoretical arguments have no consequences. This pragmatism, whose complacency seems altogether appropriate to the Age of Reagan, subsists only by a theoretical argument of the kind it in principle opposes, as an ahistorical 'preformism': what one does must be based on one's beliefs, but since there are no foundations outside the system of one's beliefs, the only thing that could logically make one change a belief is something which one already believes. We have abundant evidence, however, that critique is one of the historical forces that produces change – in beliefs, in practices and in institutional arrangements – and we can therefore seek, by our own arguments and other activities to demonstrate, as Christopher Norris puts it, 'that

[12] Richard Rorty, *Consequences of Pragmatism* (Minneapolis: University of Minnesota Press, 1982).
[13] See Steven Knapp and Walter Benn Michaels, 'Against Theory', in *Against Theory: Literary Studies and the New Pragmatism*, ed. W.J.T. Mitchell (Chicago: University of Chicago Press, 1986).

enlightened critique is *not* a concept disposed of by pragmatist arguments; that cultural forms of life *can* be understood and criticized on terms not their own; and that the powers of theoretical reflection are *not* exhausted in the recounting of first-order myths and narrative'.[14] A more serious obstacle than pragmatist objections are the difficulties of predicting the consequences of our actions, of imagining what projects might succeed and what will fail – difficulties compounded by any doubling or division of an imperative.

How are divided imperatives to be obeyed? One may explore the possibility of heeding both parts of an injunction in substantial projects of research, reflection and teaching, but one may well have to choose one side or the other. In *Professing Literature* Gerald Graff proposes that we make our theoretical disagreements the subject of discussion in teaching the humanities, that we teach not the texts themselves but how we situate ourselves in reference to those texts and thus exploit the disagreements about theoretical assumptions and frameworks that animate humanistic fields. Such a reflexive turn is by no means a general solution, but for the several double imperatives that I have put forward, the future is perhaps best imagined as an ongoing debate, where the conflicting members of each pair are pursued and their conflicts explored. This is not an easy condition, since whatever work one did in following one imperative would be vulnerable to the critiques of the other, but instead of the complacency of the new pragmatism, one would at least have the continuing argument that encourages reflection and prevents the reification of the humanities into given truths or lifeless texts.

---

[14]   Christopher Norris, *The Conflict of Faculties* (London: Methuen, 1985), p. 163.

3

The Call to History

A common theme these days in the realm of critical theory is the call for literary criticism and theory to take up a relationship to history, both by confronting the question of their insertion in social and political history and by taking account of their own history. Most often, this call to history comes from those who proceed not to show how this could be done but rather to accuse others of failing to attend to history, charging them, finally, with 'privileging literature' (a curious complaint, when one reflects that people do not accuse physicists of privileging physics). Indeed, the favorite way of making criticism political these days is to write articles attacking other critics for ignoring history or politics.

I wish, however, to discuss issues arising from the work of two writers who have risked doing what others merely evoke: Terry Eagleton, whose history of contemporary criticism, *Literary Theory: An Introduction*, has achieved a deserved popular success, and Michel Foucault, who in the United States is most often cited as the model for a historical and political criticism. Taken together, they illustrate some of the difficulties attendant on this call to history and identify problems that particularly deserve our attention.

Eagleton's witty narrative, a lively account of major developments in literary theory since what he calls 'The Rise of English', has a simple story to tell: each new method or critical orientation is one more bourgeois attempt to paper over the contradictions of capitalism or to flee 'the nightmare of modern history'. 'Literature, we are told, is vitally engaged with the living situations of men and women. . . . The story of modern literary theory, paradoxically, is the story of the flight from such realities into a seemingly endless range of alternatives: the poem itself, the organic society, eternal verities, the imagination, the structure of the human mind, myth, language, and so on'.[1] For Eagleton, these alternatives are almost equally deluded, so that the history of criticism, which to others seems chaotic and difficult, has for him a certain predictable simplicity.

Nevertheless, there is a concerted attempt to place theory and criticism in history. The call to history takes three forms: first, the demand that criticism and theory take some responsibility for the historical plight of their societies and work for change; second, the claim that literary works should be studied as products of historical circumstances; and third, the demand that criticism should take account of its own historical character, as a product of the society to whose culture it contributes. There is considerable movement among these three ways of 'being historical', but they can be considered in turn.

The first emerges in Eagleton as a concluding complaint about each mode of literary theory: whatever its virtues, it proves unhistorical, neglects concrete social and political issues. This reproach not only provides a way of bringing together otherwise disparate activities, which become different styles of evasion, but is also responsible for much of the easy, engaging tone of the exposition. Eagleton can dip into New Criticism, or phenomenology, or reader-response criticism for a reasonably sympathetic account, and then disengage swiftly and easily with the observation that this is all very well, but 'will reading Mallarmé bring down the bourgeois state?' (p. 190). Or thus: 'it became less and less clear how responding to Marvell around the seminar table was to transform the mechanized labour of factory workers' (p. 43). Again: in following Leavis one seemed to be addressing fundamental questions relevant to the lives of the oppressed, 'but it was also conceivable that you were destructively cutting yourself off from such men and women who might be a little slow to recognize how a poetic enjambment enacted a movement of physical balancing' (p. 35). In Eagleton's history, most critical movements begin in some promising way, but the greater the prospect of social and political relevance, the more bathetic the failure he ends by proclaiming. 'The whole *Scrutiny* project', he writes, 'was at once hair-raisingly radical and really rather absurd' (p. 34).

This call to history is what enables Eagleton to write easily about each of the movements he identifies and then pull free without engaging the more difficult evaluative questions, such as how far and

---

[1] Terry Eagleton, *Literary Theory: An Introduction* (Oxford: Blackwell, 1983), p. 196. Quotations from this work will henceforth be identified in the text only by page numbers.

in what ways one critical movement really differs from another; are these differences advances, or are they ideological shifts that cannot be easily evaluated? But this perspective, responsible for whatever cogency and continuity his critical history has, also makes it impossible for him to include a chapter on Marxist criticism – though Marxism has been a significant mode of twentieth-century literary theory. Marxist criticism would be immediately vulnerable to the reproaches directed at other modes of criticism: can a Marxist reading of *Clarissa* prevent the exploitation of workers? Will discussion of Fredric Jameson around the seminar table help stop the arms race? Eagleton complains that 'the great majority of the literary theories outlined in this book have strengthened rather than challenged the assumptions of the power system' (p. 195), but this is a difficult test to apply. It would certainly be hard to determine whether the criticism of Terry Eagleton or Fredric Jameson has strengthened or weakened the power structure, given the argument that the university and its pluralistic ideology are strengthened to the degree that Marxist discourse becomes an internal variant rather than external opposition. If we look to Eagleton's discussion for help in applying the test, we do find an example: the power system, he claims, is strengthened by the assumption of most literary theory that 'at the center of the world is the contemplative individual self, bowed over its book, striving to gain touch with experience, truth, reality, history, or tradition' (p. 196). But this would make deconstructive critiques of the subject a subversive form of literary theory – something Eagleton seems disposed to deny.

The first call to history thus not only renders most critical approaches equivalent but raises a more serious problem: it seems to transform into an initial test or point of departure the exceedingly difficult question of the political effects of a theoretical orientation – a question requiring broad understanding and a good deal of hindsight. The evident difficulties of calculating the social effects of well-known critical work of the past indicates the unreliability of any advance judgments we would make in trying to choose a historically responsible approach to literature.

In fact, the question of whether literary theory or criticism can have strong social and political effects is somewhat murky in Eagleton. Swift to dismiss any such pretensions of twentieth-century criticism, he is strangely eager to grant claims for the social effect of literary study put forward in the nineteenth century. The study of English literature, his opening chapter argues, was devised in order to prevent social revolution by providing a pacifying substitute for religion and by giving women and the children of the working classes a sense of a stake in the culture and instruction in timeless truths that would distract them from their immediate circumstances. 'If the masses are not thrown a few novels, they may react by throwing up a few barricades' (p. 25). While rejecting later theorists' claims that avant-garde literature and theory might disrupt bourgeois ideology, he seems to accept at face value the claims of conservative Victorian ideologues that literary study 'will promote sympathy and fellow-feeling among all classes'. Can one not retort, in Eagleton's own mode, that you won't keep the working classes from throwing up barricades by throwing them a few novels?

Eagleton does not consider the relation between his two views of the political efficacy of literary theory and literary study. In fact, given the intractable difficulties of determining, either in the past or the present, which forms of literary theory strengthen and which challenge the assumptions of the power system, Eagleton falls back on another standard of evaluation, which I earlier identified as the second form of the call to history. The test becomes what he calls 'the flight from real history': theories are found wanting for their 'obstinate, perverse', endlessly resourceful refusal to countenance social and historical realities' (p. 196) – a test which doubtless seems much easier to apply. But Eagleton offers us surprisingly little evidence of what form this countenancing of history in literary studies should take, except when he describes Eliot's *The Waste Land* as a response to the crisis of European society (global war, severe class conflict, failing capitalist economies) – a response suggesting that these 'might be resolved by turning one's back on history altogether and putting mythology in its place. . . . Eliot accordingly published *The Waste Land* in 1922, a poem which intimates that fertility cults hold the clue to the salvation of the West' (p. 41).

This sort of contextual interpretation does not seem especially promising – certainly not revolutionarily so – and this is one of the major problems in the 'history' so frequently evoked in contemporary theory. Indeed, in his Conclusion Eagleton calls not for more historical interpretation of this kind but for a *rhetoric* which would study the kinds of effects discourses produce and how they produce them. The first call to history (the call to political commitment) runs the twin risks of making most critical theory pretty much equivalent, on the one hand, and of treating as a point of departure the complicated calculus of political effects that can only be made after considerable analysis and with benefit of hindsight. The second call to history founders on the vagueness of 'countenancing' and encounters all the old problems of contextual interpretation.

The third form of the call to history emerges in Eagleton's attempt to show that critical theory arises from historical circumstances. A strong argument is made in his opening chapter, which focuses less on a particular version of critical theory than on the rise of literary study; but in later chapters the connections become less specific and convincing; theoretical approaches are presented as responses to the 'nightmare of modern history' or as imaginary solutions to real historical dilemmas. 'Phenomenology sought to solve the nightmare of modern history by withdrawing into a speculative sphere where eternal certainty lay in wait; as such it became a symptom, in its solitary, alienated brooding, of the very crisis it offered to overcome' (p. 61). 'In recentering the world on the human subject, phenomenology was providing an imaginary solution to a grievous historical problem' (p. 58). Or again, Heidegger's philosophy 'provided one imaginary solution to the crisis of modern history as fascism provided another' (p. 66). As for post-structuralism, it was 'a product of that blend of euphoria and disillusion, liberation and dissipation, carnival and catastrophe, which was 1968' (p. 142). Structuralism, he argues,

was not just a matter of shutting out something as general as the world; it was a question of discovering some toehold of certainty in a particular world where certainty seemed hard to come by. The lectures which make up Saussure's *Course in General Linguistics* were delivered in the heart of Europe between 1907–1911, on the brink of a historical collapse which Saussure did not live to see. These were precisely the years when Edmund Husserl was formulating the major doctrines of phenomenology, in a European center not far removed from Saussure's Geneva.[2]

If the historical analysis of his first chapter is more convincing than these later historical explanations, which make these theoretical movements interchangeable, deluded responses to something called 'historical crisis' or 'historical collapse', it is no doubt because of the greater specificity of the connections made and because of Eagleton's concern there with the institutions of literary study – a concern

[2] Ibid., p. 110. This example of historical explanation scarcely inspires confidence in the results of taking account of history. One should also note in passing that Eagleton's discussion of structuralism devises so bizarre a caricature that he cannot find examples to illustrate it. For instance, he claims that for the structuralist 'all surface features of the work could be reduced to an essence, a single central meaning which informed all the work's aspects' (p. 112), when in fact structuralism is distinguished by its anti-essentialism and its interest in discovering how a work means rather than what it means. Eagleton must caricature structuralism, it seems, because the task he assigns his new Marxist rhetoric, of analysing signifying practices in general ('studying how discourse is structured and organized, and examining what kinds of effects these forms and devices produce in particular readers' [p. 205]) is that of structuralism and semiotics, which thus must be set aside as a preposterous sort of essentialism.

generally lacking in the later chapters. The problem, it might seem, is that he lacks a well-thought-out model of critical history but is content for the most part to accept current notions of major critical schools – New Criticism, reader-response criticism, structuralism, post-structuralism – and see each as a response to the major wars or crises of civilization that occurred prior to their appearance, or at least in the same decade.

The person who has taught us to analyse history through institutionally situated discursive practices is, of course, Michel Foucault, whose accounts of the formations of disciplinary discourses, and whose identification of historical investigation first with the analysis of the formation rules for discourses of a period, and then with the study of relations between knowledge and power, have inspired new sorts of history. In an article entitled 'The Problem of Textuality: Two Exemplary Positions', Edward Said sets Foucault against Derrida in what he calls a 'collision' that 'has, I think, a remarkably significant bearing for contemporary criticism'. 'Derrida's criticism moves us *into* the text, Foucault's *in* and *out*'.[3]

Here Foucault is used to stage a decision for American criticism – whether to follow Derrida into the text or Foucault in and out. The situation is frequently presented in these terms: Derrida says 'il n'y a pas de hors texte' [there is no outside-the-text] and Foucault is said to reply, 'there is so! – there's history, there's power'. Foucault is seen as providing a call to or model for historical and political criticism that would relate texts to historically-defined forces. He encourages this view by, for example, what he calls a principle of exteriority: 'we must not go from discourse towards its interior, hidden nucleus, towards the heart of a thought or a signification supposed to be manifested in it; but, on the basis of discourse itself, its appearance and its regularity, go towards its external conditions of possibility'.[4] There is a rejection of hermeneutics in favor of an investigation of what makes a discursive practice possible.

Foucault seems to be used in two ways here. First he is praised for making the investigation of discourse a historical enterprise, looking at conditions of possibility, systems of rules, disciplinary practices of a period. This conception of his historical project goes along with a story about Foucault as a structuralist who converted, abandoned a

---

[3] Edward Said, *The World, the Text, and the Critic* (Cambridge, Mass: Harvard University Press, 1983), pp. 214 and 183.

[4] Michel Foucault, *L'Ordre du discours* (Paris: Gallimard, 1971), p. 55.

privileging of language or literature, turned, shall we say, from words to things, or at least to what those who promote him are inclined to regard as real historical forces: 'reality' rather than writing. 'The history which bears and determines us', Foucault declares at what is seen as a moment of conversion, 'has the form of a war rather than that of language, relations of power, not relations of meaning'.[5]

The theory thus installs us in a sphere that is explicitly conceived as historical and political: a space of power relations. But what sort of critical enterprise does this produce? There are several puzzles here. First, those who celebrate Foucault's recourse to history seem to believe that this establishes a model of historical interpretation, enjoins us to interpret texts by relating them to the situation in which they were produced, but Foucault gives scant warrant for any hermeneutical enterprise; for literary criticism his work promotes, rather, such projects as the task of situating literary studies in the history of knowledge. Foucault is not interested in interpreting texts and provides no method. It is possible, of course, that this may be a secret of his attraction: he can be set against Derrida as another model of textuality, but one which invokes history and then leaves critics free to do historical interpretation – with Foucault's writings providing an extraordinarily rich conception (which he would reject) of the 'background' against which literary works might be interpreted. The Foucauldian archeological project would serve as backdrop for the hermeneutical quest, as the critic, in defiance of Foucault's principles, sought a thought or a signification manifested in the work. And this criticism could be seen as political since the Foucauldian space in which it locates itself has been defined as a sphere of power relations. There is, however, a real oddness in making Foucault the warrant for a historical hermeneutics.

Second, Foucault is celebrated as leading us out of texts into something else, but there is a further difficulty here. What Foucault gives us is not History or Reality (as opposed to language) but *histories*; not accounts of what the 'real' conditions were at a particular moment but 'histories of the terms, categories and techniques through which certain things become at certain times the focus of a whole configuration of discussion and procedure'.[6] He does not claim to give us History, but argues that what 'events, periods, sources, accepted inferences, styles or problems are recognized in history are determined by the order that is imposed on the entangled

[5] Michel Foucault, *Power/Knowledge*, ed. Colin Gordon (New York: Pantheon, 1980), p. 114.
[6] John Rajchman, *Michel Foucault and the Freedom of Philosophy* (New York: Columbia University Press, 1985), p. 51.

mass of "documentation" with which a society is already bound up, and it is vain to seek some further basis for them in an independent reality'.[7] Foucault is a brilliant inventor of new historical objects, but it is difficult to get from this powerful historical practice either a method for interpreting texts or a conviction that we have moved outside of discourse to plant our feet firmly in 'reality'.

The most insistent use of Foucault in recent years in the United States, though, is as apostle of the political. This substantive, 'the political', is itself somewhat puzzling. In discussions of literary theory and criticism, invocation of 'the political' seems to involve, first, the claim that everything is political, including literary criticism of all sorts (so there is a political aspect to any claim that something is not political) and, second, the assumption that literary criticism should *become* political and work for change. The relationship between these two propositions is not altogether happy – whence perhaps the special usefulness of Foucault. Foucault shows that everything is political: power, the 'Method' chapter of *The History of Sexuality* tells us, is everywhere; power is not something one holds; power comes from below.[8] Foucault shows that everything is political, and if we follow Foucault, literary study will become political and hence potentially emancipatory.

The difficulty here is one Foucault's commentators are abundantly aware of. One of Foucault's most original and influential contributions is his critique of what he calls the repressive hypothesis – the notion of power as force exercised from above to repress or contain. Power is not something which is exercised and which therefore has limits; nothing escapes power. 'Power is everywhere not because it embraces everything but because it comes from everywhere. And 'Power', insofar as it is permanent, repetitious, inert, and self-reproducing, is simply the overall effect that emerges from all these mobilities . . .it is the name that one attributes to a complex strategical situation in a particular society'.[9] This certainly makes literature and criticism political (in the sense of involving power) but it raises a problem about how literary criticism can be a systematic agent of liberation, which is what critics want when they want criticism to be political. If one were casting around for the theorist who did most to indicate that criticism could *not* structurally or systematically be an instrument of liberation, one might well pick the late Foucault, for whom apparently oppositional practices belong to the network of

[7] Ibid.
[8] Michel Foucault, *The History of Sexuality*, vol.1 (New York: Random House, 1980), p. 94.
[9] Ibid., p. 93.

power: regulation masks itself by producing discourse which is apparently opposed to it but sustains the network of power. 'Power is tolerable', he writes, 'only on condition that it mask a substantial part of itself'.[10] Power needs domains which seem outside power and which thereby serve it. New Critics, Jamesonian Marxists, and deconstructionists all seem to give literature and criticism more emancipatory potential than Foucault. This difficulty is not just an accident; it is tied to the most revolutionary contribution of his thinking about power.

The kind of critical practice that emerges from an astute and resourceful use of Foucault can be seen in Mark Seltzer's *Henry James and the Art of Power,* which examines 'how both the content and the techniques of representation in James's works express a complicity and a rigorous continuity with the larger social regimes of mastery and control that traverse these works'.[11] Taking up the writings of the most 'aesthetic' of novelists, who to many has seemed particularly remote from the realm of political forces, Seltzer shows a continuity between the techniques of representation that the novelist devises and the technologies of power that his fiction censors and ostensibly disavows: systems of supervision and regulation. The connection is made through detailed accounts of contemporary discourses of power: the discourses of spying and policing (related to techniques of narrative point of view, which reproduce social modes of surveillance and supervision and make realism a mastery and policing of the real), the discourses of professionalism and social managerialism, and of the technologization of the caring professions. In a Foucauldian criticism, the novel becomes part of the system in which the everyday is brought into discourse. The notion that literature stands apart from power is one of the ways in which power masks itself and may thus reinforce the system it ostensibly resists.

Such criticism is immersed in discourses defined as political but could be said to demystify claims about the emancipatory potential of literature and criticism rather than advancing them. The question of the ultimate political and institutional effects of this kind of criticism seems to me one that we cannot now answer, except by ill-founded guesses, but it would certainly be wrong to abandon such projects on the grounds that their emancipatory force is not clear. On the other hand, the excitement of working in what can be called 'the political' should not prevent critics from remaining alert to possibilities of local

[10] Ibid., p. 86.
[11] Mark Seltzer, *Henry James and the Art of Power* (Ithaca: Cornell University Press, 1984), p. 13.

and concrete political criticism. Points or possibilities of resistance, Foucault maintains, are irregularly and unpredictably distributed. They follow no rule; 'instead there is a plurality of resistances, each of them a special case', depending on the configurations of discourses in the network of power at a particular moment.[12] The conclusion would be, in short, that an emancipatory or effectively resistant political criticism is necessarily ad hoc and does not have a theoretical basis or grounding.

Precisely this conclusion, however, is what admirers of Foucault and apostles of the political most strenuously deny, even when their own discussions provide compelling evidence that Foucauldian analysis of power does not produce an emancipatory critique. It is striking that commentators such as John Rajchman, whose book is called *Michel Foucault and the Freedom of Philosophy*, describe Foucault's thinking about power yet cling tenaciously to the idea that the political is necessarily linked to freedom, in effect setting aside the central arguments of the texts expounded. Foucault, for Rajchman, is a skeptic, whose 'philosophy does not aim for sure truths but for the freedom of withholding judgment on philosophical dogmas, and so acquiring relief from the restrictions they introduce into our lives and our thought'.[13] This seems to reinvoke the repressive hypothesis – the notion of power as a force imposed from above to restrict – which it has been Foucault's great originality to reject. Again, Rajchman writes, 'Foucault advances a new ethic: not an ethic of transgression but the ethic of constant disengagement from constituted forms of experience, of freeing oneself for the invention of new forms of life'.[14] Critical thought is seen as disengagement (though Foucault has taught us to see it otherwise), and literature, one imagines, could be seen as the most resolutely disengaged form of thought. It is as though traditional ideas of the liberating force of imaginative discourse were reintroduced to supply the systematic emancipatory possibility that Foucault questions. 'We are really free', writes Rajchman, 'because we can identify and change those procedures or forms through which our stories become true, because we can question and modify those systems which make only particular kinds of actions possible'.[15]

What is remarkable is that these comments accompany discussion of the fact that for Foucault talk of sexual liberation is part of a long history of internalizing domination. Indeed, one of the methodological tips one quickly picks up from *The History of Sexuality* is that an

---

[12]   Foucault, *History of Sexuality,* vol. 1, p. 96.
[13]   Rajchman, *Michel Foucault,* p. 2.
[14]   Ibid., p. 37.
[15]   Ibid., pp. 62 and 122.

impression of freedom or the belief that one has disengaged from a particular system of categorization is likely to be the manifestation of another regulatory practice.

In an article summing up Foucault's career, Edward Said declares that 'his work will retain its anti-utopian dimension for generations'.[16] This prediction, false almost before it was made, underestimates the strength of a contrary desire in the call to history and the attempt to use Foucault to imagine a political criticism: his work often seems unable to retain this anti-utopian dimension even in his own time. The paradox of Foucault's writing is that in exciting the reader to rethink – to identify constraining or regulatory practices where we had been unaware of them – it provokes a feeling of freedom at the moment that it demonstrates the pervasiveness of power and rejects the repressive hypothesis.

The strange use of Foucault as model for a politically engaged criticism seems to avoid the problem that his work ought to make us face: about the roles and effects of discourses, such as literature and criticism, which belong to the network of power they seek to oppose or resist. Eagleton evades these questions in his refusal to discuss Marxist criticism and his inclination simply to assume that all other critical modes strengthen the power structure. Foucault's work both directs our attention to the historical functioning of discourses and institutions and, with its critique of the repressive hypothesis, offers an antidote to accounts of institutions and disciplines as simply repressive: the formation rules of disciplines do not simply homogenize and exclude but create discursive possibilities. In going beyond recognized disciplines to describe new historical objects – the body, criminality, insanity, the medical gaze – and the discourses that constitute them, Foucault offers myriad prospects for a criticism that seeks to be historical, identifying a range of discourses that can be read with literature. If critics were to treat these discourses as what he has shown them to be – complex practices with formation rules, relations to the constitution of the subject, rhetorical strategies, and lines of force that need to be elucidated – if they were to read them with all the attention and rhetorical skills they can muster, the results might be very interesting indeed, but the bizarre reception that transforms the critic of the repressive hypothesis into a prophet of liberation suggests that a similar inversion may happen here. Critics may treat the non-literary discourses to which Foucault has directed them as simple and univocal 'background' material, and use them to control the meaning of literary works, as if the only meanings works could have were those

---

[16] Edward Said, 'Michel Foucault, 1927–1984', *Raritan* (Fall 1984), p. 10.

involving references to contemporaneous non-literary givens. The other danger, as one might call it if there seemed any possibility of avoiding it, is that Foucault's identification of the space of analysis as a region of power relations will convince critics that their Foucauldian projects are *ipso facto* political criticism and their pleasure in this will prevent them from looking for opportunities for more local and theoretically unfounded critical projects of a political cast.

4

Political Criticism: Confronting Religion

I have suggested in earlier chapters that since we have no convincing model of critical change on which we can base our predictions for the future or our arguments about what should happen in criticism, we are frequently led to adduce social and political circumstances to which the future of criticism might be linked. Discussions of the future seek to connect criticism directly to social and political goals, since we need something outside criticism to justify our choice of a future.

It is by no means evident that most important developments in criticism will derive from reflections of this sort – as opposed, say, to the single-minded pursuit of the consequences and ramifications of a particular line of thought or theoretical project – but the attempt to place criticism in the broadest possible context and to imagine the justifications which consideration of the future seems to require is of interest in itself, quite apart from its success in effecting the developments it imagines. Sometimes, however, theoretical reflection on the political implications of critical modes or schools is carried on as though this reflection on the future should determine the direction of criticism and lead people to abandon modes in which they had been working. It is quite a popular pastime these days to argue about whether the theoretical orientation of Foucault, or Lacan, or Derrida, or de Man, or Habermas, or Benjamin, or Kristeva is politically progressive or conservative. There is intrinsic interest in such debates, which can bring out aspects of a theoretical view or orientation that had been hitherto ignored, but in at least one respect they seem misdirected. It is notoriously difficult to calculate the political effects of even the best-known theoretical projects of the past, where we have the benefit of hindsight and ought to be able to judge. Was Kant, or Freud, or Wittgenstein progressive or regressive? If we cannot even give confident answers in these cases but can imagine developing either answer, we can scarcely expect that we could make reliable predictions about the political effects of general theoretical orientations of our own day. Such debates, I want to suggest, while they create an aura of political engagement by focusing on questions of political implications, are not the way to develop a political criticism. They run the double risk of ruling out of court for ill-conceived reasons theoretical approaches whose ultimate consequences are quite unpredictable and of distracting attention, through their theoretical debates, from more immediate possibilities of political criticism.

As we saw in chapter 3, the lesson we can learn from Michel Foucault – the theorist most often cited as offering criticism entry into 'the political', as it is called – is that no particular theoretical enterprise or orientation assures emancipatory criticism or exteriority to the power system. Possibilities of resistance, Foucault writes, 'are distributed in irregular fashion: the points, knots, or focuses of resistance are spread over time and space at varying densities, at times mobilizing groups and individuals in a definitive way, inflaming certain points in the body, certain moments in life, certain types of behavior'. There is no law of resistance or liberation; 'instead there is a plurality of resistances, each of them a special case', depending on the configurations of discourses in the network of power at a particular moment.[1] An emancipatory or effectively resistant political criticism is necessarily ad hoc and may lack a theoretical basis or grounding. It is symptomatic of the attraction Foucault's work has had that the gap between the account of power and the idea of an emancipatory critique is repeatedly denied, though it may well be that recognition of that gap, and of the fact that political criticism is local, specific, and theoretically problematic, will prove crucial to emancipatory political criticism. If political criticism is ad hoc, it cannot encompass the field of literary studies. Alongside other critical projects which rigorously pursue an idea or hypothesis without knowing where it will take them, a political criticism may derive above all from attention to the institutions with which criticism is involved. Where we think we can identify effects of critical approaches, we can attempt to bring about changes.

There are many potentially worthwhile projects, where theoretical problems about ultimate goals do not reduce the political desirability of intermediate measures, such as expanding the canon to bring to attention in teaching and writing what has been excluded in operations of canon formation: writings by women, blacks, and minorities, and other sorts of discourses deemed sub-literary. As we saw in chapter 2, there are serious questions about overall goals – are

---

[1] Michel Foucault, *The History of Sexuality*, vol.1 (New York: Random House, 1980), p. 96.

we seeking a multi-racial international canon or, rather, some other way of approaching non-canonical texts – but while debating questions of ends, a political criticism can work to promote awareness of cultural difference. This seems especially important in a political context where 'family values' means the reinforcement of patriarchy and where best-sellers call for a return to a 'traditional' education.

The example I wish to discuss, however – a case where I believe literary criticism bears some responsibility for a contemporary political situation – involves religion and the way in which the teaching and criticism of literature may work to legitimize religious discourse and strengthen its political power rather than to foster a critique of religion and religious authoritarianism. Literary studies may bear some responsibility for socially and politically dangerous conditions, in which an uncriticized religious discourse helps to legitimate a variety of repressive and reactionary movements. If that is so, then a political criticism ought to promote the critique of religion, not through systematic theory but through diverse challenges, including satire and mockery, in its dealings with literature and with cultural issues.

This is not, I stress at the outset, a theoretical enterprise concerned to explore the logocentrism of criticism or other possible affinities between criticism and theistic thought or sacred interpretation. Rather, it is a political project interested in the position of religious discourse in our culture, seeking out what might strengthen or weaken it. Although in many respects we may have a 'godless', secular culture, as proponents of religion tirelessly tell us, religious discourse and religious belief seem to occupy a special, privileged place, as though it went without saying that any sort of challenge or critique were improper, in bad taste. One of the few challenges, through which I wish to approach the problem, occurs in the work of William Empson.

Although Empson is generally admired as one of the great critics of our century, the world has inclined to praise his genius while dismissing most of his work since 1960 – from *Milton's God* to the essays of *Using Biography* – as hopelessly eccentric. Empson certainly cultivated the tone of the eccentric Englishman – writing with a briskness and coziness, as if he knew his audience, engaging in spirited critical battles without professional solemnity, and speculating with a winning novelizing zaniness about the doings of his authors – but it is too easy to dismiss him in this way. I myself recall vigorously condemning his eccentricity after hearing his 1971 Clark Lectures in Cambridge on Coleridge and the 'spirits of electricity'. I am now inclined to think, however, that what is regarded as eccentric in his writings in fact gives us a valuable perspective on literary criticism and its institutional effects. The very fact that we are so inclined to dismiss his views as eccentric shows how reluctant we are to confront the aspects of academic criticism that he reveals to us.

Most of Empson's biographical essays combat an underlying imperative of contemporary criticism: to interpret works as reflections on or of eternal truths and hence to deny authors their idiosyncratic views. In 'Natural Magic and Populism in Marvell's Poetry', seizing upon an obscure, evasive sentence by Emile Legouis, Empson writes,

> Excellent, but what can this mean when translated out of High Mandarin except that Marvell was still able to believe in fairies. Modern Eng. Lit. is extremely shy of making this admission about any serious author, but it was not considered so ludicrous then. From as early as 1590, at least ten of the Cambridge colleges, including Marvell's own, had the *De Occulta Philosophia* of Cornelius Agrippa in their libraries; and this tells you how to call up nymphs in water-meadows.[2]

Empson's main targets are the Christianizing interpretations fostered by the critical ideology of the Eng. Lit. establishment, which eliminates fairies and other unorthodox beliefs, drawing quasi-Christian meanings from anything that seems spiritual or transcendental. In 'The Variants for the Byzantium Poems' he observes that 'English and American critics interpret Yeats's poems as implying Christian doctrines whenever that is possible, and when they find it impossible, they treat the passage with a tactful sigh, as merely a lapse, because they cannot conceive of a good man, with a good heart, holding any other religious belief. . . . he cannot really believe in Theosophy; at best that would be a kind of play-acting' (UB, p. 163). Working with the drafts and Yeats's statements about the poems, Empson reconstructs a more interesting narrative about a city which is not heaven at all but a 'bustling metropolitan stage, for the ghosts of many periods and many nations arrive there and purge themselves, much as an Edwardian gentleman, after the excesses of the season, would purge himself in Baden-Baden' (UB, p. 164).

' "Neo-Christian" seems the right way to describe those recent literary critics', writes Empson, 'some of whom believe in Christianity and some not, who interpret any literary work they admire by finding in it a supposed Christian tradition. . . . I think they are chiefly wrong in not realizing that Christianity has always needed to be kept at bay, by people with civilized consciences'.[3] This neo-Christian tradition has been particularly strong in medieval studies, but critics of other periods too

---

[2] William Empson, *Using Biography* (London: Chatto, 1984), p. 12. Henceforth cited as UB.

[3] William Empson, *Milton's God* (London: Chatto, 1965), pp. 229–30. Henceforth cited as MG.

have assumed that to explicate literature is to find in it Christian themes, despite the fact that the authors have frequently resisted or opposed important aspects of the reigning Christian ideology of their day.

Empson urges attention to authors' deviations from or resistance to orthodox religious doctrine, but he also takes their religious views as positions open to criticism (one should argue about religious opinions expressed in poems, as one argues about other moral or political views). Critics frequently assume that since the Christian God, whose ways Milton seeks to justify, is by definition all-knowing, all-powerful and all-loving, it is inappropriate to cavil at his actions or remarks. For Empson, however, Milton's project is ambitious – of epic proportions – precisely because this God is so extremely hard to justify. Moderns accustomed to thinking vaguely and benignly about Christianity may not confront what Empson rightly sees as a central problem: the divine legitimation of unending punishment for all who disobey divine commands, and the identification of this demand for retribution with divinity and goodness itself. Christianity is, after all, centered on the crucifixion of Christ, from whom come its name and major symbol; the claim is that God the Father himself – not some external power but a God synonymous with Goodness – required the punishment of all mankind but accepted in its place the torture and death of his son. It is not, as Nietzsche claimed, that Christianity is the morality of the hangman. Rather, as Empson puts it,

only if this God had a craving to torture his Son could the Son bargain with him about it. In return for those three hours of ecstacy [while his Son was undergoing crucifixion], the Father would give up the pleasure of torturing for all eternity a small proportion of mankind [those who would be saved]; though such a tiny proportion, it has usually been agreed, that his eternal pleasure can scarcely be diminished. God's justice has regularly been said to be what required this peculiar satisfaction, but no man who was himself accustomed to administer justice, and to come away from the work feeling himself recognized to have done it decently, can ever have felt the picture of God's justice to be literally true. Such is the extremely basic objection to the Christian God which Milton tried to handle . . .[4]

[4]   MG, p. 246. Empson notes that reviewers have deemed his view of the Atonement crude. 'It is indeed, but I had to consider the belief that Milton shared with Aquinas, the operative view of the Atonement in the history of Christianity. This is the doctrine that the Son, as advocate for mankind, satisfied or propitiated the Father by accepting a vicarious punishment; and it is now rightly called "crude" because it always ascribed bad motives to the Father . . . one must go to the crude view, whether the founders intended it or not, to understand what has given the religion such fearful strength, and why it could make good men do so much evil' (MG, p. 283).

Aquinas even insists in the *Summa Theologica* ('Of the Relations of the Saints Toward the Damned') that the blessed will share God's pleasure and 'will rejoice in the punishment of the wicked': 'Nothing should be denied the blessed that belongs to the perfection of their beatitude. . . . Wherefore in order that the happiness of the saints may be more delightful to them and that they may render more copious thanks to God for it, they are allowed to see perfectly the sufferings of the damned' (MG, p. 248).[5]

Christians may begin by imitating Jesus Christ, as they are supposed to, Empson notes, but when they find themselves in positions of power, they may turn to imitating God the Father, satisfying Justice by persecuting the heathen. Such inclinations were more often indulged in Milton's time than in our own: 'The Wars of Religion so disgusted sensitive and intelligent people with the cruelty of all Christian sects that, after about a century of effort, they managed to prevent the religion from burning people alive any more' (MG, p. 14). Since the Enlightenment most societies have prevented the religious from expressing their devotion to their God by killing those who do not share it, and such behavior only emerges when religious bigotry is allied to other grievances, as in Northern Ireland or India. Unlike moderns, who can be induced to forget the violent role of religions by doctrinal subtleties and persistent talk of God's love, seventeenth-century intellectuals were surrounded 'by what seemed unbreakable proofs, of a very external kind, for morally unwelcome conclusions, such as "Thou shalt not suffer a witch to live". . . . Learned and responsible characters like Donne and Milton could therefore become hag-ridden by the moral objections to the religion without giving it up; they regarded it as an inescapable fact, and wrestled with it enormously' (MG, p. 267).

Empson's critique focuses on Christianity and the potential effects of its conceptions of God and of punishments. Since other religions, such as Judaism, do not celebrate a crucifixion or the justice of eternal punishment, they might escape his strictures; but a visitor to Israel finds Orthodox Jews just as determined to ban any activity that does not conform to their interpretation of scripture as any Roman Catholic or Protestant or Muslim fundamentalist. As political

---

[5] Empson is quoting from Question 94 of the Third Part (Supplement) of the *Summa Theologica*, which draws on such Biblical verses as 'The Just shall rejoice when he shall see the revenge'. Commentators have debated why the Papacy was slow to condemn the Nazis' persecution of the Jews, but one wonders whether the eschatological doctrine of the religion – its injunction that the blessed in glory contemplate with pleasure, or at least accept with equanimity, the endless suffering of the wicked – does not create structural resistance to condemning the systematic punishment or destruction of heretics.

divisions in Israel have given power to the Orthodox and they have set about forbidding Sabbath activities and seeking to impose their beliefs by law, they give one reason to suspect that, in this case as well, a religion in power will be sorely tempted to oppress others.[6] The rule of thumb seems to be that religion can be a positive force when there is another oppressive system in place, as the Catholic Church in Poland or Liberation Theology in Latin America have shown, but that as it gains power it becomes oppressive in its turn; tempting occasions for righteousness are bound to arise, and a likely outcome of divine revelation is the oppression of those who do not conform.

Milton's attempt at justification, which succeeded in making his God 'morally very much better than the traditional God of Christianity', is one of the 'Things unattempted yet in Prose or Rhyme' that Milton undertook (MG, p. 272). Milton specifically rejects the idea that the loyal angels will gloat over the tortures of the damned, and though God seems indifferent to the sufferings he causes, 'Milton's God is not interested in torture, and never suggests that he uses it to improve people's characters – here we reach the point of difference, however it is interpreted' (MG, p. 273). In emphasizing such differences, Empson wishes not only to open skeptical debate about Christian principles that are articulated in literature but to challenge the complicity with religion which neglects authors' opposition to theological orthodoxies, 'ignoring the text to improve its theology', as it glosses their works in religious terms (MG, p. 32).

'When I was young', Empson writes, 'literary critics often rejoiced that the hypocrisy of the Victorians had been discredited, or expressed confidence that the operation would soon be complete. So far from that, it has returned in a peculiarly stifling form to take possession of critics of Eng. Lit.' (UB, p. 203). Among other things, there is

a strong drive to recover the children for orthodox or traditional religious beliefs; well, showing them how those beliefs operated in standard authors of their own tradition is of course a good way to do it, providing an actual use for the Eng. Lit. with which the schools have been saddled. The material is processed with confident firmness to suit this intelligible policy, and when you

---

[6] The remarks of Orthodox rabbis, as well as Meir Kahane, about the Palestinians include citations of the most gruesome passages of the Hebrew Bible, such as Numbers 31: 14–17: 'And Moses was wroth with the officers of the host, with the captains over thousands, and captains over hundreds, which came from the battle. And Moses said unto them, "Have ye saved all the women alive?" "Now therefore kill every male among the little ones, and kill every woman that woman that hath known a man by lying with him." "But all the women children that have not known a man by lying with him, keep alive for yourselves,"' See Christopher Hitchens, 'Shahak in Israel', *Raritan* 6:4 (Spring 1987), p. 26.

understand all that, you may just be able to understand how they manage to present James Joyce as a man devoted to the God who was satisfied by the crucifixion. (UB, p. 203).

He calls this 'the Kenner smear', after the most energetic and resourceful of the recuperators. 'The chief claim of this theory is that Stephen Dedalus is not presented as the author when young (though the book title pretends he is) but as a possible fatal alternative, a young man who has taken some wrong turning or slipped over the edge of some vast drop, so that he can never grow into the wise old author (intensely Christian, though in a mystically paradoxical way), who writes the book' (UB, p. 204). Empson marshals internal evidence and biographical materials to oppose the American spiritualizers of Joyce, the basic purpose of whose interpreting, he writes, '(I take it no one would be eager to deny this) has been to prove that Joyce was not really opposed to Christianity. . . . From the evidence of the letters and the Ellmann biography, his critics would be more sensible to blame him for an obsessional hatred of the religion' (UB, p. 213). In any event, 'he would regard it as an enormous betrayal that, since his death, everything he wrote has been twisted into propaganda for the worship of the torture monster' (UB, p. 216).

Readers have found such remarks in rather poor taste, signs of an unfortunate obsession – 'the most tedious part of his mind', as Catholic Denis Donoghue smugly calls it.[7] No doubt the sharpness of Empson's language comes from the frustration of being dismissed as merely eccentric when he is trying to combat precisely the unreflective acceptance of Christianity that makes attacks on it seem odd and tedious behavior. It is the blitheness of critical Christianizing that irritates: 'Mr Wilson', he writes of one critic, 'invents his ghastly insertion with easy confidence, because the only Heaven he can conceive is the Christian Heaven', which he unthinkingly foists upon Yeats (UB, p. 173). Empson, whose years in the East made him alert to the pervasiveness of an unreflectively-assumed Christianity in our critical tradition, forces us to confront the complicity of literary study with religion in what the future will doubtless call the Age of Eliot.

In a postscript to Christopher Norris's excellent *William Empson and the Philosophy of Literary Criticism*, Empson registered dissent from the view that 'anything I had printed for the last quarter century was irrelevant nonsense, to be dismissed briefly with a sigh'. 'I have not', he maintained,

---

[7]   Denis Donoghue, Review of *William Empson: The Man and His Work,* ed. Roma Gill, *Times Literary Supplement,* 7 June 1974, p. 597.

been entertaining myself with frippery in my old age; . . . I have continued to try to handle the most important work that came to hand. In 1953, having returned from China, I started teaching in England, so that I had to attend to the climate of opinion in Eng. Lit. Crit., if only because of its effect on the students. This was the peak of the neo-Christian movement . . . perhaps it was already subsiding by the time I was prepared to attack it, but even so I was not making a fuss about nothing.[8]

If religion has subsided in England, it has not in the United States; on the contrary, it has become a formidable public force. And what is most striking is the extraordinary protection religious discourse enjoys. If a television evangelist is caught in scandalous behavior, he will be satirized, but religious views and beliefs are treated as sacrosanct. There is practically no public anti-religious discourse. In debates about prayer in the schools, no one champions the view that prayer is a superstition that should be discouraged; emphasis falls instead on how a particular prayer would offend the sensibilities of others with different beliefs – as though the crucial thing were to avoid offending anyone's beliefs. Not only is there no public critique of religion; there is no vital tradition of anti-religious satire that would keep the sanctimonious in check – no American Monty Python. Jokes about religion are thought in bad taste or, even worse, pointless – as though this particular set of beliefs and social practices should lie beyond criticism and ridicule. In the absence of any mockery of religion, politicians of all stripes can appeal to God without fear of ridicule; and indeed, no public figure would dare come out against religion, so widespread is the conviction that religion must be respected.

There has even arisen in our day an assumption that one should not argue about religion. This is sometimes taken as evidence that we pay lip service to religion but grant it no importance. However, it contributes to the impression that religious discourse and beliefs are of a special kind and should be protected from all challenge. One even encounters the strange conviction that religious freedom or religious toleration means not simply that no one should persecute people for their religious beliefs but that no one should say or do anything that offends a religious belief – as though Americans had a constitutional right to encounter nothing that ridicules or attacks their beliefs. The Catholic League for Religious and Civil Rights appears to act on the view that any discourse that fails to treat Catholic doctrine with

<hr>

[8]   William Empson, 'Postscript' to Christopher Norris, *William Empson and the Philosophy of Literary Criticism* (London: Athlone, 1978), p. 205.

proper respect should be forbidden. Catholic groups have expended great energy in attempting to ban such plays as Christopher Durang's *Sister Mary Ignatious Explains it All for You* and Jean-Luc Godard's film *Hail Mary*, whose portrayal of a modern Mary is deemed disrespectful of Catholic beliefs. No other group in our society is so arrogant as to claim that any discourse or representation that satirizes its beliefs ought to be banned. Whatever their wishes, Republicans have not sought to proscribe jokes about Star Wars or supply-side economics; but religious discourse, religious belief is deemed of a superior order, intrinsically worthy of respect, above mockery and ridicule. That this idea should be possible indicates just how far education has abandoned its historic tasks, of combating superstition, encouraging skeptical debate about competing religions and their claims or their myths, and fighting religious dogmatism and its political consequences.

Obviously this state of affairs is not the fault of literary critics alone, but it is hard to believe that there is no connection between this convention of respect for religion and the respectful treatment accorded religious doctrine in American education. If schools and universities are at fault, then much of the responsibility must fall on teachers of literature, for it is we, not the philosophers and historians, who spend the most time explicating literary works in religious terms and declining to challenge or contradict their teachings. To urge us to take up a critique of religion is not to deny that Christianity in particular has been the inspiration for many great works of art but to ask us to reflect on the consequences in our own day of criticism's relation to religious discourse. The complicity of literary studies with religion today is a subject that has scarcely been broached but cries out for attention, not least because religion provides a legitimation for many reactionary or repressive forces in the United States and is arguably a greater danger today than ideological positions critics do spend their time attacking.

'For the majority of Eng. Lit. critics, especially in America', Empson writes, 'it seems to have become a convention to pretend that one has never heard of the opinions of the Enlightenment' (UB, p. 208). Indeed, literature departments these days contain people with all manner of views – Marxists, Lacanians, deconstructionists, feminists – but seldom anyone who seriously attacks religion. One who did would laughingly be asked why he is 'playing the village atheist' – as though attacking religion were beneath the dignity of the urban sophisticates professors like to imagine themselves to be. Marx and Freud, who lie behind militant critical theories of our time, began powerful analyses of religion, but their followers have for the most part neglected to pursue this. Critics and theorists pride themselves on their questioning of orthodoxies and ideologies, but they characteristically hesitate to produce even the mildest critique of religion, with a curious result: our students are not much shocked by nihilistic texts of the twentieth century; critiques of meaning and value do not surprise them; but they can be profoundly shocked by a good, vigorous attack on religion from the eighteenth or nineteenth century. They have not heard anything like this from their most radical professors. And, as I have mentioned, there is no public anti-religious discourse in their culture to supply what their teachers fail to provide.

The complicity of literary study with religion takes various forms. Empson particularly resists the presumption, fostered by T.S. Eliot's and Northrop Frye's identification of Tradition with Christianity, and the New Critics' association of poetic language with the paradoxes of religious discourse, that the most powerful and appropriate interpretation is one which relates elements of the work to a symbolic order structured by the oppositions and values derived from an aestheticized Christianity. Even critics who do not explicitly identify tradition with Christian values blithely explicate literary works in religious terms and assume that any critique of religion would be in bad taste. Students are taught not to question the religious principles or values adduced in literary interpretation (to argue about religion is immature). Recently, there has been a striking revival of interest in the sacred. Instead of leading the critique of dogmatic mythologies, literary criticism is contributing to the legitimation of religious discourse. Geoffrey Hartman, one of the leaders of the attempt to bring together literary and religious studies, jokingly proposes that literature departments should be rechristened 'Departments of Mystery Management'.

Yet the critique of religion is, I submit, the proudest heritage of comparative literary studies, and certainly one region in which literary criticism has helped transform Western culture. At the beginning of the eighteenth century, one might say without greatly oversimplifying, Protestants took the Bible to be the word of God; by the beginning of the twentieth century, this belief was untenable in intellectual circles. What had been responsible for this change was scholars' and critics' insistence that techniques of textual and critical analysis which had been developed for classical literature be applied to biblical writings. Both the lower and higher criticism (textual criticism and historical criticism) were based on a comparative principle, that Old and New Testament writings should be analyzed in the same way as other ancient texts. The discovery that biblical writings consisted of textual strata from different periods undermined, for example, the assumption that Moses had been the author of the Pentateuch. Lowth's *De Sacra Poesi*

Hebraeorum showed that the prophetic books were poetical, and should be regarded as literary expression. Eichhorn treated the Bible not just as literature but as oriental literature, identifying different strands from different periods. Bultmann derived from his literary analysis of New Testament materials and sources the conclusion that only the sayings of Jesus are historical. The tales, along with the framework of the Gospel history, are a product of the missionary needs of early Hellenistic Christianity. Radical skepticism, it has been suggested, is a characteristic result of the literary criticism of the Gospels.

This is a worthy legacy of comparative literary research, which I fear we have abandoned, as literary criticism today works to legitimate rather than criticize and situate religious discourse. Most teachers of literature, I dare say, do the work of legitimation quite unknowingly, explicating literature in religious terms and believing that to articulate their own religious skepticism or promote debate would be inappropriate, unseemly. I myself came to see what was happening only through the sustained 'eccentricity' of Empson's later work, when reflecting on the nature of the orthodoxy that has succeeded in imposing this label. In our unconscious complicity, we may regard religion as a curious, irrelevant survival but all the while honor the Fryes, Hartmans, Girards, Booths and Kenners – our most famous critics – who are in their different ways promoters of religion. Let me emphasize that I am not objecting to their particular and different approaches to literature but to the fact that their work confers a legitimacy on religion which contributes to its unassailability in the social and political arena.

What, then, should be done? How should critics proceed? Doubtless in different ways, as befits our varied interests and talents. The critique of religion will obviously raise difficult theoretical problems, such as what are the viable forms of humanism in a post-Enlightenment age, but a political criticism need not wait upon an answer. The essential step is to take up the relation of our teaching and writing to religious discourse and to maintain a critical attitude when discussing religious themes – that is, not to assume that theistic beliefs deserve respect, any more than we would assume that sexist or racist beliefs deserve respect. This might involve us in comparing Christianity with other mythologies when we teach works imbued with religion, or making the sadism and sexism of religious discourse an explicit object of discussion, as we now tend to do when teaching works containing overtly racist language.

Indeed, a possible model might be our treatment of such classics as *The Merchant of Venice* or *The Taming of the Shrew*. When teaching these plays today, we do not hesitate to distance ourselves from their overt anti-Semitism and sexism but make this an issue for debate, asking whether the plays are endorsing these attitudes of the day and how this might affect our response to them. We would, I imagine, frown upon a pedagogical approach that treated sexism or anti-Semitism with the respect we give Christian doctrine or that ruled irrelevant arguments about how far they are pernicious. When teaching *Paradise Lost* we ought not to draw back from suggesting that this account of creation is a myth and initiating discussion of its implications. Perhaps we should study the Hebrew Bible not as poetry or as narrative but as a powerfully influential racist and sexist text. In addition, when we are debating the politics of criticism, we should discuss our own relation to the religious discourses abroad in our culture, which may be far more important than the popular question of whether this or that theoretical perspective is politically progressive or regressive. Above all, we should work to keep alive the critical, demythologizing force of contemporary theory – a force which a considerable number of critics are striving to capture and to divert to pious ends. *Down with the priests!* is an unlikely motto for literary studies these days, but we ought to ask why this is so and turn some of our analytical energies on our own relation to religious discourse and ideology – not as a theoretical investigation asking whether literary studies could ever free itself from the theological weight of the hermeneutic tradition or the idea of authority invested in a special text, but as a practical, political way of challenging the authority of a potentially repressive religious discourse and insuring that we do not encourage respect for it.

We may find, as we experiment with responses, that we encounter considerable resistance, both from colleagues who prove more committed to religious values than we had thought possible and from institutions themselves. We might discover that universities and those who govern them will wish to protect 'respect for religion' or 'the religious beliefs of our students', seeking ways to discourage the critique of religion and proving themselves less committed to academic freedom than we had imagined. It is at least possible that American universities might prove more tolerant of and more able to assimilate Marxism than a militant atheism. Arguments about the conservative effects of institutionalization have not touched upon this matter, which might well prove of more immediate political relevance than those they do debate. We know that critics seeking to debunk religion will feel personal discomfort, since we have internalized the injunction to respect religion, but if they also encounter institutional constraints and sanctions, as seems likely, we will learn something of the political realities that we are seeking to change and of the political character of this sort of critical work.

Political criticism can take many forms, depending on one's analysis of the cultural and institutional situation in which one seeks to intervene. It may involve the questioning of hierarchical oppositions working within our culture or the study of those texts and discourses that our canons and institutions have set aside in constructing their identity. Debates about the ultimate political implications of this or that theoretical model can be pursued not as the way to establish a political criticism but as an exploration of the models themselves. Political criticism will be more varied and opportunistic, and the critique of religion seems at this moment in our history a particularly appropriate task. The role religion plays in the discourses of our culture makes it imperative that it not escape serious intellectual challenge. And since literary works embody and portray all kinds of religious views and many of their consequences, both beneficent and nefarious, literary studies is particularly well placed to promote such critical debate.

PART II

Critics Reading

5

Empson's Complex Words

William Empson, I have contended in chapter four, should be honored for his attempt to expose the unreflective complicity with Christianity that has reigned in literary criticism in our century and for his perseverance in this attack on superstition, even when none dared to join him and he saw everything he wrote dismissed as the sad aberration of a once great mind. Perhaps one day this aspect of his work will commend him to critical memory, but it is likely that his achievement will continue to rest on his earlier criticism. Good arguments could be made for the importance of *Some Versions of Pastoral*, which shows the potential scope and subtlety of a criticism attuned to ideology and puts forward valuable concepts that suddenly bring a rhetorical phenomenon into focus, such as *pseudo-parody to disarm criticism*. But what makes Empson the greatest English critic of the century is the analysis of language in *Seven Types of Ambiguity* (1930) and *The Structure of Complex Words* (1951).

His contribution is better savored in individual discussions than in theoretical summary. Every page of *Seven Types* could teach someone a good deal about the workings of language in literature. Indeed, Empson seeks 'to show how a properly-qualified mind works when it reads the verses, how those properly qualified minds have worked which have not at all understood their own workings'.[1] Energetically expounding possible ambiguities, he seeks to articulate in explicit, cognitive terms the meanings which readers may only dimly grasp yet which are responsible for poetic effects. 'I have continually employed a method of analysis', he writes, 'which jumps the gap between two ways of thinking; which produces a possible set of alternative meanings with some ingenuity and then says it is grasped in the preconsciousness of the reader by a native effort of the mind. This

---

[1] William Empson, *Seven Types of Ambiguity* (Penguin: Harmondsworth, 1961), p. 248. Henceforth cited as 7T.

must seem very dubious; but then the facts about the apprehension of poetry are in any case very extraordinary. Such an assumption is best observed by the way it works in detail' (7T, p. 239). Empson characteristically explicates sentences or passages rather than entire poems and is more interested in the clash or concatenation of meanings than in harmonious resolutions, in the puzzles of ambiguity more than in focused paradoxes towards which all the constituents of a poem might be said to point. Consequently, he describes problems or mental processes more than solutions, as in his comments on a strange image from the third act of *Hamlet*:

> but 'tis not so above;
> There is no shuffling, there the Action lies
> In his true Nature, and we ourselves compelled
> Even to the teeth and forehead of our faults
> To give in evidence.

In the penultimate line here 'all we are given is two parts of the body and the Day of Judgment; these have got to be associated by the imagination of the reader. There is no immediate meaning, and in spite of this, there is an impression of urgency and practicality' due in part to the sense that 'the words themselves in such a context include, as part of the way in which they are apprehended, the possibility of flashes of fancy' in various directions (7T, 92). Thus 'a *forehead*, beside being a target for blows, is used both for blushing and frowning . . . *Teeth*, besides being a weapon of offence, are used in making confessions, and it is a mark of contempt . . . that you are struck there . . . the *forehead* covers the brain where the *fault* is carried out, while the *teeth* are used in carrying it out'. The structure, 'compelled even to the X of our faults' suggests that the main meaning must be something like 'the most determined, vicious, essential aspects of our faults', but the poetic effect depends upon the interaction of various half-formed senses derived from contextual implications of words in the line. Focus on figurative language involves, for Empson, a pursuit of literal possibilities (what do teeth and foreheads do?) which jostle and combine in the figurative structure.

Seven Types is often cited as the beginning of Anglo-American New Criticism, and it was without doubt a book of considerable influence, but American New Critics, with their desire to distinguish poetic language sharply from the language of science and associate it with the mysteries of religious language, were always suspicious of Empson's thoroughgoing rationalism. As Christopher Norris writes, 'The problem was that Empson insisted in *rationalizing* poetry, not merely seeking out multiple meanings but attempting to fit them into some kind of logical structure. This led the New Critics to view with suspicion Empson's habits of homely prose paraphrase and his constant drawing out of underlying philosophical arguments'.[2] Like Paul de Man, Empson presses his 'analysis of figurative language to the point where it offers a maximal resistance to the habits of straightforward rational thought. But where New Criticism simply suspends those habits – accepting that poetry just *is* paradoxical, and quite beyond the reach of logic – Empson and de Man make a point of keeping the logical problems in view'.[3]

Empson keeps these problems most squarely in view in *The Structure of Complex Words*, which has always occupied a curious place in the corpus of his critical writings: more praised than read, more honored than cited. It has not captured the general literary imagination as the earlier *Seven Types of Ambiguity* did, and it may be worth asking why this should be so, as a way of clarifying the distinctive character of Empson's project in *The Structure of Complex Words* – his most ambitious achievement – and of bringing out assumptions about language that may have produced resistance to it.

Seven Types works by taking the language of poems more seriously than is customary, showing that many great lines of poetry, when looked at closely, prove surprisingly puzzling or enigmatical, ambiguous in ways that contribute to their power and richness. *The Structure of Complex Words*, on the contrary, explores not Nashe's 'Brightness falls from the air' or Keats's 'Then glut thy sorrow on a morning rose' but the complexities of *quite* or *honest*, or *sense*. It lacks the immediate attractiveness of *Seven Types*, but this lack may be only the symptom of a deeper difference. Resistance to *The Structure of Complex Words* may be traced to the greater ambitiousness of its attempt to describe the complexities of meaning that quite ordinary words acquire in use. In *Seven Types*, Empson offers the spectacle of an ingenious, unpredictable mind engaging poems in an intense, irreverent encounter, trying to find out how they mean what they are thought to mean, brilliantly and resourcefully exploring how multiple meanings and the relations between them might contribute to their beauty and impact. Though this once seemed irreverent – making poetry a matter of words and meanings rather than feelings – it is now broadly accepted and deemed aesthetically enriching if not exactly reverent. The method focuses particularly on poetic imagery, where

---

[2] Christopher Norris, 'Some Versions of Rhetoric: Empson and De Man', *The Conflict of Faculties: Philosophy and Theory after Deconstruction* (London: Methuen, 1985), p. 78.
[3] Ibid., pp. 78–9.

several strands of meaning can be woven together, as in Empson's notorious opening discussion of 'Bare, ruined choirs, where late the sweet birds sang' from Shakespeare's 73rd sonnet:

> the comparison [of leafless trees to ruined choirs] holds for many reasons; because ruined monastery choirs are places in which to sing, because they involve sitting in a row, because they are made of wood, are carved into knots and so forth, because they used to be surrounded by a sheltered building crystallized out of the likeness of a forest, and coloured with stained glass and painting like flowers and leaves, because they are now abandoned by all but the grey walls coloured like the skies of winter, because the cold and Narcissistic charm suggested by choir-boys suits well with Shakespeare's feeling for the object of the Sonnets, and for various sociological and historical reasons (the protestant destruction of the monasteries; fear of puritanism), which it would be hard now to trace out in their proportions; these reasons, and many more relating the simile to its place in the Sonnet, must all combine to give the line its beauty, and there is a sort of ambiguity in not knowing which of them to hold clearly in mind. Clearly this is involved in all such richness and heightening of effect, and the machinations of ambiguity are among the very roots of poetry. (7T, p. 3)

If this exfoliation of meaning is excessive, as many readers have felt it to be, such manic glossing is nevertheless deemed excessive zeal in a good cause – compulsive ingenuity exercized on a special kind of language thought in fact to require a good measure of ingenuity, if not quite this much. *The Structure of Complex Words* seldom treats poetic imagery of this sort. While it takes many examples from literary texts, they are not treated as strikingly different from imagined utterances of maiden aunts: 'Yes, it's *quite* a nice day'. The ingenious unfoldings of *Complex Words* cannot therefore be wryly accepted as products of a fine but excessive literary passion. Its preoccupation with words such as *all, honest, dog, fool* or *man* makes its investigations bear inexorably on the operation of language in general, linking literary and non-literary discourse, despite the absence of general theoretical claims on this actual subject.

The problem that *Complex Words* brings into view is whether we are justified in granting a special complexity to literary language but refusing it to other sorts of discourse. We willingly concede that poetic language requires close attention and detailed explication of the myriad associations that must be held in the mind at once or of the numerous possible directions in which poetic formulations lead thought, but may not other kinds of language be just as complex and bring into play a range of associations and links with potential contexts? What is at stake in our distinction here? If we accept the idea of a special literary realm where language can be as complex, evasive, ambiguous as it likes, we perhaps do so precisely to preserve a realm of so-called 'everyday speech' or 'ordinary language' where words have simple meanings and make assertions about familiar states of affairs. It is as though we had a stake in believing that the basis of speech is a set of referential utterances with simple meanings, and that to this normal speech complexities may accrete in special circumstances. The acceptance, even celebration of *Seven Types*, despite the fact that many readers think it 'goes too far' in excavating ambiguities, may be the sign of our desire to create a realm of ambiguous, rhetorical language in order to maintain the simplicity of ordinary speech.

What is most radical in Empson's *Structure of Complex Words*, then, is his busy exploration of the intricate assumptions at work in the use of quite ordinary words, his demonstration of the weight of social implication that they carry, or can be made to carry. His examples deny a hierarchy of complexity and persuasively identify a vertiginous rhetorical dimension to everyday language use. At a time when the specificity of literary discourse is no longer taken for granted, and we are repeatedly reminded that what literature does may be something ordinary language does also – when we can no longer conceive of ordinary language on the model of declarative statements about middle-sized particulars, such as *The cat is on the mat* – Empson's book in particularly pertinent.

The most vigorous explicit resistance *The Structure of Complex Words* has provoked comes in objections to what Empson calls his machinery: a set of symbols for representing meanings and pregnancies of words, introduced in the opening chapter and exercised for about fifty pages thereafter. Thus one use of *wit*, whose implications Empson paraphrases as 'Even in authoritative writers one must expect a certain puppyishness' is represented '3b+=1a−.1£1'.[4] This is an extreme example, the sort of thing the author occasionally produces with a certain perverse glee. Indeed, it is far from clear how seriously Empson himself takes his notation – which no doubt heightens the reader's irritation. Still, since the machinery is used infrequently, and then only to represent senses that have already been paraphrased, one might well wonder whether the objections to it registered by nearly every reviewer may not be a displaced resistance to other aspects of the book, particularly to the idea of the excessive complexity yet analysability of ordinary language. Indeed, in the final analysis, the symbols seem to have no other significant function than to connote

---

[4] Empson, *The Structure of Complex Words* (London: Chatto, 1951), p. 89. Henceforth cited as CW.

analysability, proclaiming that meaning is complex yet rationally analysable, not a mysterious set of nuances that can only be grasped by delicate sensibilities. The combination of good old-fashioned rationalism and home-made machinery using, Empson explains, the symbols on the top row of an English typewriter is what prompts Hugh Kenner's comparison of Empson to a Victorian scientist 'whom the public could always surprise, as Alice did the White Knight, obliviously head down in his suit of armor, hung with bellows and beehives, "patiently labouring at his absurd but fruitful conceptions"'.[5]

To readers put off by the bellows and beehives they encounter in the first chapter, one might note that there is no need whatever to learn the system of symbols, any more than readers of *Seven Types* need to learn and apply the distinctions between the types of ambiguity. It will not repay the effort – unless students should wish to produce Empsonian formulae to annoy their teachers. But as in *Seven Types*, the machinery, the distinctions, serve above all to suggest the range and significance of discriminations that can be made: affirming that there are recognizably different things happening when language is used, the machinery claims that these rich, history-laden discriminations are definable as terms in a rational calculus.

Empson's project begins in opposition to the claim that literary language is essentially emotive and therefore not to be analysed in terms of meanings and shades of meanings. (He was working at a time when logical positivists maintained that non-verifiable propositions should be regarded as emotive only.) Taking issue in the mildest possible way with the ideas on emotion and sense of his teacher I.A. Richards, he convincingly argues that, at least in the interesting cases, emotive effects can only be produced by structures of sense. Empson is so respectful of Richards that one could miss the radical contrast between their views, and indeed the struggle to avoid rejecting Richards while in fact disagreeing with him on central points accounts for some of the prolixity of his opening chapter, 'Feelings in Words'. Here Empson is the precursor of recent criticism, which presumes that literary affect or emotion should be analysed in terms of structures of meaning. So-called 'reader-response criticism', for instance, treats reading not as a process of feeling intense emotions but of making sense – positing meaning, hesitating between alternatives, even feeling confused about whether something makes sense.

Empson's most striking and important claim here is that words carry assertions or equations: compacted doctrines, underlying

5   Hugh Kenner, 'Alice in Empsonland', *Hudson Review*, 5:1 (Spring, 1952), p. 144.

propositions, not just meanings. This is a key step in the discussion of complex words – which are not recondite words but often the most common. 'He was a man', says Hamlet of his father, 'take him for all in all,/ I shall not look upon his like again'. We are able to understand this statement only by virtue of the equation that takes as the defining case (for 'man') an ideal case (here one whose virtues, it is suggested, are so simple and obvious they can be left unspecified). It would be wrong to say that *man* has a special meaning and so does not designate the class of men here, for the point of the utterance seems to be precisely that to be a member of the class of men should be to have the ordinary virtues uniquely exemplified in Hamlet *père* (CW, pp. 321–6).

Moving from single equation-bearing words to sentences that are themselves equations, such as 'Work is prayer', one finds, as Empson wryly notes, that 'all we have done by our trustful effort to explain one "A is B" is to land ourselves with three of them'. That is, the surface equation puts together the equations or assertions implicit in each key word. 'The equation inside *work* . . . must, therefore, be of the form "honest work is the norm of all kinds of work", whereas the equation inside *prayer* must be of the form "the most general kind of prayer deserves the same feelings as the narrow kind" ' (CW, pp. 354–5). The overall result is something like 'proper work is general-but-real prayer'.

It is not clear how far the notion of equations in words should be extended, but the principle is an interesting confirmation of a curious property of language: the analyst's attempt to break language down into its constituents generally does not produce simplification but rather the discovery that the same structures, the same problems, reappear at the lower level. Words are broken down into morphemes and morphemes into phonemes, the supposedly minimal units, but phonemes themselves are the product of differences, and the problem of determining when two sound sequences count as the same phoneme is the same as that of determining when they count as the same sentence. The sentence itself, consisting of subject and predicate, can be broken into its constituents, but modern grammatical analysis has treated the constituents of sentences as themselves the product of minimal subject–predicate forms, which are embedded or presupposed: *The grey cat clawed the brown dog* contains the embedded propositions 'the cat is grey' and 'the dog is brown'. If, as Empson's analyses suggest, to account for meanings produced in discourse we must analyse individual words as carrying assertions or propositions, this is only the sort of dizzying endless regress we ought perhaps to expect of language.

Empson, however, deals playfully or wryly with the perverse systematicity of language and reserves more serious attention for the historical character of complex words, maintaining that the most interesting changes in meaning are changes in the equations. His remarkable discussion of *honest*, with equations such as 'simple people are true to the facts of our nature' and 'A frank rogue is a good fellow, fit for our set' instantiates with amazing efficiency a great deal of social history and is the most interesting account of a word that I know. No one has written so insightfully as Empson about words such as *rogue, fool, honest* or *dog*, and the historical layers of their usage, which involve a 'humor of mutuality', as he calls it: subtle implications about relations between speakers, listeners, and those spoken of. Such words, 'used both to soften the assertion of class and to build a defense against Puritanism', often bring into play a down-to-earth skepticism about absolute values and a recognition of the interlocutors' common human condition – implications which Empson brilliantly spells out (CW, pp. 159).

The study of ambiguities in *Seven Types* is often seen as the source of Anglo-American New Criticism's theory of the special, paradoxical character of poetic language, but for Empson ambiguities derive precisely from the continuity between language in poems and language in other situations. 'There is always an appeal to the background of human experience', and words are imbued with the contradictory features of experience and attempts to come to terms with it. 'The *use* of words, in fact', Empson writes, 'is to sum up your own attitude to the practical questions that they raise, and it is their business to be fluid in meaning so that a variety of people can use them. This is widely recognized, I think. "E's what I call thrifty", the charlady will say, with a rich recognition of the possibilities of using the other word' (CW, p. 30).

Empson has never subscribed to the notion of a special literary language or even literary use of language. The notes to the *Collected Poems*, which unashamedly paraphrase, elucidate, and identify experiences behind the poems, claim a continuity between this condensed, opaque, poetic language and the language in which one may continue reflection on the problems it treats. The complexities of poetic language come from its explorations of social issues, feelings, and intellectual problems entwined in words, its continuity with social exchange. Some of the most splendid passages of *The Structure of Complex Words* treat ordinary, socially weighted uses of language, as in the famous account of *quite*[6] or this example of *honest*,

when one elderly lady says about another, 'Really, Maria is getting more and more eccentric. I hardly know what to say. Well, really, it's scarcely honest'. A disinterested observer may feel that what Aunt Maria did was quite farcically dishonest, in its petty way, but the suggestion here is that *honest* is such a very elementary virtue that Maria cannot be conceived not to possess it; if you thought of her as not honest you might next have to envisage her going to jail, a thing quite outside her style of life. The sense of the word *honest* here, I think, must be given as something like 'not a member of the criminal classes'. (CW, p. 17)

What can make the literary use of language special is not its removal from the social sphere – something that never happens with language – but rather readers' willingness to assume that something engaging is being said, despite difficulties of comprehension, and therefore to attend more closely to structures that may impart a new torque to a word.

No other critic keeps so firmly in view the social character of language, but Empson's greatest originality here lies in his continuous demonstration that to refer to social and contextual use of words is not to simplify interpretation or to cut down ambiguity. In current critical debates, invocation of the social character of language and of the need for reference to context is invariably a reductive move, based on the assumption that the contextual determination will in fact produce more determinate meaning and thus cut down on the play of meaning, which is thought to be a function of decontextualization. The appeal to social experience and to context is a reductive move designed to rule out of court possibilities of meaning. But for Empson, the contrary is the case. Recourse to social attitudes and usage – or to authorial intentions, which are themselves divided, multi-layered – generates more complex explanations and realistically sagacious reflections than does reference to the symbolic dimensions favored by the critics he opposes. History opens complexities rather than closing on univocal meanings. Empson provides evidence of an unexpected sort that one cannot oppose text to context, as if context were something other than more text, for context is itself just as complex

---

[6]   The discussion is too complex to summarize here, but one main use of *quite* involves what Empson calls the 'cozy mood': *quite a scandal* or even *quite a nice day* implies 'We agree about this, we who know, don't we?' In *not quite nice* the cozy mood imposes a context of social convention: 'I speak as moderately as I can about this person's faults, though one could feel strongly. This much can't be denied.' *Quite* used alone for an answer is more independent: 'You deserve praise for saying what I knew already' CW, pp. 23–6.

and in need of interpretation. Reference to social usage does not end exploration of meaning but, for Empson, initiates it.

Despite its posture of eccentric rumination, which one can find winning or maddening depending on one's mood, *The Structure of Complex Words* therefore has considerable pertinence today for its special contribution to debates about meaning and context, about the literary in its relation to the social and the historical. Empson's brilliant discussions of words that express complex social attitudes towards one's fellows or towards moral principles open rich chapters of social and literary history and possibilities of textual investigation that remain to be explored. Here, all his evidence suggests, literary discourse conceived not as poetic language but as the discourse in and of literature, has more to teach about life in language than social materials, conceived as background, have to teach about literature.

A further connection with contemporary critical debates comes in such discussions as 'Sense in the *Prelude*', which invite comparison with Jacques Derrida's treatment of *pharmakon* in Plato, *hymen* in Mallarmé, and *supplement* in Rousseau. Derrida and Empson both take up terms which do not seem to be the author's chosen focus – *Imagination*, for example, initially seems more of a key word for the argument of the *Prelude* – but whose double meanings or whose sets of conflicting equations make them key textual constructions and thus agents of deconstruction. In Wordsworth's *Prelude* the 'flat little word', *sense* turns out to play a crucial role in establishing equations central to the poem's claims. Wordsworth does not use the term *sensibility*, and this, Empson writes, 'put a lot of extra work on *sense* and made it more fluid' (CW, p. 292). Frequently used to mean 'a feeling of', 'an intuitive perception', as in 'a sense of' or 'the sense of', and occasionally substituting for 'common sense', *sense* also appears in a new form, *the sense*:

> I have felt,
> Not seldom even in that tempestuous time,
> Those hallowed and pure motions of the sense
> Which seem, in their simplicity, to own
> An intellectual charm; that calm delight
> Which, if I err not, surely must belong
> To those first-born affinities that fit
> Our new existence to existing things . . .

The sense retains its connections with 'the senses' or sensation, but seems to rely on some such equation as 'sensation is imagination'. Empson writes, 'The effect is that, though Sensation and Imagination appear to be two extreme ends of the scale in view, so that one might expect them to be opposites, the word [*sense*] is placed so that it might equally apply to either. And the middle of the scale, the idea of ordinary common sense, is cut out from these uses no less firmly than the idea of sensuality' (CW, p. 298). More compactly, the word 'means both the process of sensing and the supreme act of imagination, and unites them by a jump' (CW, p. 304).

Paul de Man writes of this chapter of *The Structure of Complex Words*, 'one essay stands out from the fundamentally harmonious consensus that unites, for all apparent disagreement, all contemporary writers on Wordsworth'.[7] What Empson tactfully, modestly illuminates is the way language is exposed to a fundamentally rhetorical organization, even at moments when the most important cognitive claims are being made. 'Commentators', de Man maintains, 'have had to forget Empson in order to carry on'. Empson remarks that for Wordsworth *sense* appears to be 'a convenience of grammar' – as though high poetical discourse were generated by grammatical processes, in whose terms the operations of the imagination would need to be explained. 'It seems to me very likely', writes Empson, 'that there is an inner grammar of complex words like the overt grammar of sentences'. Some of the most interesting works of recent criticism and theory pursue precisely this insight: exploring the grammar of *supplement, promise* and *excuse* in Rousseau, of *pharmakon* in Plato, *parergon* in Kant, *face* in Wordsworth and others. Words prove not to be tools, as is often suggested, but machines, with complex internal structures that can generate results not always predictable to their users. Empson's eccentric investigations, which seem by turns charming, sensible, fussy, or mannered, may be especially important today when many readers have come to associate the play of language with difficult theoretical explorations and philosophical claims. Empson's practical tinkering or puzzling out may thus have even more to teach us about language now than it did in 1951, when *The Structure of Complex Words* was first published.

7 Paul de Man, *The Rhetoric of Romanticism* (New York: Columbia University Press, 1984), p. 88.

6

Bachelard's Images

At the time of his death in 1962, Gaston Bachelard was France's leading historian and philosopher of science as well as one of its most original and influential literary critics; but to pupils and colleagues he was a moral and philosophic example, a patriarch, majestically bearded, who had mastered the art of happiness and practiced it among books and friends. Rejecting Existentialism and its cognates with the simple credo, 'L'angoisse est factice' [anguish is factitious] he taught the delights of poetic reverie and the difficult beauties of mathematical physics as the two principal strains of 'une pensée heureuse'. He was, one colleague wrote, 'L'être le plus humain que j'ai jamais connu' [the most human being I have ever known].

The diversity of his accomplishments makes Bachelard difficult to assess and contributes to the neglect of his ideas. Such a range of competence and originality is almost unprecedented, and whenever one tries to engage with some part of it one senses, looming behind the work and exceeding whatever categories one might invent, the mythical figure of the man himself.

Bachelard's personal history gives him, indeed, a special aura. Born in Champagne in 1884, son of a shoemaker of Bar-sur-l'Aube, he spent nine years after leaving school as a postal clerk – first in the Vosges and then, after military service, in Paris. Studying part-time, he took a *licence* in mathematics and, after serving in the trenches in the First World War, became a teacher of natural sciences in his native village. 'Toute ma vie est sous le signe du tardif' [belatedness is my sign]: *licencié* in philosophy at thirty-six, *agrégé* at thirty-eight, he took his doctorate at forty-three with his *Essai sur la connaissance approchée*, an incisive attack on Bergsonism and Cartesian epistemology and a contribution to the problem of induction. Two years later he began his university career as professor of philosophy at Dijon and in 1940 was called to the Sorbonne.

The circuitous route to academic fame, a persistent love for his native countryside and the objects of rural life, a simplicity of manner and habit, and a playful bonhomie which delighted lecture audiences are all elements of the myth which now surrounds Bachelard, as are his own lyrical evocations of a life of reading. He is the true man of books ('Lire beaucoup, lire encore, lire toujours'), who conceives no higher form of contentment: 'là-haut, au ciel, le paradis n'est-il pas une immense bibliothèque?' [Is not paradise an immense library?] A voracious writer as well as reader, he enriched the celestial library by thirteen scientific studies and ten of a literary kind.

To the history and philosophy of science Bachelard's contribution seems to have been five-fold. First of all, beginning in his 1928 thesis, he asserted firmly and repeatedly the importance of providing a philosophy adequate to a science in constant transformation, of which contemporary physics was only the most striking example. Instead of starting from a theory of the relationship between consciousness and the world, determining what can in general be known, and then asking whether science can attain objective knowledge, philosophers should reverse their perspective: 'L'esprit doit se plier aux conditions du savoir' [The mind must conform to the conditions of knowledge]. This is an elementary but radical inversion. Instead of deciding what can in theory be known, one should begin with what science in fact knows. Objective knowledge is nothing other than the interpersonal knowledge produced by science over a given period, and the philosopher's task is to provide the theory of scientific practice, the epistemology or epistemologies of actual knowledge. Since knowledge is something constantly in production, philosophy must be dynamic, dialectical, even plural or 'dispersée'.

This attempt to account for scientific knowledge prompts Bachelard's second contribution: the attack on Cartesian epistemology. In erecting science on a foundation of clear and distinct ideas and in treating analysis as a reduction of the complex to its simple elements, Descartes asserted a continuity between immediate knowledge of a common-sense kind and the refinements of scientific knowledge. But there are two problems here. First, Bachelard argues, there are no simple phenomena; 'every phenomenon is a fabric of relations', and the simple is not an irreducible building block but a construction and reduction. 'Simple ideas are not the ultimate basis of knowledge'. Second, the history of science demonstrates that science advances only by refuting empirical experience. Alchemy, for example, is psychologically very concrete. It takes as prime the elements fundamental to immediate experience. The task of science is to replace these objects with its own constructs: 'Rien n'est donné; tout est construit'

[Nothing is given; everything is constructed]. Playing on the ambiguity of the French *expérience*, he declares, 'une expérience scientifique est une expérience qui contredit l'expérience commune' [a scientific experiment is an experiment/experience that contradicts common experience].

Common experience, in the form of intuitions, conscious and unconscious models, and psychological preferences, constitutes a series of 'epistemological obstacles' which Bachelard charts with verve and subtlety in *La Formation de l'esprit scientifique* and elsewhere (the most compact and elegant example is perhaps the discussion of changing intuitions and conceptions of mass in *La Philosophie du non*). Animist, substantialist and rationalist models or intuitions focus scientific discourse but also limit it. Each is eventually replaced by a new conception which becomes an epistemological obstacle in its turn. Descartes' sponge, a heuristic device, circumscribed possible insights, so that in Descartes 'la métaphysique de l'espace est une métaphysique de l'éponge' [the metaphysics of space is a metaphysics of the sponge].

If science works by refuting immediate experience and transcending its own theoretical frameworks, this has implications for the problem of induction. Like Karl Popper, whose *Logic of Scientific Discovery* appeared six years after *Essai sur la connaissance approchée*, Bachelard argued that nothing is decisively verified inductively and that knowledge is therefore primarily produced by negation, by falsification. Repeated positive results do not verify a hypothesis, while a negative result forces one to investigate failure and leads to more proximate knowledge (this is, Bachelard says, the philosophy of 'why not?'). One must seek partial negation, 'fine negation'. A truly scientific observation is polemical; the atom, for example, is nothing but the sum of falsifications to which its original image has been subjected. The production of knowledge through progressive falsification is what makes science a dynamic, dialectical enterprise to be ranged under the banner of 'la philosophie du non'.

This dialectical rather than inductive conception of science leads to Bachelard's most influential contribution to contemporary French thought: the demonstration that science (and by implication other disciplines) is a discontinuous rather than a continuous process; not a gradual movement towards truth but a series of differential stages separated by 'coupures' or 'ruptures épistémologiques'. Change occurs when epistemological obstacles are eliminated in favour of other models which provide new conditions of knowledge.

The notion of historical discontinuity has not only inspired notable French work in the history of science, by Georges Canguilhem and Michel Foucault among others, but is also central to Louis Althusser's

Marxist revisionism and to the semiological study of modes of discourse which succeed one another in time. Bachelard has helped to promote the conception of history as a series of synchronic stages rather than a diachronic continuum. There are similarities, too, between the epistemological discontinuities described by Bachelard and the more sociological notion of successive 'paradigms' of scientific research proposed as a development of Popper's theory of science by Thomas Kuhn. But, while Kuhn seems inclined to make epistemological stasis ('normal science') the condition of scientific productivity, Bachelard, with his emphasis on the polemical nature of scientific statements and the need for a 'poly-philosophisme' to account for the open character of science, is in some ways nearer to the epistemological anarchism advocated by Paul Feyerabend as the condition of scientific progress.

Finally, Bachelard articulates what he called in *Le Nouvel Esprit scientifique* 'a new way of looking at ambiguity', which becomes a structure constitutive of science rather than what scientific analysis eliminates. Writing in the wake of the twentieth-century revolution in physics, he argues that everyone who learns science must make use 'of not one but two metaphysical systems. Both are natural and cogent, implicit rather than explicit, and tenacious in their persistence. And one contradicts the other'. Scientists are by turn realists and rationalists, treating scientific truths as constructions and as discoveries. 'It would not be difficult to show that in forming scientific judgments the most determined rationalist daily submits to the instruction of a reality whose ultimate structure eludes him, while the most uncompromising realist does not hesitate to make simplifying assumptions just as if he believed in the principles on which the rationalist position is based'.[1] One must conclude that 'science is divided, in actuality as well as in principle, in all its aspects', and that ultimately the dualisms, the incompatible perspectives not only structure scientific thought but that 'the ambiguity is found to reside in the scientific phenomenon itself', which is not something given with a Cartesian immediacy but constituted by the interplay of rationalism and realism, or logic and experimentation. The influence of this radical conception extends beyond the history and philosophy of science, for if scientific observations and science itself are shown to be constituted by the interplay of contradictory principles, then there is no reason to expect a simpler, more unitary configuration in other intellectual domains.

In France Bachelard's importance can scarcely be overestimated, but, despite the fact that his work contains, at least in embryo, the positions later developed by Popper, Kuhn and Feyerabend, it has had little

---

[1] Gaston Bachelard, *The New Scientific Spirit* (Boston: Beacon Press, 1984), pp. 1–2.

influence elsewhere. The reason seems, alas, quite simple. Those who were exposed to the man and his teaching value his books. Philosophers outside France, exposed to the books alone, find their fundamental conceptions overlaid by a prose which, in its quest for the image or aphorism, belongs to another age of science: that leisurely and *mondaine* science of the eighteenth century which Bachelard so often analyses. Reading him is strenuous in a way wholly different from what one now expects of either scientific or philosophic writing.

The relationship between Bachelard's scientific and literary investigations is a question which always exercises commentators, who are professionally inclined to look for unity. Jean-Claude Margolin, for example, brings them together in a transcendental theory of the creative imagination, whose adventures Bachelard is said to place under the headings of *animus* and *anima*: the masculine principle of science and the feminine principle of poetic reverie. Not only is this an application of Bachelard's most insipid categories; it nullifies M. Margolin's more astute observation that imagination interests Bachelard precisely at the point where it ceases to be the prerogative of the individual subject: in poetic reverie, where the subject is wholly absorbed in an object whose universal mythic potential is released, and in science, where the 'thought' is implicit in a conceptual framework.[2] Mathematics, Bachelard asserts, is not the *language* of physics but the *thought* of physics; tensor calculus knows physics better than the physicist does.[3]

The important point, no doubt, is that Bachelard prefers both science and poetry at their purest and most extreme. He disdains a comfortable interdisciplinarity which would teach literary folk the second law of thermodynamics and produce or enjoy novels about scientists. He always maintained that his two enterprises were separate, though perhaps complementary. In fact, one is the converse of the other: the psychologically privileged images which Bachelard studies as obstacles to science become, with a change of perspective, manifestations of a basic affective and mythical universe explored by poetry.

Biographically this is indeed their relationship: Bachelard's study of epistemological obstacles, especially those of alchemy, provoked a series of books on the psychological and poetic qualities of the four elements. The earliest and best, *La Psychanalyse du feu* (1938), is fascinating in its hesitation between the scientific and the literary.

2   Jean-Claude Margolin, *Bachelard* (Paris: Seuil, 1974).
3   Bachelard, *The New Scientific Spirit*, p. 55.

Finally Bachelard chooses to revel in the imaginative possibilities of fire but draws on scientific writings for proof of the resilience of, for example, the sexual associations of fire and electricity. Though the psychoanalytic concepts he employs are personal and diffuse, he introduces psychoanalysis into literary studies as a way of analysing not authors but images, whose power is said to derive from their exploitation of a primordial and archetypal experience – not unlike that of a nineteenth-century village childhood.

The task of the poet, Bachelard writes, is to liberate in us 'une matière qui veut rêver' [matter that would dream], and for him, as for the Surrealists, the instrument of liberation is the image. The analyst tries to participate in the poetic reverie and to discover, beneath the manifest images, the primitive affective experience to which they refer us. By treating poetry in this way, Bachelard not only established 'imagist' criticism in France: he put it on a sounder footing than is usual in England or America, recognizing that, if images are made the privileged elements of a poem ('the poem is a cluster of images'), critics should not simply study them as reflections of implicit or explicit themes but should develop a theory to explain why images are treated as the source of literary power.

Roland Barthes once observed that 'present-day French criticism in its most flourishing aspect can be said to be Bachelardian in inspiration'.[4] Though he was thinking primarily of Jean-Pierre Richard, Jean Starobinski and Georges Poulet who, like Bachelard, made criticism a participation in the affective universe of an author, Bachelard has also had immense dialectical influence: much recent French criticism is an attempt to transcend his limitations. His theory of poetry has the virtue of falsifiability. We dispute it by showing that the force and significance of images depend more on specific ideological or differential functions within a text than on universal associations: that images of earth are not always 'stables et tranquilles' nor walls and houses welcoming and protective.

Moreover Bachelard's hypothesis leads us to argue that much poetry does not simply evoke or invoke an immediate and 'natural' experience of the world but works much as Bachelard claims science does; breaking down immediate intuitions, deconstructing a universe of archetypical clichés, and reinventing the world by giving it an order which is discursive rather than immediately affective. Bachelard's work, by its explicitness, has provoked a more adequate account of poetry.

---

[4]   Roland Barthes, 'The Two Criticisms', *Times Literary Supplement*, 26 September 1963.

If it seems excessively paradoxical to claim that a thematic, atomistic and sentimental approach to poetry should stimulate a formalism centred on notions of languages, codes and structure, one might look at Bachelard's most accomplished piece of criticism, his *Lautréamont* of 1939. This is both a judicious appreciation of an author previously ignored, except by the Surrealists, and a series of methodological suggestions. Investigating the energy and aggression of *Les Chants de Maldoror*, Bachelard tries to define the 'algebraic weight measuring the vital action of the diverse animals' and constructs a system of valencies relating crab to louse, eagle and vulture.[5] The notion of an underlying system of forces enables him to treat Kafka's bestiary (based on coagulation and petrification) as an inversion of Lautréamont's and to see Leconte de Lisle's as an 'adjectival' version of what is 'substantivized' in *Maldoror*. In this investigation he perceives that a psychologically or psychoanalytically astute literary criticism 'would come to pose in different terms the problem of influences, of imitation. For this, it ought to replace reading by *transference*, in the psychoanalytic sense of the term'.[6] Psychoanalytic criticism has indeed gone in this direction, thanks to Lacan rather than Bachelard, but Bachelard may have helped to establish a link between a linguistically-oriented psychoanalysis and poetic structures. But above all he seems to have grasped the formal mechanisms of modern poetry. Arguing that an elementary 'poésie primitive' is always a late conquest, a deformation of existing forms, just as the more fundamental projective geometry is founded on the systematic deformation of geometrical forms, he speaks of a 'poésie projective' based on the question: 'What are the elements of a poetic form which can, with impunity, be deformed by a metaphor while allowing a poetic coherence to remain?'[7] This is a question that seems to determine a good deal of twentieth-century literature.

Bachelard offers many observations which, when pursued, yield conclusions diametrically opposed to the conception of poetry he puts forward. He speaks, for example, of the need to understand works 'in their own systematicity', as one understands a non-Euclidian geometry in terms of its own axiomatic system, or of the need for a diagram that would indicate the direction and symmetry of a poet's metaphorical coordinations; but when Gérard Genette studies the network of imagery in baroque poetry in these terms, or Claude Lévi-Strauss formalizes the relations among images in myths, they produce not a

---

5   Bachelard, *Lautréamont* (Paris: Corti, 1939), p. 30.
6   Ibid., p. 145.
7   Ibid., p. 70.

Bachelardian *profondeur*, in which each image reaches downwards towards some primordial experience of being, but a system of elements whose functions are purely oppositional or differential. Far from having intrinsic archetypal meaning, 'sun' and 'moon' function as metaphorical operators which, so long as they are opposed to one another, can be used to express almost any thematic opposition. The universality Bachelard tried to discover in individual images now becomes a property of the system itself, operating through the displacement of one binary opposition by another. Bachelard is a seminal influence, but what is reaped is very different from what he sowed.

In his last works Bachelard's method changed. His interest in formal networks or systems wanes and instead of tracing images to their psychological sources so as to explain their power, he rejects psychoanalysis and seeks to experience phenomenologically the image's direct manifestation of being. His writing becomes somewhat insipid and sentimental, the poetic examples more banal, as he seeks in reverie 'un confort mental'. Even here, however, the sustained pursuit of a poetic image or complex of images may yield surprising results, which display the insufficiencies of his explicit account of poetry better than polemic could. In *La Poétique de l'espace*, for example, while expounding a theory of the poetic image as 'independent of causality', without a past, 'referable to a *direct* ontology', in which it is the immediate manifestation 'of the heart, soul and being of man, apprehended in his actuality', he takes up Baudelaire's use of the term *vaste*.[8] *Vaste* designates, he argues, not a property of the external world but an inward intensity in which man becomes conscious of the immensity of his own being: 'It transmits to our ears the echo of the secret recesses of our being'. Bachelard's examples do indeed show that *vaste* in Baudelaire seldom has a geometrical, objective meaning; it works to intensify while uniting inside and outside, thought and world. Bachelard calls it 'a metaphysical argument by which the vast world and vast thoughts are united'; 'always, in Baudelaire's poetics, the word *vast* evokes calm, peace, and serenity'. In the most famous example, from the poem 'Correspondances', 'Vaste comme la nuit et comme la clarté' [Vast like night and luminosity], it reconciles contraries: 'under the banner of the word *vast*, the spirit finds its synthetic being'. Moreover, its sound is crucial: 'in the word *vast* the vowel *a* retains all the virtues of an enlarging vocal agent. . . . Like some soft substance, it receives the balsamic power of infinite calm.

---

[8]   Bachelard, *The Poetics of Space* (Boston: Beacon, 1969), pp. xii–xiv. The discussion of *vaste* is on pp. 190–8.

With it, we take infinity into our lungs, and through it, we breathe cosmically, far from human anguish'.

The affective power of that syllable is indeed considerable, but 'Correspondances' identifies the synthesis Bachelard celebrates as blending which is also confusion:

> Comme de longs échos qui de loin se confondent
> Dans une ténébreuse et profonde unité,
> Vaste comme la nuit et comme la clarté,
> Les parfums, les couleurs, et les sons se répondent.
> [Like long echoes which from far merge
> In a shadowy and profound unity,
> Vast like night and luminosity,
> Smells, colors and sounds answer each other.]

The vastness of night and of brightness is both an unbounded extension and the effacement of distinctive contours – night and brightness share the property of making it difficult to distinguish, as in a night *où tous les chats sont noirs* (*vaste* itself here seems a syntactic operator that intensifies and unifies by effacing the difference between night and day). A vast unity is one whose immensity of scope effaces difference, and this unity, we are told, is produced by a distance which makes things seem similar.[9] The model for this is the phenomenon which Bachelard's analysis emphasizes, *sound*; but where Bachelard sees an echo of the infinity of Being, 'Correspondances' identifies a confusion, an impression of unity produced as echoes heard from afar blend together. And Bachelard himself illustrates the functioning of echoes when at the end of his discussion, calling *vaste* 'a vocable of breathing', he is led by an echo in his poetic memory to append a note: 'for Victor Hugo the wind is vast. The wind says: "Je suis ce grand passant, vaste, invincible, et vain"' [I am this great passer-by, vast, invincible and vain]. Hugo's example locates the value of *vaste* in a play of echoes – the repetition of the *v* and the modulation of oral and nasal *a* sounds – which produces the sequence. While Bachelard's response relates *vaste* to a calm of being 'far from human anguish' and from human rhetoric as

---

[9] In 'L'Exposition universelle de 1855' Baudelaire describes how 'tous les types, toutes les idées, toutes les sensations se confondraient dans une vaste unité, monotone et impersonnelle, immense comme l'ennui et comme le néant' [all types, all ideas, all sensations, would blend in a vast unity, monotonous and impersonal, as immense as boredom and nothingness], *Oeuvres complètes*, ed. Claude Pichois (Paris: Gallimard, 1975), II, p. 578. Here the word *vaste* appears in a passage emphasizing that unity is produced by confusing the distinct. *L'ennui* suggestively echoes *la nuit* of 'Correspondances'.

well, both the structure of the poem and the intertextual echo Bachelard hears from Hugo identify the rhetorical operations that produce effects of unity.

Bachelard remarks, 'If I were a psychiatrist I should advise my patients who suffer from "anguish" to read this poem of Baudelaire's whenever an attack seems imminent. Very gently, they should pronounce Baudelaire's key word, *vast*. For it is a word that brings calm and unity'. Although critics will smile at the idea that this poem in particular, of which Paul de Man has given a most unsettling reading, should have therapeutic potency, Bachelard's claim highlights the problem that his late critical career poses. Before one rejects out of hand the divagations of *La Poétique de l'espace* or *La Poétique de la rêverie* one ought to consider the implications: this late prose, like therapeutic use of 'Correspondances', is the direct manifestation of Bachelard's *art de bonheur*. When disturbed late at night by Paris traffic, he tells us, he induces reverie and transforms the traffic noise into the sound of a furious storm at sea, through which, safe in the tranquil harbor of his bed, he can sleep.[10]

This is scarcely reprehensible, nor is reverie an improper use of poetry. However, Bachelard's criticism, which explores and champions this use, provokes critical readers to insist, rather, on the disparity between pleasurable reverie and critical analysis – a disparity at which Bachelard's own examples sometimes hint. Bachelard thus reveals a division within literary studies and literary objects which may be analogous to the constitutive division or contradiction he earlier discovered in science. The literary work and literary study are perhaps constituted by the conflict between affective response and critical analysis, which the notion of the aesthetic presumes to bring together but which are in contradiction. His pursuit, in his late criticism, of the inherent signification of images, when set against his earlier interest in systems of relations, can provoke reflection on the conflict between affective response and analytical investigation and the extent to which literature and criticism are generated by this conflict, whose harmonious resolution may be a goal or an illusion rather than an effective possibility.

Bachelard's own writing evokes this problem in a peculiar way. His prose, which addresses the reader as a friend, works out its verbal fascination in hyperbole and exclamation, and constantly invokes, in a minor Proustian mode, memories of the muscle, hand and eye, poses the question of the relationship between the pleasurable use of literature and writing criticism. In *Le Nouvel Esprit scientifique* he

[10]   Bachelard, *Poetics of Space*, p. 28.

speaks of intellectual happiness that comes in moments of synthesis or comprehension: 'this intellectual happiness is the first sign of progress'. But in his reading of literature and writing about it happiness seems to come from reverie and a poetic evocation of the delights of reverie rather than from rigorous analysis. Bachelard read and wrote with greater pleasure and enthusiasm than most critics. Must we disqualify this attitude and make persistent *angst* the necessary critical temperament? Should we sneer at the man who spoke of the library as paradise and formulated as a daily prayer the prayer of the reader: 'Give us this day our daily hunger'? These are not easy questions. They suggest that critical theory should perhaps devote more attention to investigating the conception of the aesthetic as the harmonious reconciliation of affect and knowledge and the literary disruption of that supposed harmony in poems and in criticism.

Doubtless the best way to approach Bachelard's remarkable oeuvre is to read and quarrel with *La Psychanalyse du feu* and *Lautréamont*, but one could also to make the late works a topos for reflection on the possible relations between writing and happiness, and on the way that a critical method may prove oblivious to the insights it makes possible.

7

De Man's Rhetoric

Paul de Man has been a major influence on American literary criticism and theory since the 1960s, first through his teaching at Cornell, Johns Hopkins, and Yale, where the authority of his way of reading marked several generations of graduate students, and then in the 1980s by his writings, whose impact was increased once they were seen as illustrating a major critical movement. When de Man's work became a signal example of deconstruction in literary criticism, it became important for critics and theorists who might otherwise have ignored it.

De Man was known above all for his uncompromising critique of pieties in the study of literature and for his insistence on both the demystifying potential of close reading and the dubiousness of thinking one achieves demystified knowledge. His work is best characterized as rhetorical reading, which means not only the study of tropes or rhetorical figures in a text but also the exploration of the rhetorical force of language which cannot be captured by or reduced to a grammar-like code. His studies of Rousseau, Hölderlin, Words-worth, Shelley, Keats, and Baudelaire have been crucial to the revaluation of European romanticism: literature that the New Criticism was inclined to treat as wishful or sentimental, de Man and others have shown to be the boldest, most self-conscious writing of the Western tradition. Above all, his work raises philosophical issues in literary criticism, concerning the status and functioning of language – its positing of meaning, its relation to cognition – and the use of the category of the aesthetic to relate knowledge and action, epistemology and ethics.

The discovery in 1987 that de Man had in his early twenties, at the beginning of the Nazi occupation of Belgium, written two hundred reviews and articles in collaborationist newspapers, and that one of these articles, from a special anti-Semitic section of *Le Soir* early in the period of de Man's employment, adopted the language and premises of anti-Semitism, both shocked those who had known de Man and found him exceptionally just and upright in his dealings with students and colleagues, and provoked intense discussion of the man and his work.[1] It is appalling that he should have adopted the language of anti-Semitism, even for a moment. This discovery will block an inclination to idealize the man and will no doubt give many a reason to ignore his work. For others, the existence of these collaborationist juvenilia will lead to an intense, suspicious reading both of them and of the later work – a critical reading giving special attention to political contexts, as well as to the literary and philosophical contexts in which his work has usually been read.

It seems important that the discovery of the wartime juvenilia, written ten years before he entered graduate school, not prevent one from learning from de Man's theoretical and critical writings. The early journalism may in some cases illuminate and complicate his later writing, giving aspects of it a different resonance. The fact that de Man in a journalistic piece of 1942 criticized French literature as apolitical and called for a more political literature may have made him more wary of this term in his later writings. References in 1941 and 1942 to this 'revolutionary' period may have prevented this term from playing a role in his later thinking. Above all, one understands more plainly

---

[1] Some 170 articles and reviews, mostly of current literature, which appeared in *Le Soir*, the leading Belgian daily, (a 'moderate collaborationist paper' – G. Carpinelli, *Fascism in Europe*, ed. S. Woolf (London: Methuen, 1981), p. 305), along with articles for the *Cahiers du libre examen*, which was closed by the Nazis, and several from *Het Vlammsche Land*, are collected in a special issue of the *Oxford Literary Review* (April 1988). In view of the rumors that have surrounded this material, it is worth emphasizing three points: (1) The deplorable anti-Semitism of the one early essay does not reappear in the other articles, and was scarcely characteristic of de Man's thought at the time. A Jewish friend, a Belgian who knew him well during the war, reports that he is 'not surprised that Paul de Man should have produced some statements against the Jews to please his employers. He was extremely proud that the literary column of *Le Soir* should have been put in his hands at barely age twenty. Moreover, I believe that our man also contributed texts to a Resistance publication' (*Le Soir*, 3 December 1987). The anti-Semitic column, which the young critic may have deludedly thought would be all right since he argued that European literature had *not* been corrupted by Jewish influence, was published on March 4, 1941. Such anti-Jewish measures as a curfew and the yellow star were introduced in October 1941 and June 1942, respectively. (2) In the fall of 1942, when the Nazis extended censorship to the cultural sections of the paper, de Man ceased writing for *Le Soir* and abandoned critical writing for a decade (working in publishing after resigning from *Le Soir*, he arranged for the publication of a volume of Resistance poetry, *Exercises du silence*). (3) Although de Man never discussed his past, he acknowledged his writings for *Le Soir* in a letter to the Harvard Society of Fellows in 1955 (when asked to explain his wartime activities), and in 1969 he told an emissary of Yale University, which was offering him a senior position, of the one anti-Semitic article.

what is implied by de Man's continuing critique of the aesthetic ideology and his linking of it to violence, as in late essays on Kleist and Schiller. 'Since fascism can be characterized formally as an entry of aesthetic criteria into the political and economic realms', Alice Kaplan writes, taking up Walter Benjamin's famous observation that fascism is the introduction of aesthetics into politics, de Man's critique of the aesthetic ideology resonates also as a critique of the fascist tendencies he had known. In her study of fascism in French literary and intellectual life, Kaplan's opening definitions stress fascism's revolt against alienation and conception of the state as an organism: 'Against the distance between the state and the people, they hoped for immediacy; against alienation and fragmentation, they hoped for unity of experience...Their fascism involved a new poetic language, an immediate vocal presence, an entirely new way of writing and speaking about the state and the world'.[2] This political context gives a new dimension to de Man's attempt – from his earliest critiques of Heidegger to his late critiques of phenomenality – to undo totalizing metaphors, myths of immediacy, organic unity, and presence and combat their fascinations. His later writings offer some of the most powerful tools for combatting the ideology with which he had earlier been complicitous. In the light of the situation of the wartime juvenilia, arguments in de Man's later writing that have generally been read only in a context of literary theory take on a clearer political aspect.

The discussion of the importance of de Man's work and of the bearing on it of these newly discovered juvenilia will take time. This essay seeks to assist that process by offering what has so far been lacking in writing about de Man. Particular aspects of his writings have been brilliantly analyzed by a number of critics, including Hans Jost Frey, Neil Hertz, Werner Hamacher, and Jacques Derrida, whose *Memoires: for Paul de Man* weaves together a number of strands from

---

[2] Alice Jaeger Kaplan, *Reprodictions of Banality: Fascism, Literature, and French Intellectual Life* (Minneapolis: University of Minnesota Press, 1986), pp. 26 and 3. De Man's uncle, Hendrik de Man, President of the Belgian Workers' Party and a leading socialist theorist, welcomed the Nazi occupation as a destruction of the old order and played an important collaborationist role in 1940 and 1941, seeking to build a new socialist order that might also free the Flemish from French domination. Flemish collaboration, writes Carpinelli, 'was based in no small measure on (illusory) "nationalist" motivations, which were in fact merely regional' (p. 305). A number of Paul de Man's articles of this period, speaking of these 'revolutionary times', are marked by an idealizing nationalist language linking the fortunes of the Belgians to the German resurgence.

his work.[3] But there has been no general survey of his writing, from the essays of the 1950s to the work left unpublished at his death in 1983.

Much of de Man's writing of the 1950s belongs with the French reception of Heidegger by a group of writers associated with surrealism, particularly Georges Bataille and Maurice Blanchot. Among the most prominent Heideggerian questions are the ontological status of poetic language and its relation to temporality. 'Impasse de la critique formaliste' (1956), written to introduce French readers to Anglo-American New Criticism, argues that such questions must eventually arise in the work of the best critics in the formalist tradition, such as William Empson: 'true poetic ambiguity proceeds from the deep division of Being itself [the 'eternal separation' of the mind from the originary simplicity of the natural], and poetry does no more than state and repeat this division'.[4] Even Empson, who starts 'from the premises of the strictest aesthetical formalism, . . . winds up facing the ontological question. . . . The problem of separation inheres in Being, which means that social forms of separation derive from ontological and metasocial attitudes. For poetry the divide exists forever' (BI, p. 240). Poetic ambiguity is not a supplementary technique; it is what poetry has to teach. 'The ambiguity poetry speaks of is the fundamental one that prevails between the world of the spirit and the world of sentient substance . . . The spirit cannot coincide with its object and this separation is infinitely painful' (BI, p. 237).

Conceiving of poetic consciousness as essentially divided, sorrowful and tragic, de Man distinguishes three critical approaches: historical poetics, which 'would attempt to think the divide in truly temporal dimensions, instead of imposing on it cyclical or eternalist schemata'; salvational poetics – much the most common – which imagines redemption or fusion of contradictions through poetic imagination; and naive poetics, 'which rests on the belief that poetry is capable of

[3] See in particular Cynthia Chase, 'Giving a Face to a Name', in *Decomposing Figures: Rhetorical Readings in the Romantic Tradition* (Baltimore: Johns Hopkins University Press, 1986); Jacques Derrida, *Memoires for Paul de Man* (New York: Columbia University Press, 1986); Hans Jost Frey, 'Undecidability', *Yale French Studies* 69 (1985); Rodolphe Gasché *'Setzung* and *Übersetzung:* Notes on Paul de Man', *Diacritics* 11 (Winter 1981); Werner Hamacher, 'Lectio: De Man's Imperative', in *Reading de Man Reading,* ed. Wlad Godzich and Lindsay Waters (Minneapolis: University of Minnesota Press, 1988); Neil Hertz, 'Lurid Figures', in *Reading de Man Reading*; Michael Sprinker, *Imaginary Relations* (New York: Methuen, 1987); Allan Stoekl, 'De Man and the Dialectic of Being,' *Diacritics* 15 (Fall 1985).

[4] De Man, 'Impasse de la critique formaliste', in *Blindness and Insight,* 2nd edition with five additional essays, ed. Wlad Godzich (Minneapolis: University of Minnesota Press, 1983), p. 237. Henceforth cited in the text as BI.

effecting reconciliation because it provides an immediate contact with substance through its own sensible form' (BI, p. 244). The first exists only fragmentarily, in poems more than in criticism, but may serve as a goal. Exposing the delusions of the second and third was for de Man a major task, which continued throughout his life. Much of his writing about criticism in his last years combats apparently sophisticated forms of naive poetics that surface in the debates of contemporary criticism: assumptions that aesthetic form reconciles matter and spirit. 'Whether it be in France or in the United States', de Man concludes,

> the foremost characteristic of contemporary criticism is the tendency to expect a reconciliation from poetry; to see in it the possibility of filling the gap that cleaves Being. It is a hope shared, in very different forms, by different critical approaches: the positivist formalist, the Marxist, the salvational, and the criticism of substance [the work of Gaston Bachelard and 'the Geneva School']. (BI, p. 245)

The critique of attempts to impose a redemptive scenario on literature, on the poetic imagination, on poetic language, remains a constant of de Man's work; much of his career is staked on the premise that close reading attentive to the working of poetic language will expose these delusions. Yet some delusions are more productive than others because they come closer to the heart of the problem. 'Les Exégèses de Hölderlin par Martin Heidegger' (1955), no doubt his most important essay of the 1950s, praises the insight of Heidegger's reading, despite the fact that he gets Hölderlin precisely backward: Heidegger finds in Hölderlin the essence of poetry, which is to state 'the absolute presence of Being' (BI, p. 250). In fact, 'the poet does not say Being, but rather the impossibility of naming anything but an order that, in its essence, is distinct from immediate Being' (BI, p. 261). Because Western thought, for Heidegger, has been a forgetting of Being, he needs a witness, who has seen it and, by naming it, has preserved its memory for us. He chooses Hölderlin, de Man argues, because 'Hölderlin says exactly the opposite of what Heidegger makes him say. Such an assertion is paradoxical only in appearance. At this level of thought it is difficult to distinguish between a proposition and that which constitutes its opposite. . ... It can indeed be said that Heidegger and Hölderlin speak of the same thing', and that Heidegger's commentaries identify with precision the central concern of Hölderlin's work (BI, p. 255).

The critique of naive and salvational poetics also animates de Man's most important early essay, frequently cited in discussions of romanticism, 'Structure intentionelle de l'image romantique' (1960), which takes issue with the nostalgia for the natural object in romantic and post-romantic literature and discussions of it. Romanticism brings increasing complexity and prominence to the concept of imagination, a return to greater concreteness in poetic diction, particularly in descriptions of natural objects, and yet greater recourse to metaphorical language as

the image – be it under the name of symbol or even of myth – comes to be considered the most prominent dimension of the style . . . An abundant imagery coinciding with an equally abundant quantity of natural objects, the theme of imagination closely linked to the theme of nature, such is the fundamental ambiguity that characterizes the poetics of romanticism.[5]

Attempts to reconcile nature and imagination take the natural object as the model to which poetic form and poetic imagination aspire, as in Hölderlin's line, 'words must originate like flowers'. Using the extreme example of Mallarmé to argue that 'the priority of the natural object remains unchallenged among the inheritors of romanticism' (RR, p. 9), de Man suggests that we look to the first romantics or precursors of romanticism for moments when this assumption is open to question, not yet taken for granted; and he discusses passages from Rousseau, Wordsworth and Hölderlin, who will consistently remain his examples of undeluded romantics, 'the first modern writers to have put into question, in the language of poetry, the ontological priority of the sensory object' (RR, p. 16). They expose nostalgia for the object as 'nostalgia for an entity that could never, by its very nature, become a particularized presence' (RR, p. 15). Imagination, as in the crossing of the Alps in Wordsworth's *Prelude*, comes into play when 'the light of sense goes out'. Poetic language, de Man writes, 'seems to originate in the desire to approximate the condition of the natural object', but 'this movement is essentially paradoxical and condemned in advance to failure' (RR, p. 7). Words originate in consciousness, with negation, and are linked with 'the discontinuity of a death in which an entity relinquishes its specificity and leaves it behind, like an empty shell' (RR, p. 4). 'Poetic language can do nothing but originate anew over and over again; it is always constitutive, able to posit regardless of presence but, by the same token, unable to give a foundation to what it posits except as an intent of consciousness' (RR, p. 6). The word thus negates the literality and permanence of what it depicts, and then, as it depicts its depiction, negates *it* in the endlessly widening spiral of a

---

[5] De Man, 'The Intentional Structure of the Romantic Image', in *The Rhetoric of Romanticism* (New York: Columbia University Press, 1984), p. 2. Henceforth cited in the text as RR.

dialectic without synthesis. Language posits rather than represents something which is given; the world enters language only through negation. Language does not give the object but the negation of the object and thus the irredeemable split between subject and object.

We can say that while Heidegger's analysis of the division of Being leads him to take the poetic word as solution, as witness to the presence of Being, de Man, more Heideggerian than Heidegger, carries over the Heideggerian analysis to poetic language itself: far from offering salvation and reconciliation, a naming of being, poetic language in fact names and explores the persistence of division, the impossibility of self-coincidence or self-possession. What he would later call, in a rhetorical terminology, the figurative structure of language or the unsynthesizable relation between the performative and constative functioning of language, he now calls, in the ontological language of his early years, Being as division, as rift, a continuous conflict, which is also History. While Heidegger associates poetic language with the earth, the 'common ground' on which 'Poetically man dwells', de Man sees it as the site of division and struggle. Allan Stoekl writes,

De Man turns figurative poetic language, and the Heideggerian Being he associates with it, against the complacency of Heideggerian 'dwelling' – and against the complacency of the poetic word as natural object emerging like a flower from the earth. . . . to Being as poetic language – that is to Being as a divisive and figurative language that carries death in its repetitious movement.[6]

For De Man, Maurice Blanchot is the one critic who renounces sacramental and naive poetics. He reaches 'a level of awareness no other contemporary critic has reached' (BI, p. 62). Of all contemporary critics, he writes, 'none is more likely to achieve future prominence than [this] little publicized and difficult writer', for whom criticism

becomes a form of demystification on the ontological level that confirms the existence of a fundamental distance at the heart of all human experience. Unlike the recent Heidegger, however, Blanchot does not seem to believe that the movement of poetic consciousness could ever lead us to assert our ontological insight in a positive way. The center always remains hidden and out of reach. We are separated from it by the very substance of time, and we never cease to know that this is the case. The circularity is not, therefore, a perfect form with which we try to coincide but a directive that maintains and

---

[6] Allan Stoekl, 'De Man and the Dialectic of Being', pp. 41–2.

measures the distance that separates us from the center of things. (BI, pp. 76–7)

Blindness and Insight takes up many of these themes in a discussion of criticism. In addition to essays on American New Criticism, the phenomenological psychoanalyst Ludwig Binswanger, Blanchot, Georg Lukács, Georges Poulet and Jacques Derrida, the first edition contains three more general essays: 'Criticism and Crisis', which develops de Man's views on literary language as a demystified naming of the void; 'Literary History and Literary Modernity', on the problem posed by concepts of modernity for literary history; and 'Lyric and Modernity', on the erroneous claim that the modern lyric abandons or escapes representation. The over-arching argument is that critics 'owe their best insights to assumptions these insights disprove', a fact which 'shows blindness to be a necessary correlative of the rhetorical nature of literary language' (BI, p. 141). The Anglo-American New Critics' concentration on language (rather than authors, for example) was made possible by their conception of the work as organic form but led to insights into the role of irony that undermine the conception of literary works as harmonious, organic wholes. Poulet's criticism seeks to identify a 'cogito', a writer's originary moment of self-knowledge, but instead discovers a transcendental self which exists only in language and puts in question the status of the self: 'what is here claimed to be an origin always depends on the prior existence of an entity that lies beyond reach of the self, though not beyond the reach of a language that destroys the possibility of an origin' (BI, p. 105). Lukács defines the novel as an essentially ironic form but then treats Flaubert's *Education sentimentale* as the acme of the modern novel in which alienation and discontinuity are overcome by time, which confers on it the appearance of organic growth. The transcendental agent that is offered as the remedy is in fact the disease itself: 'the organicism that Lukács had eliminated from the novel when he made irony its guiding structural principle has reentered the picture in the guise of time' (BI, p. 58). All these critics, de Man concludes,

seem curiously doomed to say something quite different from what they meant to say. Their critical stance – Lukács's propheticism, Poulet's belief in the power of an original *cogito*, Blanchot's claim of meta-Mallarmean impersonality – is defeated by their own critical results. A penetrating but difficult insight into the nature of literary language ensues. It seems, however, that this insight could only be gained because the critics were in the grip of this peculiar blindness: their language could grope towards a certain degree of insight only because their method remained oblivious to the perception of this insight. The insight exists only for a reader in the privileged position of being able to observe the blindness as a phenomenon in its own right – the question of his own blindness being one which he is by definition incompetent to ask – and so being able to distinguish between statement and meaning. He has to undo the explicit results of a vision that is able to move toward the light only because, being already blind, it does not have to fear the power of this light. But the vision is unable to report correctly what it has perceived in the course of its journey. To write critically about critics thus becomes a way to reflect on the paradoxical effectiveness of a blinded vision that has to be rectified by means of insights that it unwittingly provides. (BI, pp. 105–6)

Blindness and Insight helped promote an interest in continental criticism and in reading critical discourses with the kind of attention given literary works; its emphasis on a complex structural relationship between blindness and insight helped to foster the development of a post-structuralist psychoanalytic criticism which reads texts as performing psychic operations they seek to theorize (such as repression, displacement, projection), even though de Man himself remained resolutely distant from psychoanalytic language and concepts. What attracted the most attention and certainly the greatest amount of commentary, however, was the essay on Jacques Derrida's reading of Rousseau.

The importance of Derrida, as de Man explains it, is on the one hand, to engage philosophical issues in a way that the close reading of the New Critics does not, yet on the other hand, unlike Blanchot, who uses categories of philosophical reflection but erases the moment of actual interpretive reading, to restore 'the complexities of reading to the dignity of a philosophical question. . . . This means that Derrida's work is one of the places where the future possibility of literary criticism is being decided' (BI, p. 111). Derrida argues that despite Rousseau's commitment to a certain metaphysics of presence, manifested in his condemnation of writing and nostalgia for a state of nature, Rousseau's works undermine the assumptions of that metaphysics. De Man explains,

Whenever Rousseau designates the moment of unity that exists at the beginning of things, when desire coincides with enjoyment, the self and other are united in the maternal warmth of their common origin, and consciousness speaks with the voice of truth, Derrida's interpretation shows, without leaving the text, that what is thus designated as a moment of presence always has to posit another, prior moment and so implicitly loses its privileged status as a point of origin. Rousseau defines voice as the origin of written language, but his description of oral speech or of music can be shown to possess, from the start, all the elements of distance and negation that prevent written language from ever achieving a condition of unmediated presence. ... Derrida's considerable contribution to Rousseau studies consists in showing that Rousseau's own texts provide the strongest evidence against his alleged doctrine. (BI, pp. 115–16)

The point on which de Man takes issue with Derrida is the status of the 'knowledge' Derrida discovers in Rousseau's text: for Derrida, Rousseau's writings escape his control and undermine the doctrine he attempts to assert. De Man maintains, on the contrary, that Rousseau was adopting a rhetorical strategy, knew exactly what he was doing. In fact, though de Man wants Rousseau to receive credit for insights that Derrida's mode of presentation may seem to deny him, the real question for de Man is not what Rousseau himself actually knew but 'whether his language is or is not blind to its own statement' (BI, p. 137). Rousseau's text, de Man roundly asserts, 'has no blind spots: it accounts at all moments for its own rhetorical mode'.

Since de Man calls ' "literary", in the full sense of the term, any text that implicitly or explicitly signifies its own rhetorical mode and prefigures its own misunderstanding as a correlative of its rhetorical nature' (BI, p. 136), and since he treats Rousseau as a 'non-blinded author', this essay has frequently been thought to define literature as a special, unblinded language, as though the disagreement between de Man and Derrida were de Man's privileging of literature. This idea is encouraged by claims in the opening essay of *Blindness and Insight* that literature 'is the only form of language free from the fallacy of unmediated expression' and that fiction or literature 'is demystified from the start' (BI, pp. 17–18). But the 'literary', like so many other categories in de Man's writings, proves elusive. To the definition of the 'literary' quoted above de Man appends a footnote, specifying that critical or philosophical texts which signify their own rhetorical mode and prefigure their own misunderstanding are 'not more or less literary than a poetic text that would avoid direct statement' (BI, p. 136), and later we are told that 'Lukács, Blanchot, Poulet and Derrida can be called "literary", in the full sense of the term, because of their blindness, not in spite of it' (BI, p. 141). Moreover, 'Criticism and Crisis', while telling us that literature is demystified, notes that when critics claim to demystify literature, 'literature is everywhere; what they call anthropology, linguistics, psychoanalysis, is nothing but literature reappearing, like the Hydra's head, in the very spot where it had supposedly been suppressed' (BI, p. 18). The literary, therefore, is neither the corpus of poems, plays and novels, nor a group of special texts without blind spots. Texts with a high degree of rhetoricity, that signify their own rhetorical mode, whether by affirming or denying it, count as literary, but this is not a test for identifying the literary but an account of what reading ubiquitously discovers. Blindness, de Man concludes, is 'the necessary correlative of the rhetorical nature of literary language', but it may be situated at various points in the circuit of original text, readers, and critical text.

The crucial claim of the essay on Derrida, in fact, is that literary language prefigures its own misreading by adopting figural strategies that are bound to be misread. To talk about language, Rousseau adopts a diachronic fiction, a fiction of origins that is an allegory about language; in exactly the same way, de Man argues, Derrida adopts the fiction of a historical period of logocentrism to which Rousseau is said to belong – 'his historical scheme is merely a narrative convention'.

Rousseau's use of a traditional vocabulary is exactly similar, in its strategy and its implications, to the use Derrida consciously makes of the traditional vocabulary of Western philosophy. What happens in Rousseau is exactly what happens in Derrida: a vocabulary of substance and presence is no longer used declaratively but rhetorically, for the very reasons that are being (metaphorically) stated. (BI, pp. 138–9)

'Rousseau's text postulates the necessity of its own misreading. It knows and asserts that it will be misunderstood. It tells the story, the allegory of its misunderstanding: the necessary degradation of . . .metaphor into literal meaning' (BI, p. 136). That is, the story about language that it tells is a story that applies to its own language: figurative language misread as literal language.

Of course the question arises whether de Man can tell us these things in a straightforward way. One of the striking features of his style is his avoidance of conspicuously oblique, playful modes, which might seem to reflect the message about the figurative nature of language. Instead, he adopts an austerely philosophical language – though that language varies during his career – and an apodictic mode of statement, asserting what is true and what it is false as one possessed of absolute knowledge. The claim to know with certainty things that are at the very least complicated and debatable, the discrepancy between the claims made about the elusive nature of language or pervasiveness of critical blindness and the confident declarations, has annoyed many commentators. How is it to be explained or defended?

The failure to argue for claims that might seem to require demonstration could doubtless be defended as a rhetorical strategy: the only way to make some truths persuasive is to make people to read as if they were true because, given the nature of what is being asserted, readers would not in any event be persuaded by argument but only by coming to see or think in this way. As de Man would later argue, language works by positing, but this takes the form of assertions that such and such is the case. Moreover, the possibility of arguing for a general claim (about literature or language or cognition) in a particular instance or for a single text would induce an error about the status of that claim, implying that it depended on the possibility of such demonstrations for every text, whereas many of these claims need to be read, rather, as general premises or horizons for discussion, figurative or allegorical rather than literal, performative rather than constative.

The emphasis on truth and error in the tone of assurance that readers can find annoying forcibly shows that there is for de Man no question of trying to stand above or outside the play of truth and falsity and pluralistically allow each competing view a validity of sorts. Such attempts to avoid truth and falsity are misguided, for 'no reading is conceivable in which the question of its truth or falsehood is not primarily involved'.[7] Modest disclaimers, invocations of possible blindness, would both mask this ineluctable claim to truth and fail to meet the issue, which is structural: one's own blindness is precisely that which one is not able to identify and take account of. Extending this pattern to Derrida's reading of Rousseau, de Man makes it clear that the structure of blindness and insight holds for the most careful and astute readings. There is an irreducible iterability to the critical process. The critic skilled in detecting the blindness of prior readings (including, at times, his own prior readings) will produce similar errors in turn. As Derrida's reading of Rousseau makes it possible for de Man to use Rousseau to identify Derrida's misreadings, so de Man's account will enable later critics to use Derrida and Rousseau against de Man, who notes in *Allegories of Reading*, 'Needless to say, this new interpretation will, in its turn, be caught in its own form of blindness'.[8]

The structure of blindness and insight does not, however, wholly account for de Man's manner. One might also apply to his discourse what he says of Michael Riffaterre's 'dogmatic assertions': 'by stating them as he does, in the blandest and most apodictic of terms, he makes their heuristic function evident. An eventual critique will have to

---

[7]   De Man, 'Foreword', to Carol Jacobs, *The Dissimulating Harmony* (Baltimore: Johns Hopkins University Press, 1978), p. x.

[8]   De Man, *Allegories of Reading: Figural Language in Rousseau, Nietzsche, Rilke, and Proust* (New Haven: Yale University Press, 1979), p. 139. Henceforth cited in the text as AR.

consider the results that such postulates allow one to reach rather than their merit as transcendental judgments'.[9] But even this would not hold for all his claims, since assertions about the eternal division of being, for instance, do not permit one to do anything. They seem to function – are necessarily made to function for readers – as allegories, as part of a story of reading and writing in which the figure of literature plays a starring role.

De Man's next book, *Allegories of Reading: Figural Language in Rousseau, Nietzsche, Rilke and Proust* (1979), goes further in describing how a deconstructive reading that identifies the errors of the tradition and shows the text exposing its own founding concepts as tropological aberrations is itself put in question by the further moments in which the text adumbrates an allegory of unreadability. In this account the terms 'blindness' and 'insight', with their references to acts and failures of perception, no longer appear, for what is involved here are aspects of language and properties of discourse which insure that critical writings, like other texts, will end up doing what they maintain cannot be done, exceeding or falling short of what they assert by the very act of asserting it. In discussing Rousseau, de Man stresses the mechanical and inexorable processes of grammar and discursive organization in remarks that also apply to critical attempts to master Rousseau's writings. *The Social Contract*, for example, discredits *promises*, yet it promises a great deal.

The reintroduction of the promise, despite the fact that its impossibility has been established, does not occur at the discretion of the writer. ... The redoubtable efficacy of the text is due to the rhetorical model of which it is a version. This model is a fact of language over which Rousseau himself has no control. Just like any other reader, he is bound to misread his text as a promise of political change. The error is not within the reader; language itself dissociates the cognition from the act. *Die Sprache verspricht (sich)*; to the extent that it is necessarily misleading, language just as necessarily conveys the promise of its own truth. (AR, pp. 276–7)

Misreading here is a repeated result of the problematical relation between the performative and constative functioning of language.

An important essay first published in 1969, 'The Rhetoric of Temporality', sums up many of de Man's early views on literature – as language that names the void with ever-renewed understanding – but, as de Man himself later wrote when reprinting it, 'With the deliberate emphasis on rhetorical terminology, it augurs what seemed to me a

[9]   De Man, *The Resistance to Theory*, ed. Wlad Godzich (Minneapolis: University of Minnesota Press, 1986), p. 30. Henceforth cited as RT.

change, not only in terminology but in substance. This terminology',
he correctly observed, 'is still uncomfortably intertwined with the
thematic vocabulary of consciousness and of temporality that was
current at the time, but it signals a turn that, at least for me, has
proven to be productive' (BI, p. xii).

It has also proven productive and influential for readers – more so
than that of *Blindness and Insight*. De Man takes up the figures of
symbol and allegory, which romantic aesthetics and subsequent
criticism have opposed as organic to mechanical and motivated to
arbitrary. The supremacy of the symbol as an expression of unity has
become a commonplace that underlies literary taste, procedures of
literary criticism, and conceptions of literary history. Looking at the
supposed shift from allegorical to symbolical imagery in late-
eighteenth-century poetry, de Man challenges the view that romantic
literature produces through the symbol a reconciliation of man and
nature and instead identifies the allegorical structures at work in its
most intense and lucid passages. Allegorizing tendencies 'appear at the
most original and profound moments. . ., when an authentic voice
becomes audible', in works of European literature between 1760 and
1800. 'The prevalence of allegory', he writes,

always corresponds to the unveiling of an authentically temporal destiny. This
unveiling takes place in a subject that has sought refuge from the impact of
time in a natural world to which, in truth, it bears no resemblance. . . .
Whereas symbol postulates the possibility of an identity or identification,
allegory designates primarily a distance in relation to its own origin, and,
renouncing the nostalgia and the desire to coincide, it establishes its language
in the void of this temporal difference. In so doing, it prevents the self from an
illusory identification with the non-self, which is now fully, though painfully,
recognized as a non-self. It is this painful knowledge that we perceive at the
moments when early romantic literature finds its true voice. (BI, pp. 206-7)

Romanticism is now seen not to center on a dialectic of subject and
object, mind and nature, but rather on a 'a conflict between a
conception of the self seen in its authentically temporal predicament
and a defensive strategy that tries to hide from this negative
self-knowledge' (BI, p. 208).

Here, as in earlier essays, the acme of literary achievement lies in the
renunciation of the temptations of reconciliation or transcendental
totalizations, in the confrontation of 'the nothingness of things
human' – 'le néant des choses humaines', as Rousseau's *La Nouvelle
Héloïse* puts it. But de Man's shift from a vocabulary of consciousness
to a rhetorical terminology brings a renunciation of renunciation: it is
no longer a question of will and lucidity but of structures of language,

as emerges in the second section of the essay, on irony as the unveiling of a split within the subject. Irony produces no positive synthesis or mastery but involves, rather, the repetitive recurrence of a self-escalating act of consciousness and

> a temporality that is definitely not organic, in that it relates to its source only in terms of distance and difference and allows for no end, for no totality. . . . The temporal void that it reveals is the same we encountered when we found allegory always implying an unreachable anteriority. Allegory and irony are thus linked in their discovery of an authentically temporal predicament. They are also linked in their common demystification of an organic world postulated in a symbolic mode of analogical correspondence or in a mimetic mode of representation in which fiction and reality could coincide. (BI, p. 222)

The tension between symbol and allegory, as Minae Mizumura writes, 'is already another name for the tension between a temptation of assuming the readability of a text, that is, of reconciling sign and meaning, and a renunciation of this temptation'.[10] It brings together this linguistic problematic with that of the self: literature comes into being in the tension between the temptation of reconciling an empirical self and a self that exists only in language and the renunciation of that temptation, or in the exposure of the discontinuity between a self that will die and a self that knows this but cannot change it.

De Man's essay, describing the symbol as a mystification and associating allegory with an 'authentic' understanding of language and temporality, contributed to a revival of interest in allegory already under way, but it went further than discussions by Northrop Frye and Angus Fletcher in effecting a reversal that made symbol a special case of figural language, for which allegory, with its explicit discrepancy between signifier and signified, seemed a better model. This revised conception of allegory and the allegorical functioning of texts of all sorts has been an important development in literary criticism of the 1970s and 1980s.

Allegories of Reading seems to pursue this interest in allegory, but here the term relates to texts' implicit commentary on modes of signification, implied second- or third-order narratives about reading and intelligibility. The principal impact of this series of dense essays is to undo various totalizations by showing how they are constructed, by focusing on ways in which the texts under consideration reveal these totalizing operations as rhetorical structures, figural impositions

---

[10]   Minae Mizumura, 'Renunciation', *Yale French Studies* 69 (1985), p. 91.

dependent on the forces or mechanisms they claim to overcome. A major instance is the concept of self or subject itself, which texts reveal as 'a mere metaphor by which man protects himself from his insignificance by forcing his interpretation upon the entire universe, substituting a human-centered set of meanings that is reassuring to his vanity for a set of meanings that reduces him to being a mere transitory accident in the cosmic order. The metaphorical substitution is aberrant but no human self could come into being without this error' (AR, p. 111). 'The possibility now arises', de Man writes in one of the climactic passages of the book, 'that the entire construction of drives, substitutions, repressions, and representations is the aberrant, metaphorical correlative of the absolute randomness of language, prior to any figuration or meaning' (AR, p. 299).

Metaphorical totalizations, which on the basis of resemblance presume to name or convey the essence of an entity, protect us from the knowledge of nothingness – 'faced with the truth of its non-existence, the self would be consumed as an insect is consumed by the flame that attracts it' – yet the critique of these notions generates a position in its turn: 'but the text that asserts this annihilation of the self is not consumed, because it still sees itself as the center that produces the affirmation. . . . By calling the subject a text, the text calls itself, to some extent, a subject . . . By asserting in the mode of truth that the self is to some extent a lie, we have not escaped from deception' (AR, pp. 111–12).

What is particularly striking about de Man's procedure is the unwillingness to remain content with – or, one should say, the procedure's inability to halt at – anything that seems a settled, demystified knowledge: one must ask how it is obtained and the status of the means. There is, for example, no question of escaping from the pitfalls of rhetoric by becoming aware of the rhetorical nature of discourse. When one asks whether a particular essay – by Nietzsche, for example – escapes from the error it denounces, the answer is no. Nor is literature 'the less deceitful because it asserts its own deceitful properties' (AR, p. 115). What was earlier described as the division at the heart of Being, and then as the complex relation between blindness and insight that prevents self-possession or self-presence, is here analysed as a linguistic predicament, the figural structure of language that insures a division variously described as a gap between sign and meaning, between meaning and intent, between the performative and constative functions of language, and between rhetoric as persuasion and rhetoric as trope.

Although the main emphasis falls on the way in which 'metaphors of primacy, of genetic history, and most notably, of the autonomous power to will of the self' are put in question by the mechanical, metonymical patterns on which they prove to depend, de Man also offers a critique of the assumption underlying this demystificatory movement, that rhetoric can be mastered by reduction to metonymical or grammar-like patterns. The opening essay, 'Semiology and Rhetoric', takes issue with the presumption of structuralist criticism that the linguistic model, which seeks to account for sentences by describing the grammatical rules that make them possible, can be extended to literature in something like a grammar of literary and rhetorical forms. Even simple examples illustrate the problematical character of this endeavor: asked by his wife whether he wants his bowling shoes laced over or laced under, Archie Bunker irritably replies, 'What's the difference?' A single grammatical form engenders two possible meanings which cannot simply coexist in a happy ambiguity, since one (which we call the 'rhetorical question') denies the relevance or even existence of the difference the other seeks to have explained, rejecting the illocutionary mode (questioning) of the other.

'Rhetoric', for de Man, names the pervasive condition of language, where one cannot decide by grammatical means between literal and figurative meanings. Insofar as understanding means determining the referential status of a text, establishing which statements refer literally and which are figures for something else, the rhetorical character of language makes of understanding a process of misreading, reveals it as an imposition, and shows reference to be not given but produced by reading and misreading. What earlier essays had treated as a human error is here described as an inevitable fact of language, which literature names and explores without being able to escape.

'The paradigm for all texts', de Man writes, 'consists of a figure (or a system of figures) and its deconstruction. But since this model cannot be closed off by a final reading', for as we have seen it displaces the figure to another position, where it must also be deconstructed, 'it engenders, in its turn, a supplementary figural superposition which narrates the unreadability of the prior narration. As distinguished from primary deconstructive narratives, centered on figures and ultimately always on metaphor, we can call such narratives to the second (or third) degree, allegories' (AR, p. 256). These are allegories of reading, or in fact, unreadability, allegories exposing the temptation to make sign and meaning coincide, to reconcile the irreconcilable. The move from the deconstruction of figure to allegories of reading is inherent in the logic of figure itself, de Man claims, but it is brilliantly elucidated and exemplified in Rousseau, to whom the second half of *Allegories of Reading* is devoted.

Six chapters take up works by Rousseau: his *Discourse on the Origin of Language*, his little known play *Pygmalion*, *La Nouvelle Héloïse*, *La Profession du foi du vicaire savoyard*, *Le Contrat social* and *Les Confessions*. The discussion of *La Nouvelle Héloïse* might be taken as exemplary here, since this novel figures in earlier essays ('Madame de Stael et Jean-Jacques Rousseau' and *Blindness and Insight*) as the text that achieves the highest wisdom through its unflinching confrontation of 'the nothingness of things human' and its renunciation of the temptations of reconciliation. Here the analysis moves a step further to focus on figure, its deconstruction, and the consequence thereof, which is no longer the detachment of renunciation but inevitable though unwarrantable involvement. Julie's rejection of love denounces it as a figure, a mystified substitution or exchange of properties between self and other, inside and outside. 'I thought I recognized in your face the traces of a soul which was necessary to my own', she writes to Saint-Preux. 'It seemed to me my senses acted only as the organs of nobler sentiments, and I loved you, not so much for what I thought I saw in you as for what I felt in myself'. This language of exalted sentiment offers in fact a precise analysis of love as a figure based on substitution, thematizing the work's deconstructive unmasking of the figure. But this primary narrative of a figure and its deconstruction does not give rise to settled knowledge: 'At the moment when Julie acquires a maximum of insight, the control over the rhetoric of her own discourse is lost, for us as well as for her' (AR, p. 216). The first narrative cannot be closed off by assured knowledge and generates in turn a superposed story that narrates the unreadability of the prior narration, in a second order narrative or allegory, an allegory of reading or unreadability.

In this case the unreadability emerges in several ways: first, Julie is unable to understand her own deconstruction; she immediately begins to repeat the deluded figural involvement she has so lucidly exposed, this time substituting God for Saint-Preux. She is, de Man writes, 'unable to read her own text, unable to recognize how its rhetorical mode relates to its own meaning' (AR, p. 217). Second, there emerges an insistent ethical discourse that readers have found hard to read. Allegories are always ethical, de Man writes; 'the passage to an ethical tonality does not result from a transcendental imperative but is the referential (and therefore unreliable) version of a linguistic confusion', the inability to read and calculate the force of a deconstructive narrative (AR, p. 206). Finally, the claim in the Preface of the speaker R. allegorizes the necessary unreadability of this narrative: 'R.'s statement of helplessness before the opacity of his own text is similar to Julie's relapse into metaphorical models of interpretation at her moments of insight' (AR, p. 217n). This allegory of unreadability figures the inability of deconstructive narratives to produce settled knowledge. 'Deconstructions of figural texts engender lucid narratives which produce, in their turn, and as it were within their own texture, a darkness more redoubtable than the error they dispel' (AR, p. 217). The problem is 'that a totally enlightened language . . . is unable to control the recurrence, in its readers as well as in itself, of the errors it exposes', any more than the self that exists in language is able to prevent the death of the empirical self (AR, p. 219n).

De Man's readings focus on elements that are glossed over by readings intent at achieving a humanistic, thematic recuperation, at fitting Rousseau's texts into any of the totalities that dominate literary education: schemes of literary history, conceptions of the thought of a period or of the beliefs or the development of an author, not to say the thematic unity of a work. Usually explication is seen as an attempt to overcome difficulties and make them fit presumed totalities, but, de Man asks, what if one were to reverse the ethos of explication? What if one were to attempt 'a reading that would no longer blindly submit to the teleology of controlled meaning', but rather would explore resistance to meaning? The result is a demonstration that the text deconstructs the totalizations it puts forward. In Nietzsche's *The Birth of Tragedy*, for instance,

the deconstruction of the Dionysian authority finds its arguments within the text itself, which can then no longer be called simply blind or mystified. Moreover, the deconstruction does not occur between statements, as in a logical refutation or in a dialectic, but happens instead between, on the one hand, metalinguistic statements about the rhetorical nature of language and, on the other, a rhetorical praxis that puts these statements into question. (AR, p. 98)

As he explained in an interview, 'if it is true that texts always undo readings, it is equally true that texts constitute meanings. So the real theoretical question is what it is in language that necessarily produces meanings but that always undoes what it produces'.[11] This is a continuing burden of his investigation of literary and philosophical texts.

Indeed the power of texts to constitute meaning that they ceaselessly undermine is, for de Man, a source of history, on several levels. At the first level, we might think in terms of celebrated individual texts, such as Marx's *Capital* or Rousseau's *Social Contract*. If texts simply had

[11] 'Interview with Paul de Man', by Robert Moynihan, *Yale Review* 73:4 (Summer 1984), p. 587.

meanings determined once and for all, interpretation would not be a historical struggle, but history is in part a series of conflicting interpretations of Marx and Rousseau, the imposing of totalizing interpretations, which are then undone. 'To read the *Social Contract*, for instance and among other things, is to determine the relation between general will and particular will', and while de Man's discussion is not concerned with 'an evaluation of the political and ethical praxis that can be derived from it', his analysis of 'the rhetorical patterns that organize the distribution and the movement of the key terms' outlines the parameters for the political structures that can be seen as historical interpretations of this powerful text (AR, p. 256).

One of these structures, however, leads us to the second level, at which history is not the violent imposition of interpretations of individual texts. Here, rather, the disparate, mutually disjunctive modes of determination that are specific to linguistic structures, to texts, are determining of historical reality. History is the product of the combination of freedom and determinacy that characterizes a generalized textuality. 'The divergence which prevails, within the State, in the relationship between the citizen and the executive is in fact an unavoidable estrangement between political rights and laws on the one hand, and political action and history on the other. The grounds for this alienation are best understood in terms of the rhetorical structure that separates one domain from the other' (AR, p. 266). That rhetorical structure is the discrepancy between language conceived as grammar and language as reference or intentional action, and the ineluctability and indeterminacy of this structural relationship is what de Man calls 'text'. 'The structure of the entity with which we are concerned', writes de Man in his exposition of *The Social Contract*, '(be it as property, as national State, or as any other political institution) is most clearly revealed when it is considered as the general form that subsumes all these particular versions, namely as legal *text*' (AR, p. 267). The problematical relationship between the generality of law, system, grammar and its particularity of application, event, or reference is the textual structure Rousseau expounds in the relationship between the general will and the particular individual, or between the state as system and the sovereign as active principle. The tension between grammar and reference

is duplicated in the differentiation between the state as a defined entity and the state as principle of action or, in linguistic terms, between the constative and performative function of language. A text is defined by the necessity of considering a statement, at the same time, as performative and constative, and the logical tension between figure and grammar is repeated in the impossibility of distinguishing between two linguistic functions which are not necessarily compatible. (AR, p. 270)

The pertinence of the aporia between performative and constative emerges clearly in Rousseau's question of whether 'the body politic possesses an organ with which it can *énoncer* [articulate] the will of the people'. The constative function of stating a preexisting will and the performative positing or shaping of a will are at odds, and while the system requires that the organ only announce what the general will determines, the action of the state or 'lawgiver' will in particular instances declare or posit a general will. This is especially so in the founding of the state, for though, as Rousseau writes, 'the people subject to the Law must be the authors of the Law', in fact, he asks, 'how could a blind mob, which often does not know what it wants [promulgate] a system of Law?' The structural tension between performative and constative here in what de Man calls the text is determinative of history, with the violence of its positings, its tropological substitutions, and their 'eventual denunciation, in the future undoing of any State or any political institution' (AR, pp. 274–5).

De Man's next book, *The Rhetoric of Romanticism*, collects most of his writings on romanticism – from his earliest as well as his latest periods: 'The Intentional Structure of the Romantic Image', a long essay on Yeats from his doctoral dissertation, and chapters on Hölderlin, Wordsworth, Shelley, Baudelaire, and Kleist. Despite striking differences in terminology and technique, these pieces reveal continuities in his concerns and his view of romanticism as an exploration of the figurality of language and a critique of the priority of the natural object.

Discussion of romanticism is particularly difficult, de Man suggests, because it requires a coming to terms with a past from which we are not yet separated, a past whose most intense questioning involves precisely this interpretive relation to experiences become memories – that is, the very structure on which our relation to it depends. Descriptions of romanticism always miss the mark, for reasons which are structural rather than due to failures of intelligence. A further complication is introduced by the fact the genetic categories on which literary history depends – the models of birth, development, death – are most decisively promoted but also exposed by the romantic works that they would be used to discuss: 'one may well wonder what kind of historiography could do justice to the phenomenon of Romanticism, since Romanticism (itself a period concept) would then be the movement that challenges the genetic principle which necessarily underlies all historical narrative' (AR p. 82). As a result, 'the interpretation of romanticism remains for us the most difficult and at the same time the most necessary of tasks' (RR, p. 50).

'The Intentional Structure of the Romantic Image' suggested that one could find in the early romantics a questioning of the ontological priority of the natural object – the priority of nature to language, for example. 'Image and Emblem in Yeats', the extract from de Man's dissertation, argues that many of Yeats's images must be read as emblems which come from literary or hermetic (especially Neoplatonic) traditions and receive their meaning not by analogy with nature but by independent decree or positing, and that Yeats sees natural images as nothing but disguised, not yet understood emblems. This is a radical departure within the Western poetic tradition:

when nature itself is considered a mere sign, . . . then one has left the mainstream of the tradition and embarked on 'strange seas of thought'. We can understand and share in Hölderlin's nostalgia for a time when words will originate like flowers; but it is much more difficult to understand a conception of the emblem which reverses the process and wants flowers to originate as if they were words. (RR, pp. 168–9)

In detailed discussion of Yeats's poetic development and of changes of style reflecting a commitment to a poetry of emblems, de Man reveals a recurrent structure, in which a passage 'states the destruction of the stylistic device by means of which it functions and exists' (RR, p. 195). For instance, 'a striking natural image, "A moon . . ., in the trembling blue-green of the sky", functions also as an emblem that states the inadequacy and the downfall of precisely that type of natural image' (RR, p. 197). The most potent example comes in a reading of 'Among School Children', whose concluding stanza, with its image of the chestnut tree and the dancer indistinguishable from her dance, has been taken to glorify fundamental unity of being and doing in natural forms, to which human beings and the organic form of the poem itself aspire. If read as emblems, however, the images of the final lines – the tree, the dancer, and the dance – acquire very different connotations, to which other Yeats texts convincingly attest, and 'what appears as synthesis is only one more veiled statement of the absolute superiority of the emblem over the image' (RR, p. 201). The poem's final question, 'How can we know the dancer from the dance?', comes to be read not as a rhetorical question presuming the impossibility of distinguishing but as a genuine question about the choice between the transient world of matter (the dancer) and the renunciation of natural joys for the sake of divine revelation (the dance). 'The ways of the image and the emblem are distinct and opposed; the final image is not a rhetorical statement of reconciliation but an anguished question; it is our perilous fate not to know if the glimpses of unity we perceive at times can be made more permanent by natural ways or by the ascesis of renunciation, by images or by emblem.'[12]

Yeats's poetry of emblems provides, however, not a solution for the loss of the natural object or a synthesis between the physical and the spiritual, as critics wishfully maintain, but an oscillation that emphasizes the split or division. Where a poetry of the emblem has promised the eternal peace and ecstacy of divine presence, the poems can only explode this belief. 'Those who look to Yeats for reassurance from the anxiety of our own post-romantic predicament, or release from the paralysis of nihilism', de Man writes, 'will not find it in his conception of the emblem. He cautions instead against the danger of unwarranted hopeful solutions', but this what the highest forms of language can accomplish (RR, p. 238).

Other pieces in this volume, along with the late essays collected in *The Resistance to Theory* and *Aesthetic Ideology*, take up a related series of themes: (1) the aesthetic as an ideology which imposes, even violently, continuity between perception and cognition, form and idea, and which literature is always undoing; (2) 'disfiguration' as the repetitive process by which language 'performs the erasures of its own positions' (RR, p. 119) – a destruction, for instance, of the anthropomorphisms by which entities are given face and voice, the condition of meaning; (3) an unveiling, then, of the 'senseless' positional power of language, which like the power of death itself, must always be recuperated by acts of reading and interpretation; (4) the identification of a resistance to literary theory that is not external to the theoretical enterprise but a resistance to the rhetorical character of language that theory arises to address but ends by reducing or monumentalizing; (5) a critique of attempts to identify in language, or in the production and reception of texts, a level or moment of phenomenality, when something – words, meanings, affects, effects – would simply be given to perception rather than produced by reading.

The Resistance to Theory and *Aesthetic Ideology* have somewhat different focuses. The former is primarily a discussion of contemporary

---

[12]   RR, p. 202. Yeats's question is also discussed in 'Semiology and Rhetoric', which was reprinted as the opening chapter of *Allegories of Reading,* but since de de Man did not there fill in the reading of the poem that would follow from taking this as a serious, anguished question, he was frequently accused of arbitrarily selecting a rhetorical option without considering contextual meaning. The fuller reading given in *The Rhetoric of Romanticism* illustrates that deconstruction is not a matter of ignoring context, but that context must be read with the same intensity as the text it supposedly elucidates.

literary theory and its implications, with essays on Walter Benjamin, Mikhail Bakhtin and, perhaps most important, on Michael Riffaterre and Hans Robert Jauss, two theorists of reading or reception who can be shown to evade, in different ways, the rhetorical nature of language and the problem of reading in presuming a phenomenality of language – form or meaning given to perception. The latter collection focuses on Kant, Hegel, Schiller, Pascal, and the epistemology of metaphor, exploring in particular the character and role of 'the aesthetic' and finding in Kant a critique of the ideology of the aesthetic developed, for instance, by Schiller and applied, or misapplied, both in humanistic conceptions of aesthetic education and in fascist conceptions of politics as an aesthetic project.

Both collections emphasize and explore the tension between a linguistically-oriented or rhetorical approach to literature and an aesthetic, phenomenological, and hermeneutical approach. Two general essays, 'The Resistance to Theory' and 'The Return to Philology', describe the problem most clearly: close reading, whether theoretically inspired or not, involves attention to problematical or puzzling features of texts, and to 'the bafflement that such singular turns of phrase [are] bound to produce in readers honest enough not to hide their non-understanding behind the screen of received ideas that often passes, in literary instruction, for humanistic knowledge' (RT, p. 23). Mere reading, with its identification of rhetorical structures, upsets assumptions of literary criticism, based on an identification of literature with the aesthetic, conceived of as the harmonious fusion of form and meaning, the sensible and the intelligible.

Traditionally, the aesthetic is the name of the attempt to find a bridge between the phenomenal and the intelligible, the sensuous and the conceptual. Aesthetic objects, with their union of sensuous form and spiritual content, serve as guarantors of the general possibility of articulating the material and the spiritual, a world of forces and magnitudes with a world of value. Literature, conceived here as the rhetorical character of language revealed by close reading, 'involves the voiding rather than the affirmation of aesthetic categories' (RT, p. 10). Thus the convergence of sound and meaning in literature is an effect which language can achieve 'but which bears no relationship by analogy or by ontologically grounded imitation, to anything beyond that particular effect. It is a rhetorical rather than an aesthetic function of language, an identifiable trope that operates on the level of the signifier and contains no responsible pronouncement on the nature of the world – despite its powerful potential to create the opposite illusion' (RT, p. 10). Literary theory, in its attention to the functioning of language, thus 'raises the question whether aesthetic values can be compatible with the linguistic structures from which these values are derived' (RT, p. 25). Literature itself raises this question in various ways, offering evidence of the autonomous potential of language, of the uncontrollable figural basis of forms, which cannot therefore serve as the basis of reliable cognition, or as de Man argues in the essay on Kleist in *The Rhetoric of Romanticism*, allegorically exposing the violence that lies hidden behind the aesthetic and makes aesthetic education possible.

De Man's 'Kant and Schiller' concludes with a quotation from a novel by Joseph Goebbels, which casts the leader as an artist working creatively on his material: 'The statesman is an artist too. The leader and the led ("Führer und Masse") presents no more of a problem than, say, painter and color. Politics are the plastic art of the state, just as painting is the plastic art of color. This is why politics without the people, or even against the people, is sheer nonsense. To shape a People out of the masses and a State out of the People, this has always been the deepest intention of politics in the true sense'. This aestheticization of politics, which seeks the fusion of form and idea, is, de Man writes, 'a grievous misreading of Schiller's aesthetic state', but Schiller's conception is itself a similar misreading, which must be undone by an analysis that takes us back to Kant. Kant had 'disarticulated the project of the aesthetic which he had undertaken and which he found, by the rigor of his own discourse, to break down under the power of his own critical epistemological discourse'.[13] The fact that de Man's wartime juvenilia had themselves on occasion exhibited an inclination to idealize the rebirth of the German nation in aesthetic terms gave him a special reason for demonstrating how the most insightful literary and philosophical texts of the tradition expose the unwarranted violence required to fuse form and idea, cognition and performance.

The title essay of *The Resistance to Theory* asks what is so threatening about literary theory that it provokes attacks, and it offers several explanations: 'It upsets rooted ideologies by revealing the mechanics of their workings; it goes against a powerful philosophical tradition of which aesthetics is a prominent part; it upsets the established canon of literary works and blurs the borderlines between literary and non-literary discourse. By implication it may also reveal the links between ideologies and philosophy' (RT, pp. 11–12).

---

[13] 'Kant and Schiller', m/s pp. 42 and 9. The essay will be published in de Man's *Aesthetic Ideology,* ed. Andrzej Warminski (Minneapolis: University of Minnesota Press, 1988).

Literary theory can do this because it focuses on 'the modalities of production and reception of meaning *prior* to their establishment' (RT, p. 7). Traditional literary study based on historical and aesthetic considerations takes for granted the possibility of understanding, the phenomenal reality of literary meaning. Literary theory, on the other hand, takes this as a problem. Theory arises with the introduction of a linguistic terminology, that is, one which sees reference as an effect of language rather than something given and phenomenal, given to perception. 'What we call ideology', de Man writes, 'is precisely the confusion of linguistic with natural reality, of reference with phenomenalism' (RT, p. 11). In many cases, this is quite difficult to avoid: 'it is very difficult not to conceive of the pattern of one's past and future existence as in accordance with temporal and spatial schemes that belong to fictional narratives ...' (RT, p. 11). Such schemes or tropes produce referential effects, but ideology, which pervades our dealings with the world, involves taking a referential effect for a phenomenal reality, assuming the existence of what may be produced by the referential functioning of language. A linguistic perspective, stressing that the relationship between word and thing is not phenomenal but conventional, helps to identify the ideological inclinations to take reference as natural and perceptual and hence to assume a referent as given. 'More than any other mode of inquiry, including economics', de Man writes,

the linguistics of literariness is a powerful and indispensable tool in the unmasking of ideological aberrations, as well as a determining factor in accounting for their occurrence. Those who reproach literary history for being oblivious to social and historical (that is to say ideological) reality are merely stating their fear at having their own ideological mystifications exposed by the tool they are trying to discredit. (RT, p. 11)

Rhetorical reading exposes the ideological imposition of meaning as a defense we build against language – specifically against the inhuman, mechanical aspects of language, the structures or rhetorical possibilities that are independent of any intent or desire we might have, yet which are neither natural nor phenomenal either (RT, p. 96). There are, in de Man's accounts, two levels of imposition: 'a lie super-imposed upon an error' is his economical description. First there is the positing by language, which does not reflect but constitutes, which simply occurs. De Man speaks of 'the absolute randomness of language prior to any figuration or meaning' (AR, p. 299). 'The positing power of language is entirely arbitrary, in having a strength that cannot be reduced to necessity, and entirely inexorable in that there is no alternative to it' (RR, p. 126). Then there is the conferring of sense or meaning on this positing, through figuration. Positing does not belong to any sequence or have any status; these are imposed retrospectively. 'How can a positional act, which relates to nothing that comes before or after, become inscribed in a sequential narrative? . . . it can only be because we impose, in our turn, on the senseless power of positional language the authority of sense and meaning' (RR, p. 117). We transform language into historical and aesthetic objects, or embed discursive occurrences in narratives that provide continuities, in a process of troping that de Man calls 'the endless prosopopoeia by which the dead are made to have a face and a voice which tells in turn the allegory of their own demise and allows us to apostrophize them in their turn' (RR, p. 122). 'We cannot ask why it is that we, as subjects, choose to impose meaning, since we are ourselves defined by this very question' (RR, p. 118).

For de Man, Shelley's 'The Triumph of Life' is the text which

warns us that nothing, whether deed, word, thought, or text, ever happens in any relation, positive or negative, to anything that precedes, follows, or exists elsewhere, but only as a random event whose power, like the power of death, is due to the randomness of its occurrence. It also warns us why and how these events then have to be reintegrated in a historical and aesthetic system of recuperation that repeats itself, regardless of the exposure of its fallacy. (RR, p. 122)

The senseless and random, of which death is the best example (and Shelley's death is literally marked in this poem as what prevented its completion), is endowed with meaning – as 'senseless', for example, – and reintegrated in structures which 'reading as disfiguration' works to undo but recuperates and monumentalizes in its own way. 'No degree of knowledge', de Man notes, 'can ever stop this madness, for it is the madness of words' (RR, p. 122).

It is also the madness of literary criticism, which characteristically seeks to render language intelligible and produces generic categories, schemes of literary history, totalizing readings – all aesthetic and ethical defenses against language. 'Generic terms such as "lyric" (or its various subspecies, "ode", "idyll", "elegy") as well as pseudo-historical period terms such as "romanticism" or "classicism" are always terms of resistance and nostalgia, at the furthest remove from the materiality of actual history' (RR, p. 262). What de Man calls reading – unflagging attention to what resists intelligibility, suspicion of the myriad totalizing procedures by which language is recuperated – undoes the figurations of literary criticism but cannot itself escape the recuperative process.

Nowhere does this emerge more clearly than in one's own reading of de Man. While his analyses focus on the resistant or disruptive and insistently oppose modes of understanding that overcome textual difficulties so as to hear in the text what it is thought to say, the character of his own writing makes this the only way to understand or interpret him. One can only make sense of his writings if one already has a sense of what they must be saying and can bear with the slippage of concepts, the elusiveness of idiosyncratically employed philosophical and linguistic terms. One works to get over or around the puzzling valuations, the startling sweeping assertions, the apparently incompatible claims. To learn from his writings, one must read him also in the ways he warns us against, giving in to the teleology of meaning.

De Man's writing grants great authority to texts – a power of illumination which is a power of disruption – but little authority to meaning. This highly original combination of respect for texts and suspicion of meaning will give his writing a continuing power in years to come, though the effects of this power are not easily calculable. His works celebrate great literary and philosophical texts for their insightful undoings of the meanings that usually pass for their value. His cumbersome writing, with its tone of authority and elusive yet resonant key terms, effectively teaches suspicion of meaning and 'the danger of unwarranted hopeful solutions', or as he puts it on the final page of *The Rhetoric of Romanticism* 'the trap of an aesthetic education which inevitably confuses dismemberment of language by the power of the letter with the gracefulness of a dance' (RR, p. 290). The power of the letter, or inscription, is senseless occurrence, like death itself, which is nevertheless invested with significance, in a process of recuperation which de Man warns against but which, he concludes, occurs regardless of the exposure of its fallacy. Speaking of Shelley's death, he writes, 'The final test of reading, in *The Triumph of Life*, depends on how one reacts to the textuality of this event, how one disposes of Shelley's body' (RR, p. 121). The apparent ease with which readers evade reading by constructing monuments 'demonstrates the inadequacy of our understanding of Shelley and, beyond him, of romanticism in general'. The inevitable monumentalization of an interpretive summary is only one enactment of this general predicament. The discovery in 1987 of de Man's wartime juvenilia both illuminated and disrupted the process of idealizing monumentalization that was underway, encouraging more suspicious reading, king the temptation to invest the author with a personal authority, and forcing readers to attend to texts.

Senseless occurrence, or what is glimpsed only as that which is translated into intelligibility by tropes of various sorts, takes different guises in de Man's writings: *inscription*, 'the uncontrollable power of the letter as inscription', 'the absolute randomness of language prior to any figuration or meaning', and *occurrence* are some of the terms which abusively figure that which figuration brings into representation. In his later writings this reality is increasingly identified with 'the materiality of actual history', as opposed to schematic, redemptive and dialectical patterns of history. His own death left further to be explored the implications of his characterization of history and his engagement with ideology and the aesthetic – as a certain historical inscription, a version of the materiality of actual history, compelled those who wished to learn from his writing to work out the problem of the political stakes of the aesthetic, which otherwise they might have preferred to avoid.

PART III

Reading Culture

8

Deconstruction and the Law

The notion of 'applying' deconstruction to law or legal doctrine contains an initial problem: the very idea of post-structuralism includes a critique of the notion of application. That is, what seems to be shared by the projects and discourses deemed 'post-structuralist' is a critique of the structuralist concept of a separate metalanguage or method which could be applied to the analysis of various domains of objects. While structuralism entailed the attempt to position oneself outside a cultural practice so as to describe its rules and norms, the post-structuralist critique demonstrated, in a variety of fields, that structuralist analyses are caught up in the processes and mechanisms they are analysing.

The analytical posture, then, is not one of scientific detachment and application but of intractable involvement. This can be most clearly observed in psychoanalytic criticism, which in its post-structuralist turn has ceased to be the application of a psychoanalytic metalanguage to a set of literary objects. One must speak, rather, of a movement back and forth between literary and psychoanalytical texts, literary and psychological models, as critics read Freud's analyses as simultaneously theories and examples of textuality, arguing that the force of Freud's insights can be seen in the way his writings are themselves structured by the processes of repression, condensation, displacement and transference that they describe. Freud's own case studies make it clear that his analytical discourse is not external to the psychic forces he is analyzing and that its pertinence to literature comes not from its exteriority and scientific authority but from its own susceptibility to literary and rhetorical analyses.

If the defining feature of post-structuralism is the breakdown of the distinction between language and metalanguage – a theory of narrative is itself a narrative, a theory of writing is itself writing, a discourse on metaphor does not escape metaphor, a theory of repression involves repression – then the project of 'applying' post-structuralism or deconstruction to the law encounters right at the outset an engaging paradox: the defining feature of what one wishes to apply is its critique of the notion of application. There are two points to note here, though. First, the critique itself produces discourse that functions metalinguistically. Jacques Lacan's dictum, 'Il n'y a pas de metalangage' – meaning that any supposed metalanguage proves to be more language, worked by the forces it purports to describe – is itself a metalinguistic statement, and the claim that post-structuralist projects share a critique of the notion of application provides a post-structuralist concept to apply to some further domain. The lesson is not that application cannot take place but rather that it is no different from other activities of interpretation, and that one cannot expect to produce a grand theory which would stand outside the domains to which it might apply. Second, if there is a problem about application it is not because deconstruction is too pure to be applied; it is because it is already applied. One of the distinctive features of Jacques Derrida's writing has been its refusal to develop a general and consistent theoretical metalanguage but its exploration instead of the logic of particular terms within the texts he is analysing: *pharmakon* in Plato, *supplement* in Rousseau, *hymen* in Mallarmé, *parergon* in Kant. You start wherever you are, Derrida writes. Discursive argument does not clear the ground to build from the ground up, on a foundation. You start wherever you are, *in medias res*.

Suppose, then, that we find ourselves in the domain of law. What happens here that can be brought into a relation with the practice of deconstruction? One might say at the outset that since what is deconstructed in deconstruction are the hierarchical oppositions of Western metaphysics, it is entirely appropriate that deconstruction should occur in the realm of law, which to a considerable extent is based on these categorial oppositions, between essential and accidental, internal and external, private and public, substance and form. Within what is known as the Critical Legal Studies movement (CLS) one can identify both themes and strategies of argument that seem comparable to those of deconstruction, beginning with the demonstration of persistent contradictions within the system of legal doctrine, which turns out to rely on principles that are at war with each other. Roberto Mangabeira Ungar hails as a crucial feature of Critical Legal practice 'the willingness to recognize and develop the conflicts between principles and counterprinciples that can be found in any body of law'.[1] One of the founding articles of Critical Legal

---

[1]   Roberto Mangabeira Ungar, *The Critical Legal Studies Movement* (Cambridge, Mass: Harvard University Press, 1987), p. 17.

Studies, Duncan Kennedy's 'The Structure of Blackstone's *Commentaries*', argues that the history of legal discourse is a series of attempts to paper over a fundamental contradiction in our conception of the relation between the self and others.[2] Analysis is thus a matter of exposing an underlying contradiction, demonstrating its pervasiveness, showing that while the arguments of legal doctrine attempt to privilege one pole of the contradiction, the other reasserts itself.

An example which non-lawyers have no difficulty grasping is the conflict between a society's commitment to a jurisprudence of formal and explicit rules, which can be applied automatically once the relevant facts are ascertained, and a jurisprudence of informal standards, which enable judges to consider each case on its merits. By the first model, a law against speeding should take the form of an explicit rule: anyone exceeding a posted speed limit is guilty, whatever the circumstances. By the second model, the judge ought to consider each case on its merits in terms of a social goal, such as the safety of the public: was the defendant endangering himself or others? There is a conflict between rules and standards, in that rules will frequently fail to achieve the relevant social goals – a rule about speeding will permit some behavior that is in fact dangerous and forbid some that is harmless – while standards introduce the possibility of capricious, unpredictable application – drivers would have difficulty knowing whether a judge would find their speed dangerous. As Mark Kelman puts it, 'there will remain in any legal dispute a logically or empirically unanswerable formal problem, that granting substantially greater discretion or limiting discretion through significantly greater rule boundedness in the formation of the prevailing legal command is always perfectly plausible'.[3]

Duncan Kennedy maintains that the conflict between the commitment to rule and the commitment to standards reflects the contradiction between ideals of individualism and of altruism, between the conception of the self as autonomous and self-reliant and the conception of the self as inextricably involved with others whose interests are as important as its own. Whether or not this is so, it has encouraged analysts to demonstrate the pervasiveness of the conflict between standards and rules and to show that this conflict both undermines attempts at doctrinal justification and introduces a fundamental indeterminacy into legal matters. Kennedy's 'Form and

---

[2] Duncan Kennedy, 'The Structure of Blackstone's *Commentaries*', *Buffalo Law Review* 28 (1979).

[3] Mark Kelman, *A Guide to Critical Legal Studies* (Cambridge, Mass.: Harvard University Press, 1987), p. 16. I am much indebted to Kelman's book, which offers clear exposition and illuminating syntheses.

Substance in Private Law Adjudication' focuses on problems of contract law, where questions of when a contract is formed and which contracts are to be deemed enforceable are questions about the relations between rules and standards. The rule model stipulates that there is a contract when there has been an offer and an overtly communicated acceptance whose terms mirror those of the offer; but the standards model seeks to require that parties deal with one another in good faith, so that trading partners may be held to a contract 'even when critical terms (including price) are unspecified, as long as terms can be filled in in accordance with more or less vague "reasonable commercial practice" (such as past dealings or market price)'.[4] Consumers engaged in commercial transactions embrace each model in turn: they hold that a merchant who advertises a particular television set at a given price should be required to sell it without fail at that price; yet they also wish the contract to be governed by a principle of fair dealing and to be held to include various presumptions – that a television set will work as television sets are supposed to or the sale is void – even when they are not part of an explicit contract.

In criminal law the conflict between rules and standards underlies disputes both about the law and about particular cases: by the rule model a defendant who is fortuitously prevented by the police from committing a robbery might be innocent, while the standards model, focusing on intent, would ask whether the defendant has shown a clear disposition to crime and was a danger to society. Each solution has its virtues and its drawbacks, and compromises only conceal the conflict between the two clearly different principles. 'It is not possible, in fact', Kelman concludes, 'to conceive of a legal dispute in which the choice of form [i.e. rules versus standards] is not implicated. What is more important, or more controversial at any rate, is that in each case there is no clear reason to prefer one formal resolution to another. . . . when one actually gets down to disputes between 'good' versions of rules and 'good' standards, the formal arguments hardly seem resolvable' (p. 31). A rule and a standard calculated to give the same result in a particular case will give divergent results in others. Kelman concludes,

If mainstream lawyers are to make a convincing case that the Critics [the practitioners of CLS] are wrong to see a formal *contradiction* rather than a list of policy concerns to be balanced to arrive at a rational and sensible solution, they must demonstrate some general tendency for formal disputes to converge

---

[4]   Kelman, *Guide*, p. 18. See Duncan Kennedy, 'Form and Substance in Private Law Adjudication', *Harvard Law Review* 89 (1976).

toward a single balanced solution, must counter the tendency, which I believe I have demonstrated in my examples, for irreducible formal conflict to persist. (p. 32)

Legal doctrine has generally presumed that rules are the norm and that standards are supplied to supplement the rule, to soften its application and deal with exceptions; yet it can be shown that the exception devours the rule, that the supposedly supplementary principle also governs the cases regarded as normal. CLS writers have energetically demonstrated, in critiques of analyses of law as a system of rules, that the standards are what govern the functioning of the rules, their conditions of possibility. Where there seems to be a clear rule – say, that no vehicle may go more than 35 miles per hour on a particular road – it is likely that the rule will not be universally enforced, and thus that some general standard will govern its enforcement: the police will only arrest those going 'unreasonably' or 'dangerously' fast, or who look to be otherwise dangerous to the peace. In fact, the clearer the rule, the more crucial will be some standard that governs and makes possible its enforcement. Criminal laws against various forms of consensual sex could not be strictly enforced without causing great social disruption, so that effectively the law relies on standards applied at the discretion of the police and magistrates – as if the law were *Thou shalt do nothing publicly outrageous.*[5] The more explicit the rule, the more likely that in fact a principle of standards will operate, and conversely, in cases where the law is supposed to be a standard – say, that a defendant in a torts action is liable only when he has not taken 'reasonable' care – some de facto rules will develop in the legal system. Jacques Derrida has demonstrated the ubiquity of what he calls the logic of supplementarity, whereby the supposed addition or exception turns out to contain the principles that govern and make possible the supposed norm: speech proves a special case of a generalized writing (operates on the principles attributed to writing); constative utterances are a special sort of performative utterance; literal language is a special case of figurative language (figures whose figurality has been forgotten).[6] This logic, in which the operation of what is presented as the norm depends on principles embodied in the supposed exception or supplement, can be shown to operate powerfully in the domain of law.

One can thus see that work in Critical Legal Studies has affinities with deconstruction in philosophy and literary criticism and that a

---

[5]   William H. Simon, 'Legality, Bureaucracy, and Class in the Welfare System', *Yale Law Journal* 92 (1983), p. 1230.

[6]   For discussion see my *On Deconstruction: Theory and Criticism after Structuralism* (Ithaca: Cornell University Press, 1982), pp. 102–16, 164–70, 193–9.

comprehensive survey of deconstruction in the law would prove of considerable interest. While awaiting such a study, one can ask how deconstruction in law and in literary studies are related and what they might have to teach each other, taking as points of reference two fine deconstructive readings, Gerald Frug's 'The Ideology of Bureaucracy in American Law' and Clare Dalton's 'An Essay in the Deconstruction of Contract Doctrine'.

Literary critics, whether working on literary or non-literary texts, have generally convinced themselves that their fundamental task is to interpret individual works. In law, the situation appears to be different. Although frequently analysis may focus on the text of a particular judicial decision or a law, the real object of analysis is the system of legal doctrine, whose structure – whose most important functional oppositions – must be revealed. Occasionally analysts may need to argue that particular categories and distinctions of this elaborate structure are discursive constructions, not natural givens, but the coherence of the system and its success in providing foundations for its constructions are major issues. A deconstructive analysis in the field of law will not in general need to draw concepts from Derrida but can and should work on the categories through which the system of legal doctrine seeks to master a particular domain or set of problems. One of the most crucial questions is how far and in what way these models conceal and displace the problems they purport to resolve. Gerald Frug's 'The Ideology of Bureaucracy in American Law', studying the doctrines of administrative and corporate law that describe, regulate and justify the operations of bureaucracy, argues that *all* of these doctrines attempt to distinguish and to articulate the subjective and the objective, but that these attempts at distinction fail: 'every attempt to separate objectivity and subjectivity in bureaucratic thought has resulted instead in a relentless intermixing of them'. 'The facets of organizational life that need to be subjective have become so constrained by objectivity that they cannot convincingly represent the expression of human individuality. Similarly, the facets that need to be objective have become so riddled with subjectivity as to undermine their claim to represent common interests'.[7] Bureaucracy is impersonal yet capricious.

Clare Dalton's fascinating 'Essay in the Deconstruction of Contract Doctrine' analyses the functioning of the oppositions between form and substance, public and private, and intention and manifestation in the doctrine of contracts, showing how attempts to provide a solid

---

[7] Gerald Frug, 'The Ideology of Bureaucracy in American Law', *Harvard Law Review* 97:6 (April 1984), pp. 1289 and 1287.

foundation by granting precedence to one term let the other in by the back door: 'within the discourse of doctrine, the only way we can define form, for example, is by reference to substance, even as substance can be defined only by its compliance with form. . . . Each supposed "solution" to one of these doctrinal condundra, each attempt at definition or line-drawing, winds up mired at the next level of analysis in the unresolved dichotomy it purported to leave behind'.[8] There are certainly suggestive similarities here to structures deconstruction has revealed elsewhere: for instance, in the way attempts to set aside writing and ground an account of language on an idealized speech, without distance, absence, or deferral, wind up reintroducing inscription and iteration. What such examples emphasize most plainly, however, is that what is deconstructed in a deconstructive reading is not the text being read but doctrine, particularly the hierarchical oppositions which shape it and through which it functions. Oppositions such as meaning/form, inside/outside, intuition/expression, literal/metaphorical, nature/culture, positive/negative, transcendental/empirical may appear to be symmetrical but function as hierarchies: the first term is treated as prior and the second conceived in relation to it, as a complication, a negation, a manifestation, or a disruption of the first, or a supplement to it. To deconstruct these hierarchical oppositions is to expose them as constructions – impositions that can be shown to be impositions by the very discourses that rely on them. Analysis of the functioning of such oppositions in various discourses involves an interest in what's at stake in these hierarchizations and an attempt to undo it, showing that the system does not live up to its proclaimed principles. In deconstructive readings of literary and philosophical texts, one finds that the most productive and revealing analyses come when one is dealing not with mediocre texts which lack ambition and lucidity but rather with texts that are culturally the most powerful and resourceful, that pull no punches in seeking solutions to problems. Since legal doctrine sets out to bring order to a domain and to cope explicitly with problems that might arise, its imposed solutions should lend themselves to revealing deconstructive analyses.

A legal problem that literary critics may find particularly interesting is the issue of intention in contract doctrine. What is the role of intention in determining the meaning of a contract? Legal doctrine recognizes the distinction between subjectivity, substance, and intent on the one hand, and objectivity, form and manifestation, on the

---

[8]   Clare Dalton, 'An Essay in the Deconstruction of Contract Doctrine', *Yale Law Journal* 94:5 (April 1985), pp. 1002–3.

other, but in most areas contract law explicitly favors objective over subjective, form over substance, manifestation over intent. What determines the meaning of a contract are its manifest, objective terms rather than the subjective intentions of either contracting party. But in fact, writes Dalton, in contract doctrine 'the suppressed subjective constantly erupts to threaten the priority accorded to the objective, is subdued, and erupts again' (p. 1040). The 1979 *Restatement (Second) of Contracts* treats a promise as a 'manifestation of intent', specifying that it thus 'adopts an external or objective standard for interpreting conduct', but while stipulating that intention is relevant only when objective and manifest, it in fact accords subjectivity what Dalton calls

a vital and subversive supplementary role. According to the *Restatement* scheme, recognizing a manifestation requires a knowledge of intent. . . . Doctrinally we cannot, it turns out, sort or interpret manifestations without reference to an intent we have already acknowledged to be beyond our grasp save through the graspable reality of manifestations that we cannot comprehend without reference to an unknowable intent . . . and so on. (p. 1041)

Examining the turns of doctrinal argument on the problem of intention and various sorts of objective manifestation, Dalton maintains that

(1) any standard that begins by emphasizing intention winds up depending on equally unsatisfying models of formal hierarchy or responsibility; (2) any standard that begins by emphasizing formal hierarchy winds up depending on equally unsatisfying models of intention or responsibility; and (3) any standard that begins by emphasizing responsibility winds up depending on equally unsatisfying models of formal hierarchy. (p. 1042)

There is a strong parallel here to the deconstruction of speech act theory. An attempt to derive meaning from linguistic structure or linguistic conventions must contend with the fact that speakers can mean different things by the same linguistic sequence. This suggests the need for a supplementary model that derives meaning from speakers' intentions. J. L. Austin argues, however, that what makes an utterance a command or a promise is not an inner intention but rather compliance with certain conventions; and speech act theory explicates a further dimension of meaning by setting forth a formal 'grammar' of linguistic acts, the conditions of promising, commanding, and so forth. But in order to carry out this analysis, Austin must exclude the multifarious ways in which jokes, poems and other graftings or recontextualizations can alter the force of a speech act and prevent *I promise to pay you ten dollars* from being an effective promise. To do this he reintroduces the criterion of intention: 'words must be spoken "seriously" ... an important commonplace in discussing the purport of any utterance whatsoever'.[9] Yet this commonplace begs precisely those questions about the nature and functioning of language that are at issue. As Derrida writes, 'what is at stake is above all the structural impossibility and illegitimacy of such an idealization, even one which is methodological and provisional'.[10]

What makes the juxtaposition with the legal deconstruction particularly interesting is this: literary and philosophical demonstrations that arguments about meaning oscillate unstoppably between appeals to intention and convention are often seen as sophistical denials that language works, as though the critique of claims about how it works were a frivolous diversion; but in the case of law, where we have an interest in believing not just that the legal system functions but that its functioning is predictable and just, determined by coherent and defensible principles, a structurally similar critique of the system has an importance that is more difficult to deny. In contract cases it is obvious that a lot is riding on how the meaning of words is determined, but the issues are in fact similar in other areas of experience, including the interpretation of literary works, even though we cannot set a dollar figure on gains and losses.

One can also imagine fruitful exchange between legal and non-legal thinking about the relation of meaning and context. Deconstruction has often been associated with the principle of the indeterminacy of meaning (though if one reads Derrida's interpretations of texts it is actually quite difficult to see how people could claim this is his teaching). Against this, critics claim that meaning is contextually determined: a word or phrase taken by itself might seem ambiguous, especially if read perversely by a punning or etymologizing deconstructionist, but in context, the claim goes, it will generally prove to have a determinate meaning. Now what deconstruction would question initially is precisely the distinction between item and textual context or text and its context. Context is just more text, just as much in need of interpretation and in fact constituted by the same sort of inimical forces that produce the possible ambiguities it is being called

[9] J. L. Austin, *How to Do Things With Words* (Cambridge, Mass.: Harvard University Press, 1975), p. 9. For discussion see my *On Deconstruction*, pp. 115–16 and 110–28 passim.

[10] Jacques Derrida, *Limited Inc.*, Supplement to *Glyph* 2 (Baltimore: Johns Hopkins University Press, 1977), p. 39.

on to resolve. The appeal to context only displaces into a larger arena the problems at issue. Specifically, as the legal analogy makes clear, the appeal to context does not resolve disputes about meaning but displaces them into disputes about what is the relevant context and what it means.

This leads to a second point about context, however: while meaning is context-bound, context is boundless. This is something lawyers know well; context is in principle infinitely expandable, limited only by their resourcefulness, their clients' resources, and the patience of the judge. There is always more evidence that may bear in some way or another on the meaning of the act or words at issue. Even terms which ordinarily would not be thought at all ambiguous, – the name of a familiar middle-sized object, such as *chicken* – may become ambiguous under the weight of further contextual evidence, as in *Frigaliment versus BNS International Sales Corp.*, cited by Clare Dalton, where opposing witnesses were called to testify on what *chicken* meant in the chicken trade: a bird of any age or a young broiler, fryer, or roaster. Context is often thought of as a given, but lawyers know that it is produced, and that it is not saturable. Contextualization is never completed; rather one reaches a point where further contextualization seems unproductive.

The defenders of the determinacy of meaning (and in law, defenders of the determinacy of the legal situation: that the law does determine a correct answer and appropriate outcome for a given situation) often seek to bolster their case by citing the different factors that contribute to the determinacy of meaning: the author's intention, the rules of the language of the community, and the contextual information adduced by an informed and intended reader; but the attempt to combine models of determination in effect concedes the point at issue, for the question of determinacy of meaning (or of a legal result) arises precisely because of the conflict among determining factors. Apply pressure to a model of this sort, and you will discover that it simply incorporates the problem it purports to solve, as the legal examples splendidly illustrate.

A related point would be that for law, in Derrida's notorious phrase, *il n'y a pas de hors texte* [there is no 'outside-the-text']. In literature the idea of interpreting an autonomous text – a work whose being lies in a self-enclosed unity – is attractive and persistent. The fact that this work has meaning only in terms of other works, with which it forms a system, is something that must be painfully argued and which many still resist. But in law it seems abundantly evident that any case is part of an endless text: its has potential points of contact with a vast array of other cases and other data. Moreover, in the realm of law everything is textualized, comes before one in the form of discourse, tightly constrained, for example, by the rules of evidence. In law it seems clear that one is dealing with a ubiquitous textuality whose structures are those of signification, and clear also that to say this is not to deny that legal discourse has 'real effects' on 'real people'.

One might in this connection note how differently the problem of politics is posed for deconstructive discourses in law and in literature. At one level the political character of CLS can be taken for granted: because of its contestatory relation to the traditional apparatus of legal education which is a conspicuous part of the power structure (more so than the apparatus of literary education), because the students law professors teach will take jobs in government, become judges, or represent individuals and corporations in cases disputing the social allocation of power and wealth, CLS need not argue that *it* is political but can argue instead both that particular legal forms represent political choices and that the image of a functioning system of rules and doctrine presented by other legal analysts masks the operation of political choices in the radical indeterminacies of the system. For instance, Clare Dalton's consideration of the functioning of contract doctrine in cases about cohabitation contracts (both celebrated 'palimony' cases and less dramatic adjudication of similar issues) illustrates both the restrictions imposed by the polarities of contract doctrine, in whose terms argument is conducted (public versus private, manifestation versus intent, form versus substance) and the way conflicting principles permit views about women and sexuality to influence legal decisions. That is, the choice of what is deemed public and what private or what form and what substance depends to a considerable extent on ideological factors which enter the case through the interstices of conflicting principles. While deconstruction in law may concentrate on showing how the system of law conceals the operation of political choices, deconstruction in literature and philosophy must defend itself against the charge that any critique of literary and philosophical doctrine, however radical, remains effectively conservative if it only produces another way of reading texts and changes in the procedures of disciplines of the academy. Literary theory must conduct an argument, which CLS seems not to have been led to explore, about the nature of the political and distinctions between thought and action. What seems a disadvantage at one level, then, may lead to a more profound reflection at another level on the problems of history, historical totalization, and the relation of the aesthetic and the political. However, the two sorts of deconstruction, legal and non-legal, share an exposure to attacks from both the right and the left, for pursuing a critique of institutions and procedures which does not ground itself in an alternative set of values and thus undermines confidence in a system without offering foundations for action or easy recipes for change.

I have been suggesting that the encounter of deconstruction and the law may be interesting and productive, but it seems nearly preordained – they seem in some sense made for each other. Alongside the critique which asks whose interests are served by the law, there is a place for a critique which examines the operation of the hierarchical oppositions through which legal doctrine seeks to manage its domains, which disputes the well-foundedness and success of its procedures.

But there is one respect in which literary critics have an advantage – an interpretive advantage. One strategy open to literary critics and theorists does not seem to have been available to law professors. Confronted with an ambiguity, a literary critic can argue that this is precisely the point, that the work is *about* ambiguities of this sort – their nature, their function, their inevitability; it is an allegory of reading or writing, if you will. This is not simply a critic's trick to avoid struggling with a difficulty; it does not, in any case, avoid struggles, only premature resolution. But literature, by tradition and convention, is a discourse that strains at the limits of language and resists the intelligence, almost successfully; it makes us question our categories and procedures for analysis and so does indeed thematize and allegorize problems of signification and interpretation. I notice, however, that Gerald Frug does not conclude that administrative law is *about* the impossibility of separating subjective from objective and of controlling their relationship. And Clare Dalton stops short of saying that the meaning or message of contract doctrine is 'that we can neither know or control the boundary between self and other'. She concludes instead that contract doctrine deploys comparatively few mediating devices 'to displace and defer the otherwise inevitable revelation that public cannot be separated from private or form from substance or objective manifestation from subjective intent. The pain of that revelation, and its value, lies in its message that we can neither know nor control the boundary between self and other' (p. 1113). This is seen not as the message of contract doctrine but as the message of the revelation that contract doctrine energetically seeks to displace and defer. Here we have a difference between deconstructive procedures in literary criticism and in law. Is it a difference that makes a difference? Might lawyers be missing an important possibility here? Might not a systematized irresolvable dialectic between conflicting principles that we ideologically wish to preserve be precisely the point of contract doctrine or of administrative law? This is a problem that deserves further study.

Finally, I want raise questions about two curious features that appear in deconstructive readings of law. In explaining her purpose, Clare Dalton writes, 'I suggest that the demonstration of indeterminacy, and the linkage between indeterminacy and fundamental problems of knowledge and power, can clear the way for some new inquiries into how and why cases get decided as they do' (p. 1003). One learns to be suspicious of figures of 'clearing the way' or 'clearing the ground', which suggest that the real value lies in some fresh start, which could begin on a new foundation. That involves imagining a dubious discontinuity; in fact, the way or the ground is never going to be clear in law, or in literary studies. The hope that one's analysis will clear the ground, eliminating the mass of prior writings and placing one in a situation of sublime simplicity before a poem or some other social phenomenon, is a temptation to which lawyers may be even more prone than literary critics, since the latter know that they function in what is ineluctably a world of texts. Figures of clearing the way suggest the possibility of a fresh start when in fact this new enterprise will already have been – is already – under way. The question is how one can reinscribe, redirect, recombine the categories being analysed. And indeed, a revealing investigation of how judges in fact decide cases about cohabitation contracts, for instance, could not proceed without taking up the displacement of the traditional oppositions that Clare Dalton's article produces.

A striking feature of both Dalton's and Gerald Frug's articles is the way in which analyses conclude in symmetrical or reciprocal structures; I have already quoted several of these formulations, but here are two more: 'the mutual dependence of form on substance and substance on form', and 'the "objective" reading can be understood only by incorporating within its definition of objectivity a subjective supplement, and the subjective reading has no meaning without an objective supplement'.[11] The symmetries may come from the fact that each article seeks to engage comprehensively with the models that approach the problem from each pertinent angle, but still I find these symmetries surprising, for in other deconstructive analyses these oppositions function hierarchically, and hence asymmetrically; analysis does not simply identify a reciprocal relation between terms (no speech without writing and no writing without speech) but reveals an attempt to displace into the second the problematical features of the first and seeks to combat that imposition by reversing and displacing it. I wonder whether there is perhaps in the reciprocities of such conclusions a residual assumption, which would counter the

[11]   Frug, 'Ideology of Bureaucracy', p. 1341.

explicit thrust of the argumentation in these articles, that law in the United States has balanced everything very nicely? This question is provoked by a repeated formal feature, rather than by a knowledge of the work of Critical Legal Studies, but the irritant of such questioning is one thing that literary criticism might contribute to the deconstruction of the law, while the readings of legal discourse, in their turn will display the self-deconstructive functioning of hierarchical oppositions in cases where the stakes are more evident and the effects of discursive operations more patent than they generally are in literary criticism.

9

The Semiotics of Tourism

Tourism is a practice of considerable cultural and economic importance and, unlike a good many manifestations of contemporary culture, is well known in some guise to every literary or cultural critic. Some may claim ignorance of television or rock music or fashion, but all have been tourists and have observed tourists. Yet despite the pervasiveness of tourism and its centrality to our conception of the contemporary world (for most of us, the world is more imperiously an array of places one might visit than it is a configuration of political or economic forces), tourism has been neglected by students of culture. Unlike the cinema, popular romance, or even video, tourism has scarcely figured in the theoretical discussions and debates about popular culture of recent years.

The problem may be that tourism has so few defenders, constitutes an embarrassment, and seems such an easy target for those who would attack modern culture. The tourist, it seems, is the lowest of the low. No other group has such a uniformly bad press. Tourists are continually subject to sneers and have no anti-defamation league. Animal imagery seems their inevitable lot: they are said to move in droves, herds, swarms, or flocks; they are as mindless and docile as sheep but as annoying as a plague of insects when they descend upon a spot they have 'discovered'. Here is Daniel Boorstin, Librarian of Congress and guardian of our cultural heritage, on this contemptible species of American:

The tourist looks for caricature; travel agents at home and national tourist bureaus abroad are quick to oblige. The tourist seldom likes the authentic (to him often unintelligible) product of a foreign culture. He prefers his own provincial expectations. The French chanteuse singing English with a French accent seems more charmingly French than one who simply sings in French.[1]

---

[1] Daniel Boorstin, *The Image* (New York: Atheneum, 1967), p. 106.

There are perhaps interesting reasons why this should be so, but Boorstin does not stop to inquire. 'Tourist "attractions" offer an elaborately contrived indirect experience, an artificial product to be consumed in the very places where the real thing is free as air'. What could be more foolish than a tourist paying through the nose for an artificial substitute when the real thing, all around him, is as free as the air?

This discussion is not untypical of what passes for cultural criticism: complaints about the tawdriness or artificiality of modern culture which do not attempt to account for the curious facts they rail against and offer little explanation of the cultural mechanisms that might be responsible for them. If cultural criticism is to go beyond nostalgic vituperation, it needs to find ways of analysing the cultural phenomena in question, and tourism, that marginalized yet pervasive cultural practice, seems to demand a semiotic approach. If for the tourist the French chanteuse singing English with a French accent seems more charmingly French than one who simply sings in French, the reason might be not stupidity nor moral turpitude but a semiotic code. American films treating foreign people and places characteristically have minor characters speak with charming foreign accents, to signify Frenchness, Italianeity, Teutonicity, while the main characters (even though foreign) speak American English. There are mechanisms of signification here with which tourism is deeply intertwined.

Roland Barthes, who might be regarded as the founder of a semiotics aiming at demystification or culture criticism, writes in his *Elements of Semiology* that 'dès qu'il y a société, tout usage est converti en signe de cet usage' [once society exists, every usage is converted into a sign of this usage].[2] By wearing blue jeans, for instance, one signifies that one is wearing blue jeans. This process is crucial, Barthes continues, and exemplifies the extent to which reality is nothing other than that which is intelligible. Since it is as signs that our practices have reality, they swiftly become signs, even if signs of themselves. Of course, once a sign is constituted in this way – a usage become a sign of this usage – society may very well refunctionalize it and speak of it as a pure instance of use. A fur coat one wears is a sign of its category; it signifies *fur coat* as one wears it. But, Barthes says, a society may well attempt to mask this mythological function and act as if the coat were simply an object that serves to protect one from the cold.[3] This process is what Barthes in *Mythologies* calls the

---

[2]   Roland Barthes, *Elements of Semiology* (New York: Hill and Wang, 1967), p. 41.
[3]   Jean Baudrillard writes, 'Far from the primary status of an object being a pragmatic one, it is the sign exchange value which is fundamental – use-value is often no more than a practical guarantee (or even a rationalization pure and simple). Such, in its paradoxical form, is the only correct sociological hypotheses.' *For a Critique of the Political Economy of the Sign* (St Louis: Telos, 1981), p. 29.

'alibi', or the general tendency of a culture to convert history into nature.[4] The task of the semiotician, according to Barthes, is to penetrate the alibi and identify the signs.

The notion of a usage become sign of itself might remain somewhat obscure and offer the analyst little methodological instruction in how to penetrate alibis and what to look for were it not for the exemplary case of tourism, which can provide considerable guidance and illumination. The tourist is not interested in the alibis a society uses to refunctionalize its practices. The tourist is interested in everything as a sign of itself, an instance of a typical cultural practice: a Frenchman is an example of a Frenchman, a restaurant in the Quartier Latin is an example of a Latin Quarter restaurant, signifying 'Latin Quarter Restaurantness'. All over the world the unsung armies of semiotics, the tourists, are fanning out in search of signs of Frenchness, typical Italian behavior, exemplary Oriental scenes, typical American thruways, traditional English pubs; and, deaf to the natives' explanations that thruways just are the most efficient way to get from one place to another or that pubs are simply convenient places to meet your friends and have a drink, or that gondolas are a natural way to get around in a city full of canals, tourists persist in regarding these objects and practices as cultural signs. They put into practice Jean Baudrillard's claim that an accurate theory of social objects must be based on signification rather than needs or use-value.[5] Dean MacCannell, author of a superb study, *The Tourist*, records his pleasure and surprise in discovering that the tourists he was studying were in fact his allies in the sociological study of modernity: 'My "colleagues" were everywhere on the face of the earth, searching for peoples, practices and artifacts that we might record and relate to our own socio-cultural experience'.[6] In their most specifically touristic behavior, however, tourists are the agents of semiotics: all over the world they are engaged in reading cities, landscapes and cultures as sign systems.

If semioticians have not recognized tourists as their allies, it is perhaps because they are so universally maligned. Even books that celebrate travel engage in denigration of tourists. Paul Fussell, a reputable and intelligent literary critic, in a celebration of British literary traveling between the wars, attempts to convey 'what it felt like to be young and clever and literate in the final age of travel'.[7]

[4] Roland Barthes, *Mythologies* (New York: Hill and Wang, 1972), pp. 128–9.
[5] Baudrillard, *Political Economy*, pp. 29–30.
[6] Dean MacCannell, *The Tourist* (New York: Schocken, 1976). Henceforth cited as T.
[7] Paul Fussell, *Abroad* (New York: Oxford University Pres, 1972), p. vii.

'Final age of travel' because since 1939 there is no more travel, only tourism, which is totally different. 'Perhaps the closest one could approach an experience of travel in the old sense today would be to drive through Roumania or Afghanistan without hotel reservations and to get by on terrible French'. What distinguishes the tourist, Fussell continues,

is the motives, few of which are ever openly revealed: to raise social status at home and to allay social anxiety; to realize secret fantasies of erotic freedom; and most important, to derive secret pleasure from posing momentarily as a member of a social class superior to one's own, to play a role of a 'shopper' and a spender whose life becomes significant and exciting only when one is exercising power by choosing what to buy. Cant as the tourist may of the Taj Mahal and Mt. Etna at sunset, his real target today is the immense Ocean Terminal at Hong Kong, with its miles of identical horrible camera and tape recorder shops. The fact that a tourist is best defined as a fantasist equipped temporarily with unaccustomed power is better known to the tourist industry than to anthropology. The resemblance between the tourist and the client of a massage parlor is closer than it would be polite to emphasize.[8]

Fussell's hysterical smugness is puzzling until one realizes what the problem might be. When this Professor of English at the State University of New Jersey, as he then was, goes to England, the natives probably mistake him for another American tourist. Ferocious denigration of tourists is in part an attempt to convince oneself that one is not a tourist. The desire to distinguish between tourists and real travelers is a part of tourism – integral to it rather than outside it or beyond it.

The ubiquity of the distinction between travelers and tourists is quite striking. Fussell contrasts the fake travellers of the past thirty years with the real travelers of the inter-war period: young Englishmen, generally of the better classes, who went off to the south of France, or to Italy, to the Middle East, to Tahiti, and wrote about getting drunk in run-down hotels. But for Boorstin the character of travel begins to change markedly in the mid-nineteenth century, with the success of Thomas Cook and Sons: mass transportation – railways and ocean liners – brings about what he calls 'the decline of the traveler and the rise of the tourist:

The traveler, then, was working at something; the tourist was a pleasure seeker. The traveler was active; he went strenuously in search of people, of adventure, of experience. The tourist is passive; he expects interesting things

[8]   Ibid., p. 42

to happen to him. He goes 'sight-seeing' (a word, by the way, which came in at about the same time, with its first use recorded in 1847). He expects everything to be done to him and for him. Thus foreign travel ceased to be an activity – an experience, an undertaking – and became instead a commodity.[9]

Boorstin here echoes Ruskin's view that 'Going by railroad I do not consider as travelling at all; it is merely being "sent" to a place, and very little different from becoming a parcel'. This sounds strange today, when travel by rail, like travel by steamship, has become the last refuge of the traveler trying to avoid being a tourist and is celebrated nostalgically as true travel reminiscent of a bygone age. But Ruskin is not alone in denigrating the mass of nineteenth-century travellers as tourists; nineteenth-century travelers are as ferocious in their denunciation of tourists and tourism as twentieth-century travelers. Boorstin quotes an Englishman in 1865 fulminating at the race of tourists:

The cities of Italy are now deluged with droves of the creatures, for they never separate, and you see them forty in number pouring along a street with their director – now in front, now at the rear, circling round them like a sheepdog – and really the process is as like herding as may be. I have already met three flocks, and anything so uncouth I never saw before, the men mostly elderly, dreary, sad-looking; the women somewhat younger, travel-tossed, but intensely lively, wide-awake, and facetious.[10]

Even earlier, in 1826, Stendhal complained, when writing a book for tourists, *Rome, Naples, et Florence*, that 'Florence is nothing better than a vast museum full of tourists'.[11] The true age of travel has, it seems, always already slipped by; other travelers are always tourists.

This repetition and displacement of the opposition between tourist and traveler suggests that these are not so much two historical categories as terms of an opposition integral to tourism. The historical explanations are excuses for what travelers always do: feel superior to other travelers. As MacCannell notes, denigration of the tourist 'is so prevalent, in fact, that it is part of the problem of mass tourism, not an analytical reflection upon it' (T, p. 104). To be a tourist is in part to dislike tourists (both other tourists and the fact that one is oneself a tourist). Tourists can always find someone more touristy than

---

[9] Boorstin, *The Image*, p. 85. Baudrillard notes that 'the structure of the sign is at the very heart of the commodity form', *Political Economy*, p. 146.

[10] Ibid., p. 88.

[11] Stendhal (Henri Beyle), *Rome, Naples, and Florence* (London: Braziller, 1959), p. 317.

themselves to sneer at: the hitchhiker arriving in Paris with a knapsack for an undetermined stay feels superior to a compatriot who flies in on a jumbo jet to spend a week. The tourist whose package tour includes only air travel and a hotel feels superior, as he sits in a cafe, to the tour groups that pass by in buses. Americans on bus tours feel superior to groups of Japanese, who seem to be wearing uniforms and surely understand nothing of the culture they are photographing.

Tourism thus brings out what may prove to be a crucial feature of modern capitalist culture: a cultural consensus that creates hostility rather than community among individuals. Tourism is a system of values uniting large segments of the world population from the richer countries. Groups with different national interests are brought together by a systematized knowledge of the world, a shared sense of what is significant, and a set of moral imperatives: they all know what one 'ought to see' in Paris, that you 'really must' visit Rome, that it 'would be a crime' never to see San Francisco and ride in a cable car. As MacCannell points out, the touristic code – an understanding of the world articulated by the moral injunctions which drive the tourist on – is the most powerful and widespread modern consensus, yet the effect of these shared values is not to create solidarity within the international community of tourists but hostility, as each wishes the other tourists were not there. The idea of a consensus which sets members of the group against one another is a remarkable feature of modernity which demands further analysis.

Once one recognizes that wanting to be less touristy than other tourists is part of being a tourist, one can recognize the superficiality of most discussions of tourism, especially those that stress the superficiality of tourists. Tourists are inevitably reproached, by Boorstin and his ilk, for their satisfaction with the inauthentic, the spurious: 'the tourist seldom likes the authentic product of a foreign culture', Boorstin writes. 'The American tourist in Japan looks less for what is Japanese than for what is Japanesey'.[12] We shall later take up this semiotic structure, but one should emphasize that tourists do set out in quest of the authentic. Proof of that desire is that authenticity is a major selling point in advertisements and travel writing. Perhaps the most common motif in travel columns is the hotel, restaurant or sight 'just off the beaten track'. The genre is familiar: 'Only a couple of blocks from the main tourist hotels lies a street of small shops where one can see real native craftsmen at work and whose wares sell for a fraction of the prices charged at tourist

[12] Boorstin, *The Image*, p. 106.

traps on the main street'. Or, 'only ten miles further down the coast you will find an unspoiled fishing village with a few inns patronized by locals, where the innkeeper's wife will happily make you a hearty lunch to take on your rambles'.

The distinction between the authentic and the inauthentic, the natural and the touristy, is a powerful semiotic operator within tourism. The idea of seeing the real Spain, the real Jamaica, something unspoiled, how the natives really work or live, is a major touristic *topos*, essential to the structure of tourism. It is even the explicit selling point of commercial tours: 'Take "De tour", Swissair's freewheeling fifteen day Take-a-break Holiday that lets you detour to the off-beat, over-looked and unexpected corners of Switzerland for as little as $315 . . . including car. Take de tour. But watch out for de sheep, de goats, and de chickens'. Even tourists who take the most packaged package tours, who are indeed, as Ruskin predicted, sent from one place to another like a parcel, venture bravely forth from their hotels in search of atmosphere and discover something which for them is unusual, authentic in its otherness, a sign of an alien culture – say a butcher's shop with undressed fowl and rabbits hanging in the window. And characteristically tourists emphasize such experiences – moments regarded as authentic – when telling others of their travels. The *authentic* is a usage perceived as a sign of that usage, and tourism is in large measure a quest for such signs.

In their quest, tourists engage in a practice which attracts volumes of scorn: they purchase mementos of various sorts. The denigrators of tourism make fun of the proliferation of reproductions associated with tourism: picture postcards, travel posters, miniature Eiffel Towers, piggy banks of the Statue of Liberty. These reproductions are what MacCannell in his account of the semiotic structure of the tourist attractions calls *markers*. Like the sign, the touristic attraction has a triadic structure: a marker represents a sight to the tourist (T, p. 110). A marker is any kind of information or representation that constitutes a sight as a sight: by giving information about it, representing it, making it recognizable. Some are 'on-site' markers, such as plaques telling that 'George Washington slept here' or that this vial of dust comes from the moon. Some are mobile markers, such as pamphlets and brochures designed to draw people to the site, give information at the site, and serve as souvenirs or representations off the site. MacCannell quotes a brochure which marks and thus constitutes tourist sights in the state of Iowa: 'Kunkle cabin site. In 1848 Benjamin Kunkle and his family became the first permanent settlers of Guthrie County. Mr Kunkle raised the first hogs in the county. The marker is attached to a large elm tree in the Myron Godwin farmyard'

(T, p. 114). Finally, there are off-site markers, reminding one that the attraction is an attraction, such as a kewpie doll bearing a flag that reads 'Souvenir of Yellowstone'.

The proliferation of markers frames something as a sight for tourists. The existence of reproductions is what makes something an original, authentic, the real thing – the original of which the souvenirs, postcards, statues etc. are reproductions – and by surrounding ourselves with reproductions we represent to ourselves, as MacCannell astutely suggests, the possibility of authentic experiences in other times and in other places (T, p. 148). One of the characteristics of modernity is the belief that authenticity has been lost and exists only in the past – whose signs we preserve (antiques, restored buildings, imitations of old interiors) – or else in other regions or countries. 'The United States', MacCannell writes, 'makes the rest of the world seem authentic. California makes the rest of the United States seem authentic' (T, p. 155). And, of course, Los Angeles makes the rest of California seem authentic. But the semiotic process at work has a curious effect: the proliferation of markers or reproductions confers an authenticity upon what may at first seem egregiously inauthentic. The discussion of Los Angeles, the reproduction of its features in a variety of media, creates originals of which these reproductions are reproductions and a desire to see the signified of which these markers are signifiers. Describing what he calls 'sight sacralization', MacCannell writes, 'it is the mechanical reproduction phase of sacralization that is most responsible for setting the tourist in motion on his journey to find the true object. And he is not disappointed. Alongside the copies of it, it has to be The Real Thing' (T, p. 45).

The denigrators of tourism are annoyed by the proliferation of tacky representations – postcards, ashtrays, ugly painted plates – and fail to grasp the essential semiotic function of these markers. Not only do they create sights; when the tourist encounters the sight the markers remain surprisingly important: one may continually refer to the marker to discover what features of the sight are indeed significant; one may engage in the production of further markers by writing about the sight or photographing it; and one may explicitly compare the original with its reproductions ('It's not as big as it looked in the picture'; or 'It's even more impressive than I imagined'). In each case, the touristic experience involves the production of or participation in a sign relation between marker and sight.

Moreover, the sight/marker relation in the sign structure of the touristic attraction is responsible for the phenomenon that Boorstin and others deplore when they complain that 'the American tourist in Japan looks less for what is Japanese than for what is Japanesey'. This is scarcely surprising, for to be Japanesey is to signify 'Japaneseness', to be marked by various sorts of representations as typically, interestingly Japanese. Boorstin and his like assume that what is reproduced, represented, written about, is inauthentic, while the rest is authentic: tourists pay to see tourist traps while the real thing is free as air. But 'the real thing' must be marked as real, as sight-worthy; if it is not marked or differentiated, it is not a notable sight, even though it may be Japanese by virtue of its location in Japan. The authentic is not something unmarked or undifferentiated; authenticity is a sign relation. Even the sights in which the most snobbish tourists take pleasure are not unmarked; they have become for these tourists the 'real' Japan by a process of semiotic articulation, only their markers are more recondite and less tacky than the plastic reproductions or souvenirs of the most famous sights.

There is, nevertheless, a problem about the relation between these two sorts of authenticity that I have been describing: the authenticity of what lies off the beaten track and is thus apparently unexpected and the authenticity a sight derives from its markers, so that tourists want to encounter and recognize the original which has been marked as a sight. These seem rather different cases but they are in fact intimately related in a process which can be approached through a description of another talented author, Walker Percy. His book of homespun semiotics, *The Message in a Bottle*, makes naive assumptions, but its account of tourism is rich and suggestive.

Percy's 'The Loss of the Creature' begins with a myth of origins, the story of a first traveler who can experience authentically – as a pure unmediated experience – what later travelers can only experience superficially and mediately: 'Every explorer names his island Formosa, beautiful. To him it is beautiful because, being first, he has access to it and can see it for what it is. But to no one else is it ever as beautiful'.[13] This is an attractive myth but highly dubious, especially in its notion that the context in which the explorer first comes across a sight is so much the privileged context as to make the sight what it truly is. (One should note, by contrast, Prosper Merimée's astute claim that 'Rien n'est plus ennuyeux qu'un paysage anonyme' [Nothing is more boring than an unnamed landscape]. A visitor to Niagara Falls who does not know that it is 'Niagara Falls' he is seeing, will immediately demand, 'What is this place?' since a great deal of its interest comes from its relation to its marker or 'symbolic complex'.)

---

[13] Walker Percy, *The Message in the Bottle: How Queer Man Is, How Queer Language Is, and What One has to Do with the Other* (New York: Farrar, Strauss, 1975), p. 46. Henceforth cited as MB.

When Percy turns, though, to the Grand Canyon – discovered by a Spanish explorer and then set aside as a National Park so that others might see and appreciate this sight – his reflections become more pertinent. When a man from Boston takes a bus tour to the Grand Canyon, does he in fact see the Grand Canyon? Possibly, answers Percy,

> But it is more likely that what he has done is the one sure way not to see the canyon.
> Why is it almost impossible to gaze directly at the Grand Canyon and see it for what it is . . .? It is almost impossible because the Grand Canyon, the thing as it is, has been appropriated by a symbolic complex which has already been formed in the sightseer's mind. Seeing the canyon under approved circumstances is seeing the symbolic complex head on. (MB, p. 47)

This is why I suggested earlier that tourism was an exemplary case for the perception and description of sign relations. The sightseer confronts the symbolic complex head on and explores the relation of sight to its markers. 'The term of the sightseer's satisfaction', writes Percy, 'is not the sovereign discovery of the thing before him; it is rather the measuring up of the thing to the criterion of the preformed symbolic complex' (MB, p. 47).

The question for Percy, then, is 'How can the sightseer recover the Grand Canyon?' How can one escape semiotic mediation? He imagines various strategies: one might get off the beaten track and come upon the canyon through the wilderness, avoiding markers, trails and lookout spots. Or one might attempt to recover the canyon from familiarity by an exercise in familiarity, visiting the canyon 'by a Greyhound tour in the company of a party from Terre Haute'. The visitor 'stands behind his fellow tourists at the Bright Angel Lodge and sees the canyon through them and their predicament, their picture taking and their busy disregard' (MB, p. 48–9). This technique is superior to the first – getting off the beaten track, he admits, is the 'most beaten track of all' – but it is not satisfactory either, for it does not deliver an unmediated experience.

Committed to the idea of an original, authentic experience, Percy finds that the strategies he imagines all involve semiotic mediation – as any semiotician could have told him – and so falls back on the stratagem of apocalypse: a war destroys civilization and, years later, an expedition from Australia lands in southern California and makes its way east. 'They stumble upon the Bright Angel Lodge, now fallen into ruins. The trails are grown over, the guardrails fallen away, the dime telescope at Battleship Point rusted. But there is the canyon, exposed at last' (MB, p. 49). Percy here follows Victor Hugo who, in a poem of 1837 about another tourist attraction, 'A l'Arc de Triomphe', imagines that three thousand years hence, when all Paris save Notre Dame, the Vendôme column and the Arc de Triomphe has fallen into ruin, a shepherd making his way at dusk will come upon the Arc de Triomphe, and it will, at last, be truly beautiful.[14] But Hugo, more astute than Percy, recognizes that this situation of a civilization in ruins is a very particular semiotic frame which confers a conventional authenticity on what persists amid ruins. The sublimity of the Australian explorers' experience (assuming that they did not boorishly consider the canyon just an obstacle to their eastward progress) would come from the juxtaposition of the canyon with the markers which it had outlasted.

Percy tells another story which in fact illustrates very well both the impossibility of escaping semiosis and the complex relation between authenticity in touristic experience and mediating sign structures or symbolic complexes. He imagines an American couple visiting Mexico, who see the usual sights and enjoy themselves, yet feel that something is missing.

Although Taxco and Cuernavaca are interesting and picturesque as adver-tised, they fall short of 'it'. What do the couple have in mind by 'it'? What do they really hope for? . . . Their hope has something to do with their own role as tourists in a foreign country and . . . something to do with other American tourists. Certainly they feel that they are very far from 'it' when, after traveling five thousand miles, they arrive at the plaza in Guanajuato only to find themselves surrounded by a dozen other couples from the Midwest. (MB, p. 51)

Their problem, as he diagnoses it, is to find an 'unspoiled' place, an attraction that has not attracted tourists or become encrusted with renown. While driving to Mexico City they accidentally do so. Lost on back roads, they discover a tiny Indian village where an elaborate native ritual is in progress. They know at once, Percy says, that this is 'it'. 'Now may we not say that the sightseers have at last come face to face with an authentic sight, a sight which is charming, quaint, picturesque, unspoiled, and that they see the sight and come away rewarded? Possibly this may occur. Yet it is more likely that what happens is a far cry indeed from an immediate encounter with being' (MB, p. 52). The failure to have an immediate encounter with the sight, which Percy earlier attributed to symbolic encrustations with which a culture has surrounded the sight, is here recognized as a

14 Victor Hugo, *Poésie* (Paris: Seuil, 1972), I, pp. 375–81.

feature of the encounter itself – intrinsic to it and not an accidental corruption that might be put right. The village seems unspoiled; there are no signs of other tourists, so the couple ought in principle to be like Percy's explorer, coming upon an authentic sight and finding it splendid. But in fact their pleasure is anxious and divided, not a plenitude of fulfillment.

> The clue to the spuriousness of their enjoyment of the village and the festival is a certain restiveness in the sightseers themselves. It is given expression by their repeated exclamations that 'this is too good to be true', and their anxiety that it may not prove to be so perfect, and finally by their downright relief at leaving the valley and having the experience in the bag, so to speak – that is, safely embalmed in memory and movie film.
>   What is the source of their anxiety during the visit? . . .
>   We have another clue in their subsequent remark to an ethnologist friend. 'How we wished you had been with us! . . . Every minute we would say to each other, if only you were here! You must return with us'. (MB, p. 52–3)

This is not, Percy notes, a desire to share their experience with others but a need of a different sort, essential to the semiotic structure of tourism: 'They need the ethnologist to certify their experience as genuine. This is borne out by their behavior when the three of them return for the next corn dance. During the dance the couple do not watch the goings on; they watch the ethnologist! Their highest hope is that their friend should find the dance interesting. And if he should show signs of true absorption . . . then their cup is full. "Didn't we tell you?" they say at last' (MB, p. 53).

To be truly satisfying the sight needs to be certified, marked as authentic. Without these markers, it could not be experienced as authentic – whence the couple's anxiety, anxiety from the absence of markers. The paradox, the dilemma of authenticity, is that to be experienced as authentic it must be marked as authentic, but when it is marked as authentic it is mediated, a sign of itself, and hence lacks the authenticity of what is truly unspoiled, untouched by mediating cultural codes. We want our souvenirs to be labeled 'authentic native crafts produced by certified natives using guaranteed original materials and archaic techniques' (rather than, say, 'Made in Taiwan'), but such markers are put there for tourists, to certify touristic objects. The authentic sight requires markers, but our notion of the authentic is the unmarked.

Percy's idea of a friendly ethnologist who accompanies the tourist is the most positive version of this double bind. The expert here is in fact nothing other than a personalized, individualized projection of the cultural sign systems that articulate the world, attaching labels, producing reliable and unreliable markers, certifying sights as genuine instances of what one should look for. The authenticity the tourist seeks is at one level an escape from the code, but this escape itself is coded in turn, for the authentic must be marked to be constituted as authentic.

Another version of this basic semiotic mechanism is the dialectical relation between what MacCannell, following Erving Goffman, calls front and back regions. In their quest for an authentic experience, tourists want to see the inside of things, so social and economic arrangements are made to take them behind the scenes, ranging from guided tours of the Paris sewers, the morgue, or the stock exchange to schemes whereby small groups of tourists willing to pay handsomely for the privilege can stay at a ducal castle and breakfast with the duke. The authenticity markers attached to these tourist attractions indicate that they are already coded, and therefore not the true back regions, which become in turn a further source of attraction (the dream that the duke might invite one to see something he does not show to tourists). In English stately homes that are open to the public, the grandest and most attractive regions are generally turned over to the tourist parties, but visitors avidly hope to catch a glimpse, through an open door or down a passageway, of the smaller and architecturally ordinary back regions where the noble family now lives in bourgeois style. In regions frequented by tourists, MacCannell observes, the distinction between front and back, or between what is there to be shown to tourists and what is genuine, is operationally decisive but has become highly problematic: 'the continuum is sufficiently developed in some areas of the world that it appears as an infinite regression of stage sets' (T, p. 105). Every 'original' is a further representation.

A semiotic perspective advances the study of tourism by preventing one from thinking of signs and sign relations as corruptions of what ought to be a direct experience of reality and thus of saving one from the simplistic fulminations against tourists and tourism that are symptoms of the touristic system rather than pertinent analyses. Tourism, in turn, enriches semiotics in its demonstration that salient features of the social and natural world are articulated by what Percy calls 'symbolic complexes' and its revelation of the modern quest for experience as a quest for an experience of signs. Its illustration of the structural incompleteness of experience, its dependency on markers, helps us understand something of the nature of semiotic structures.

Particularly interesting are the processes by which touristic attractions are produced. We have already noted the dependency of sights on markers: 'empty' sites become sights through the attachment of markers. An unremarkable piece of ground becomes a tourist attraction when equipped with a plaque reading 'Site of the Bonnie and Clyde shootout', and as more markers are added – informative historical displays, a little museum, a Bonnie and Clyde amusement park with shooting galleries – the markers themselves quite explicitly become the attraction, the sight itself. These markers would then have further markers attached to them: postcards depicting the Bonnie and Clyde Museum, pennants depicting Bonnie-and-Clyde-Land and its more famous attractions. MacCannell notes that analysis of the touristic attraction demonstrates the interchangeability of signifier and signified: the Statue of Liberty, originally a marker – a sign welcoming travelers to New York – has become a sight; but then as a celebrated tourist attraction it has become at another level a marker, used on posters and travel displays as a marker for the United States as a country for tourism. The Eiffel Tower, a major touristic signified, represented by a variety of different signifiers, is itself a signifier which signifies 'Paris'. The Empire State Building is a sight that serves as a marker for the sightseer's Manhattan. Buildings constructed to mark and preserve sights often become the sights themselves: the Sainte Chapelle, built to contain and display for visitors the 'true crown of thorns', is now the principal sight and the crown is forgotten. The arbitrary nature of the sign, we can infer, prevents there being a difference of nature between signifier and signified, so that not only may the signified marked by a marker prove to be another marker or signifier in its turn, but – a less frequently recognized semiotic possibility – a signifier may itself function as a signified.

The production of touristic sights relies on semiotic mechanisms whose operation may seem quite local and contingent, but the general framework and product of these signifying mechanisms, the touristic code, is a modern consensus of vast scope, a systematized, value-laden knowledge of the world. Groups which disagree on a range of moral and political issues know what tourists ought to see and, when they flout the value system to 'get off the beaten track', for instance, they do so in terms that are already prescribed by that system. Our primary way of making sense of the world is as a network of touristic destinations and possibilities which we ought in principle to visit. Tourism, MacCannell writes, 'is a ritual performed to the differenti-ations of society', an attempt to overcome fragmentation by articulat-ing the world as a series of societies, each with its characteristic monuments, distinctive customs or cultural practices, and native scenery, all of which are treated as signs of themselves, non-functional displays of codes.

This touristic system accompanies and is tied in with the world system of multinational capitalism, which has created much of the infrastructure, such as airports and Western hotels, on which tourism depends. Like tourism, this capitalism seeks to make the world a series of accessible sites, equivalent as markets for goods and interchangeable as sites of production according to the momentary advantages of wage scales and local conditions. Could one not say that modern tourism, with its reduction of cultures to signs and celebration of the distinctiveness of those signs, is a mask for the capitalist world system, a celebration of signification and differentiation which conceals the economic exploitation and homogenization that underlies it; that tourism, which celebrates cultural difference, makes cultures museum pieces to conceal their destruction at the hands of the world economic system? One could certainly make this claim, but as Fredric Jameson notes when discussing the post-modern culture of the simulacrum, while this cultural practice to some extent masks the economic reality, it also reveals aspects of that system, foregrounding its mechanisms, making clear, for example, that what we visit is not an organic, autonomous native reality but attractions marked and thus constituted by an international touristic practice – signs produced within a international system of signification.[15] Moreover, there are few clearer indicators of shifting lines of force within the economic order than changes in the flow of tourists.

Tourism reveals difficulties of appreciating otherness except through signifying structures that mark and reduce it. It is tempting to see here nothing more than the result of an exploitative international order. But the Marxist condemnation of tourism as the reduction of otherness to caricature in complicity with multinational capitalism risks falling into a sentimental nostalgia for the organic or the unmediated that resembles nothing so much as the vituperative nostalgia of conservatives, who fondly imagine a time where the elite alone traveled and everything in the world showed itself truly to them. Baudrillard, in his critique of the Marxist appeal to an authentic 'use-value', maintains that 'Every revolutionary perspective today stands or falls on its ability to reinterrogate the repressive, reductive, rationalizing metaphysic of utility' so as to study sign relations.[16] Certainly in the case we are dealing with, to condemn tourism may be morally satisfying, but to do so is also, I fear, to rely on the naive postulate of an escape from semiosis and to cut oneself off from the possibility of exploring semiotic mechanisms which prove persistent and ubiquitous, central to any culture or social order.

---

[15]   See Fredric Jameson, 'Postmodernism, or The Cultural Logic of Late Capitalism', *New Left Review*, 146 (July/August 1984), pp. 53–92, especially, pp. 86–8.
[16]   Baudrillard, *Political Economy*, p. 138.

10

Rubbish Theory

Reflection on this topic might begin with one of the classics of social anthropology, Mary Douglas's *Purity and Danger*. Her discussion of anomalies, of matter out of place, of dirt, pollution, taboo, proceeds in best structuralist fashion by rejecting piecemeal diachronic or causal explanations in favor of synchronic, structural explanation, which treats dirt as the product of a differential, diacritical system. 'Where there is dirt there is system', she writes. 'Dirt is the by-product of a systematic ordering and classification of matter, insofar as ordering involves rejecting inappropriate elements'.[1] She argues that dirt is vital evidence for the total structure of thought in a culture because it is an omnibus category for everything that is out of place. To investigate what counts as dirt helps to identify the categories of the system. 'It is a relative idea', she continues.

Shoes are not dirty in themselves, but it is dirty to place them on the dining table. Food is not dirty in itself, but it is dirty to leave cooking utensils in the bedroom, or food bespattered on clothing; similarly, bathroom equipment in the drawing room; clothing lying on chairs; out-door things indoors; upstairs things downstairs; under-clothing appearing where overclothing should be, and so on. In short, our pollution behaviour is the reaction which condemns any object or idea likely to confuse or contradict cherished classifications.

As this last sentence suggests, Douglas is particularly concerned to question the distinction between cultures with supposedly superstitious notions of ritual pollution and taboo and our own culture with its supposedly rational conceptions of dirt and disorder. 'I am going to argue', she writes, 'that our ideas of dirt also express symbolic systems and that the difference between pollution behaviour in one part of the world and another is only a matter of detail' (p. 47).

---

[1] Mary Douglas, *Purity and Danger: An Analysis of Concepts of Pollution and Taboo* (Harmondsworth: Penguin, 1970), p. 48.

Her approach is extremely productive and, as the emphasis on symbolic systems suggests, it is a semiotic inquiry, assuming that to study objects and events with meaning one must proceed not in piecemeal fashion but by reconstructing the underlying system of norms and categories – the system of signification – that makes these meanings possible. Since systems of classification depend upon exclusions, one looks at what is apparently marginal to the system in order to understand the system. One must consider ungrammatical sentences in order to work out the grammar of a language, or look at what is 'unthinkable' in a particular milieu in order to discover its deepest assumptions, or at what is unfashionable in order to reconstruct the code of fashion. In developing a theory of speech acts – of how to do things with words – J. L. Austin focuses on the various ways in which speech acts can misfire, so as to discover the conventions for the successful performance of speech acts. Attending to all the factors that might prevent one from successfully promising, warning, commanding or marrying is essential to the project of describing the conventions of promising, warning, commanding, marrying. Austin writes, 'The project of clarifying all possible ways and varieties of not exactly doing things . . . has to be carried through if we are to understand properly what doing things is'.[2]

Douglas argues that since culture is the standardized values of a community, its system of categories resists easy revision, but it cannot neglect the challenge of aberrant forms. 'Any given system of classification, ' she continues, 'must give rise to anomalies, and any given culture must confront events which seem to defy its assumptions'. It will have 'provisions for dealing with ambiguous or anomalous events'; ways of labeling them (p. 52). 'Uncleanness or dirt is that which must not be included if a pattern is to be maintained' (p. 53). It is a residue, what is set aside as polluting or improper, so as to preserve the system, and thus provides a key to understanding the system. What is marginal or taboo turns out to be essential to the study of the system that excludes it.

This procedure works very well, but it often leads analysis to focus on what has been given a negative value: what is taboo, what is ungrammatical, what pollutes, what disgusts. Douglas talks a good deal about dirt, but the title of her book is *Purity and Danger: An Analysis of the Concepts of Pollution and Taboo,* and she does rather tend to press dirt in this direction. Although she defines dirt simply as matter out of place, she concentrates on what is disgustingly or objectionably out of place. So one wants to say, this is all very well,

---

[2] J.L. Austin, *Philosophical Papers* (London: Oxford University Press, 1982), p. 27.

but what about just ordinary old junk and rubbish – stuff that does not pollute or defile, that is not taboo but just junk? Most of us have quite a lot of quite ordinary and inoffensive junk, which is most simply defined as stuff that is of no real value but that you are keeping around because, well, you never know, and besides, you just haven't got around to throwing it out. We all have material of this sort which scarcely pollutes and seems quite inoffensive until someone comes along with another use for the space that it occupies: 'Look, we have to clean all that junk out of the closet in the guest room so our guests can use it', or 'We have to clear that rubbish out of the garage so that we can put the car in it this winter . . .'

This stuff also seems to lie on the margins of systems of value, but it is passed over in discussions of dirt, disorder, anomaly, taboo. My question is, what is the semiotic role of this relatively innocent sort of junk or rubbish? If dirt is evidence for a system of signification, what about junk and rubbish?

A good deal of my own junk and rubbish – and I discover that this is true for other people as well – falls under the general heading of mementos or souvenirs: college term papers, postcards, brochures and leaflets from trips, old conference programs, photographs and clippings, old letters. This is a familiar kind of junk: leavings of various sorts that one hasn't thrown away because it might be of interest some day. If one formulates the thought that it might be of interest some day, one imagines something like showing these materials to one's grand-children (since it is difficult to imagine that one's children would be interested). One imagines it functioning as a representation of the experience of which it is a memento. And one imagines, or at least tries to imagine, an audience who might exclaim over the *authenticity* of the experience that is represented or memorialized: 'You've been *there*!' or '*That*'s how people dressed in the sixties?'

A good deal of this junk functions much as do touristic souvenirs. As we have seen in chapter nine, denigrators of tourists and tourism make fun of the proliferation of reproductions and souvenirs associated with tourism, but all these postcards, stolen ashtrays, pieces of native fabrics and other mementos function as markers, which are crucial to the semiotic structure of tourism: by representing the sight, the marker constitutes it as a touristic attraction. Souvenirs are mobile, off-sight markers, which work to mark the sight as an original, making it *the real thing*, of which the postcards, statues and other souvenirs are imita-tions. Analysts with pretensions to sophistication sneer at the junk that surrounds and suffuses tourism – the tacky representations and souve-nirs – but they fail to understand its function as markers which, through their very tackiness, reaffirm the sight itself as original and authentic.

This example is pertinent because a lot of the junk that people collect is of this sort: relics, remnants and representations of things done, seen and admired. This is rubbish because it has no use-value, nor any value in an economic system of exchange; it has only the signifying function of a marker, and its very inferiority to what it marks makes it rubbish. Moreover, the semiotic functioning of touristic markers seems to illuminate the functioning of other rubbish. One collects a certain amount of junk in the hope that it might one day come to function as marker and make the event, experience or whatever a truly significant one. One may secretly hope that if one has enough junk the past it marks will become truly memorable. There is, at least, a feeling that if we throw out this junk we are being disrespectful to the past it memorializes, as though our discarding decreed that it was not authentic, for what constitutes the past as notable and significant are the markers that mark it as the original.

Clearly, rubbish is not irrelevant to value. If one is interested in meaning and value one must think about rubbish. However, the touristic analogy works only for one sort of rubbish, and though it suggests a semiotic function for rubbish, it does not lead towards a general theory of rubbish. For assistance in this project, one might turn to a book by an English sociologist, Michael Thompson. *Rubbish Theory: The Creation and Destruction of Value* provides a conceptual framework for value theory: a framework in which rubbish plays a prominent part.

Thompson begins by identifying two general categories in which we place cultural objects, the *transient* and the *durable*. Objects placed in the transient class are thought of as having finite life-spans and as decreasing in value over time. Objects viewed as durable are endowed with, ideally, infinite life-spans and retain their value or even increase in value over time. A ham sandwich is transient while a diamond is durable, this much is obvious, but for a wide range of objects class membership is determined by social forces as much by the physical character of an object: a vase may be placed either in the transient category or in the durable category (viewed as secondhand or as an antique).

Since durable objects are more desirable and valuable than transient objects, groups with wealth and power will try to keep their objects in the durable class and keep others' transient objects in the transient class. Thompson's initial question is how change can occur within this system.

We are all familiar with the way despised Victorian objects have become sought-after antiques; with bakelite ashtrays that have become collector's items; with old bangers transformed into vintage motor cars. So we know that change takes place, but how? The answer lies in the fact that the two *overt* categories which I have isolated, the durable and the transient, do not exhaust the universe of objects. There are some objects (those of zero and unchanging value) which do not fall into either of these categories, and these constitute a third *covert* category: rubbish.

My hypothesis is that this covert rubbish category is not subject to the control mechanism (which is concerned primarily with the *overt* part of the system, the valuable and socially significant objects) and so is able to provide the path for the seemingly impossible transfer of an object from transience to durability.[3]

A transient object, decreasing in value, becomes rubbish, where it exists in a timeless limbo, without value, but where it has a chance of being discovered and suddenly transformed into a durable. In such situations we encounter not a continuum of value but the radical discontinuities or flip-flops of fashion. (Indeed, Thompson is interested in using the mathematics of catastrophe theory to model the movements of value.) The utterly unfashionable has a better chance of suddenly becoming fashionable than does something mildly out of fashion. It is never the relatively new chair, which has only lost some of its value, that suddenly becomes a priceless durable but rather the old-fashioned, uncomfortable wooden monstrosity that has been gathering cobwebs in an attic. It is not the transient that becomes durable but rubbish. One notes a certain kinship between durables and rubbish: both partake of a certain timelessness (as opposed to the time-bound quality of transients) and both can be thought of as in a sense priceless: the Mona Lisa and a relative's hideous watercolors both lie outside the ordinary economic system constructed around transients. There is a relation between the piece of junk and the collectors' item. As Mary Douglas writes, 'there is energy in the margins and unstructured areas'.[4] Here the category of rubbish is the margin of and point of communication between categories of value.

Now it happens that the first example Thompson uses to describe this process is a particular sort of touristic souvenir from the Victorian era, though manufactured until just before the Second World War: woven silk pictures called Stevengraphs, manufactured by Thomas Stevens of Coventry. First sold at the York Exhibition of 1879, they depicted such scenes as 'Dick Turpin's Ride to York on his Bonny Black Bess', or 'The London and York Royal Mail Coach', with

---

[3] Michael Thompson, *Rubbish Theory: The Creation and Destruction of Value* (Oxford: Oxford University Press, 1979), p. 9. Henceforth cited as RT.

[4] Douglas, *Purity and Danger*, p. 137.

legends such as 'Woven at the York Exhibition' – though they were later sold in other contexts. Today's versions of this sort of object are doubtless the pennants or cloth banners ('Souvenir of Nashville') which people buy as decorative mementos and which quickly become rubbish. Thompson is not interested in Stevengraphs for their place in the structure of tourism, however; he adopts them as examples of the movement from transient, through rubbish, to durable.

In this case, the switch from transient to rubbish is quite swift: until nearly the 1960s there is no evidence for any sort of market for secondhand Stevengraphs. Once purchased and taken home, or presented to someone as a souvenir of a trip on which he or she had not gone, they quickly became rubbish – sometimes left hanging on walls, more often consigned to drawers, trunks, attics, much as this sort of thing is today. Antique dealers who had acquired them in batches of Victoriana report that no one was interested. 'The most convincing proof', writes Thompson, 'that the rubbish category occupied by the Stevengraph between 1881 and 1960 is indeed covert is the fact that when one comes to look for the history of the Stevengraph during this period, there isn't any' (RT, p. 20). One eccentric collector started buying in 1937, but it was not until 1965 that he had enough fellow collectors to found the Stevengraph Collectors Association. Apparently some Americans started to buy them and helped to start a market in the 1960s. The first monograph was published by an American in 1957. Within a decade prices had shot from zero to more than a hundred pounds, and, of course, it swiftly became meaningless to speak of the price of a Stevengraph in general, as numerous distinctions arose. Rubbish is undifferentiated, while the very essence of durables is their differentiation. A body of specialist knowledge developed, revealing hitherto unsuspected variants. (Some Dick Turpin Stevengraphs lack a signpost reading 'To York'; others say 'Woven at the York Exhibition' rather than 'Manufactured at the York Exhibition'.) The first exhibition of Stevengraphs took place in 1963; the first sale devoted entirely to Stevengraphs in 1967. One decisive moment in the transmutation of rubbish into durable was the enshrining of the original pattern book in the Coventry City Museum (anything in a museum is marked as durable). Other less happy but distinctly significant events include the first reproduction, the first planned robbery, the first dealers ring, and the first fake Stevengraph.

Thompson's discussion of Stevengraphs focuses on the way in which the transfer from rubbish to durable occurs. We might be tempted to say that it is all a matter of taste: one man's rubbish is another man's collectable. Indeed, the word *collectable* suggests as much, since any reasonable-sized physical object is collectable. The question is, which collectables are collectors' items and why? The answer – scarcely satisfying – seems to be, first, that collectors' items are collectables collected by collectors. Prior to the emergence of a market for Stevengraphs, there were a few eccentrics who bought them, they said, for their charm or decorative value. Only when some American collectors began buying them and asking dealers to find more did they become collectables. Noting that American interest preceded British interest – as it did with other collectables such as paintings by Stubbs and other eighteenth- and nineteenth-century sporting and animal paintings, Thompson writes,

> Various reasons might be advanced for this tendency, the most attractive of which, since it hints at the inherent superiority of the Old World over the New, is that the States, having been in existence for a much shorter time than Europe, has a much smaller repertoire of rubbish to choose from. Alternatively, it can be seen as an example of the principle of a prophet being without honor in his own land. The most likely and much less palatable reason is that the power of the United States is very much greater than that of Britain, that durables are in the hands of the most powerful, and that when there is a shift in power there is a shift in durables as well. (RT, p. 25)

This last phrase seems to me not quite right. As he says, durables are in the hands of the most powerful. The point is that Stevengraphs were rubbish, not durables, until they were purchased and collected by collectors. To take another, perhaps more interesting example which illustrates the same principle, London Bridge was a transient – very famous as a transient; but finally it was in such a state of falling down that it became rubbish, of no value, and was about to be scrapped. At which point it was made a collectable, bought by Americans and established in Arizona as a durable, a combination of antique and touristic souvenir (it is, in fact, a semiotically complex object: a memento of London Bridge, which is also London Bridge.)

In the case of American collectors who transformed Stevengraphs from rubbish to durables, the point is not just that the most powerful get the most durables but rather that what the powerful collect become durables. One of Thompson's anecdotes illustrates this nicely. When working as a mason and carpenter in London, he and his coworker installed a discarded mid-Victorian fireplace grate and marble surround (rubbish) in a Regency townhouse being renovated by a well-to-do businessman and charged the owner what they took to be an exorbitant price for this supposed antique. They felt pleased with themselves, but 'a few weeks later, while we were doing some more work on the same house, the owner proudly showed the drawing room to a friend, who exclaimed, "Oh, isn't that splendid! Whatever you do, you *must* keep that marvellous fireplace". At that moment I realized that we were the exploited ones. The fact that we knew that the fireplace had just been installed and was of the wrong period was irrelevant . . . Already the value of the house had risen by very much more than £30' (RT, p. 53). The fireplace, that is to say, was no longer a piece of rubbish. Simply by being installed in the renovated house of this well-to-do Londoner, the mid-Victorian monstrosity had become a durable.

There are various lines of inquiry one might explore in pursuing these structures. The value systems of transients and durables, and the residual, marginal category of rubbish, form a major semiotic structure in which a great deal of social force is invested and through which socio-economic power operates. A Marxist analysis of power and class focuses on ownership of the means of production, but it is striking that in most societies the powerful classes are not by any means satisfied with owning the means of production; indeed, this may not be the most prominent features of class identity. A *New Yorker* cartoon widely circulated on flyers advertising Christmas gift subscriptions to the magazine, represents a man in pajamas kneeling, presumably in prayers beside his bed. The caption: 'I don't ask for much, but what I get should be of very good quality'.

Since the semiotic categories of durables, transients and rubbish are clearly related to class, one might even hazard a direct correlation and imagine three classes: those whose possessions are durables, those whose possessions are transient, and those whose possessions are rubbish – or perhaps one should say, rather, those who think of their possessions as durable, those who think of their possessions as transient, and those who think of their possessions as rubbish. If you think your possessions are or should be durables, you will, of course, act differently from the way you would if, given an equal amount of money, you assumed that your possessions were transient. You might buy an antique desk rather than a new desk. You would expect your Volvo to run forever and would sink corresponding amounts of money into its maintenance, instead of buying a new car every three years. The expectation of durability is neatly summed up in the motto of the aristocratic Curzon family: 'Curzon hold what Curzon held'. The goal is astonishing: everything they have should be a durable, a collectable. If a Curzon were to develop a perverse, wholly eccentric interest in mid-century oven mitts, this would increase their chances of becoming collectors' items.

Semiotics attempts to make explicit the categorial systems which underlie behavior, the structures of signification which govern the assignment of meaning to objects and events, and this particular categorial system has, I have found, considerable power to elucidate various aspects of everyday life. For instance, the countryside around Ithaca, New York, has what one might call an extremely varied housing stock, ranging from elegant Federal and Greek Revival houses to particularly shabby trailers. According to the usual economic model, all housing is transient: it has a value when new and loses value as it ages, until eventually it becomes worthless (when it costs more to repair than it could be sold for). If one takes a tax deduction for rental property or a home office, for example, one employs this economic model, giving one's house a life of fifty years, for instance, and claiming depreciation on this basis.

There are many houses in the region which are treated so as to fit this model: they are unmistakably transient, losing value, gradually declining into ruins, likely to become rubbish in a little while – by which time their inhabitants will have moved into a new little ranch house, or perhaps a house trailer. Just as obviously, however, there are houses whose value is stable or increasing, not just because of inflation but because they function as durables. Their owners assume that the houses ought to be durable and treat them accordingly, devoting perhaps quite exorbitant sums of money to repairs and preservation. We have these two models – houses as transients and houses as durables – which go some way to accounting for behavior. Those who are sufficiently well off to afford two snowmobiles may not paint their houses, since they see them as transient and bound to fall apart anyway. If they should repair the front door, they will most likely put on a modern flush door with chrome fittings. In repairing the transient one tries to arrest its transience by making it newer. The owners who define their houses as durables, on the other hand, would, in repairing them, try to make them look more authentically old by installing imitation period front doors with old-fashioned fittings.

The residual, marginal category of rubbish is the point of connection between the two conflicting codes: as the transient moves toward rubbish, it can either be torn down to make way for something new (this is the transient view, the view from the system of transience) or else be salvaged as durable: rebuilt, reconstructed. Struggles are always being waged over rubbish – struggles whether the system of transience or durability should prevail. This situation of conflicting codes was marvelously summed up in a statement by British politician Richard Crossman when he was Minister of Housing in a Labour government and announcing a decision to proceed with a controversial housing project (tearing down old terraced or row houses to build modern high-rise apartments): 'These rat-infested slums must be demolished. Old terraced houses may have a certain snob appeal to members of the middle class, but they are not suitable accommodation for working class tenants'.[5]

In the system of transience – here that of the working class – this housing has become rubbish and must be replaced by something new. In the system of durability, it is a candidate for restoration. Crumbling eyesore or glorious architectural heritage – we are familiar with such battles and they are, of course, code struggles. It is in such battles that the discontinuity between our systems of value and the importance of the category of rubbish become most apparent, for there is seldom any compromise that could possible satisfy *either* side, much less both. There is a radical opposition between two incompatible valuations, and the social and political system will decide one way or another, reinforcing the views and authority of the winners. That is a point to stress here. If this rubbish is torn down, that will go to prove that it was indeed transient; if preserved, that will show that it was durable, as the other side contended.

Thompson is interested in rubbish – covert category and point of transition between transients and durables – as a key to understanding the dynamic processes by which value is created and destroyed. The next step, for him, is a demonstration that the mathematics of catastrophe theory, whose three-dimensional graphs model sudden and discontinuous change at the same time that they describe gradual change, can represent a wide range of social phenomena that involve both continuity and discontinuity. He opposes his 'dynamic theory of rubbish' to semiotics, which he sees as necessarily static, unable to distinguish change from noise. He argues that 'the conventional response of the semiologist, that he is not concerned with such changes in the rules but simply with the rules, implies that he is not concerned with anything at all, for the class of phenomena with which semiotics cannot cope includes all those phenomena to which it addresses itself' (RT, p. 62).

The solution is catastrophe theory, which can model indeterminacy as well as determinacy and thus in principle map situations, like the struggle over old terraced houses, where there are two codes in play, one or the other of which will be made to apply. In fact, semioticians such as Thomas Sebeok, who desire above all that semiotics distance itself from literary theory and become a science, have seen in René Thom's work on catastrophe theory not an opponent of semiotics but its future. Since in the cases that interest semiotics, which include those that interest Thompson, there are seldom ways to collect

---

[5] Quoted by Thompson, *Rubbish Theory*, p. 35.

relevant numbers that would actually enable one to plot a pertinent curve, the role of catastrophe theory is in fact to offer assurance that phenomena which present striking discontinuities (such as the radical flip-flops of fashion) and indeterminacies (such as the difficulties of predicting which transients will be selected for durability once they become rubbish) may still be systematic, not random or subject entirely to individual tastes. The model catastrophe theory provides works above all to suggest that there is no reason for the semiotician not to be interested in changes in conventions, since these changes may be cultural phenomena that themselves involve or are produced by semiotic mechanisms.

In his concern with the applicability of catastrophe theory, Thompson does not consider what, if anything, rubbish theory might have to say about the condition of a society whose everyday cultural products – television, best-sellers, the mass media generally – are frequently judged to be rubbish. Since he proves to have shrewd things to say about many cultural phenomena, one regrets that the fleshpots of formalization, so fatally alluring to the social scientist, prevented him from taking up this topic; but one might speculate that one aspect of the problem of cultural rubbish is the conflict between the value systems of transience and durability.

To put it simply, we are accustomed to think – tradition urges us to think – of two sorts of compositions: those which, utilitarian and transient, transmit information in a world of practical affairs and those which, not tied to the time- or use-value of information, are part of the world of leisure – our cultural heritage – and belong in principle to the system of durables. Newspapers and magazines are transient, but symphonies, paintings and short stories are in principle durable. Of course, it has always been the case that many symphonies, paintings and stories have vanished quickly and thus proved quite as transient as newspapers and magazines, but this was thought to be something of an accident, and symphonies, paintings and short stories were still in principle and in essence of the system of durables.

What may have changed recently is that innumerable cultural compositions – visual, verbal and musical – which do not carry transient information, nevertheless clearly belong to the mode of transience. Television programs are not supposed to be remembered and treasured but swiftly replaced by the next program or next episode. Not only are cultural compositions associated with leisure functioning in the system of transience rather than durability, as we expect, but even the concept of fame, which is supposed to belong to durability if anything does, has been claimed for transience, as in Andy Warhol's dictum that in the future everyone will be famous for ten minutes.

With the predominance in our culture of the system of transience, *rubbish* has come to be more important, since it is the point of interchange, the only way the transient can become durable. Rubbish has thus become an essential resource for modern art. At one time in the Tate Gallery in London the point of greatest interest in the museum, drawing by far the largest crowds, was an artifact consisting of, I believe, forty-eight old bricks, arranged in a rectangle, six bricks long and eight bricks wide. The crowd's view seemed to be that this was a load of rubbish. Indeed, recent newspaper articles had made fun of the Tate for paying a large sum for this artwork (the museum had bought it as a durable rather than as transient or as rubbish). Doubtless many of the spectators felt annoyed that they had not themselves hit upon the scheme of arranging some bricks in a rectangle and selling them to the Tate, but of course not just anyone has the power or authority to transform rubbish into durable. And to those who claimed that the artist had bamboozled the Tate, one might reply that this piece of rubbish was at the moment provoking more intense interest than any other art object in the museum. Such examples suggest that in junk and rubbish lie possibilities for change within the artistic system. At a time when there are fewer and fewer conventions sufficiently rigorously established so that to violate them is taboo, and when it is thus more and more difficult to innovate by *breaking* rules, the possibilities of change may well lie in junk and rubbish and in the mechanisms whereby the transient and functional may, when reduced to rubbish, be discovered and become durable. There are of course numerous examples in the history of twentieth-century art, such as Marcel Duchamps's urinal: a transient piece of plumbing, detached from its function, become rubbish, and thus available for sudden elevation into art.

In literature, rubbish theory might apply to Flaubert's *Bouvard et Pécuchet*, frequently hailed as the forerunner of contemporary literary techniques and something of a rubbish dump: a collection of transient propositions which are piled up, exposed as rubbish and thus made available for durability. Marshall McLuhan once wrote a book about modern culture whose title sums up one aspect of this process: *From Cliche to Archetype*. The cliche, a piece of cultural junk, when foregrounded in a certain way, achieves durability – as archetype perhaps.

Nor is the artistic reclamation of rubbish limited to prose. Michael Riffaterre has developed a theory of poetry that relies heavily on cliches and set phrases – the flotsam and jetsam of culture. Though poems appear to be making statements about the world, they are, in fact, periphrastic transformations of cliches and descriptive systems.[6]

The example with which I conclude, however, comes from a modern novelist whose work would be a gold mine for the serious student of rubbish. Readers of Donald Barthelme come to treasure a certain pointlessness, achieved by a variety of sophisticated and not so sophisticated techniques. Sometimes he creates sequences that make language seem so much dead matter, as in this passage from *Snow White*:

> Snow White took off her pajamas. Henry took off his pajamas. Kevin took off his pajamas. Hubert took off his pajamas. Clem took off his pajamas. Dan took off his pajamas. Edward took off his pajamas. Bill refused to take off his pajamas. 'Take off your pajamas Bill', Snow White said. Everyone looked at Bill's pajamas. 'No, I won't', Bill said. 'I will not take off my pajamas'. 'Take off your pajamas Bill', everyone said. 'No. I will not'. Everyone looked at Bill's pajamas.[7]

At other times, Barthelme marshals, in a way that reveals all their flaccidness, the cliches that make up our culture.

Snow White, hailed by one critic as the most original literary exercise since *Finnegans Wake*, is presented by the publishers as shocking, scandalous. The Bantam edition sports a naked Snow White on the cover (her skin is 'white as snow') and tells us that she is a nymphomaniac who lives in Greenwich Village and makes love to each of her seven friends. Presented as pornographic trash, this novel must have disappointed many readers, for it is trash of a different species. It innovates through rubbish and also comments on books and rubbish – on rubbish as a major contemporary resource.

The dwarfs, representative moderns, are heavily into rubbish. They have a plant where they manufacture plastic buffalo humps – even more pointless than plastic Statues of Liberty. Giving a tour of the plant, Dan talks about their vocation and about language as stuffing, not to say dreck.

> 'You know, Klipschorn was right I think when he spoke of the "blanketing" effect of ordinary language, referring, as I recall, to the part that sort of, you know, "fills in" between the other parts. That part, the "filling" you might say, of which the expression "you might say" is a good example, is to me the most interesting part, and of course it might also be called the "stuffing" I suppose, and there is probably also, in addition, some other word that would

---

[6] Michael Riffaterre, *Semiotics of Poetry* (Bloomington: Indiana University Press, 1978).
   [7] Donald Barthelme, *Snow White* (New York: Bantam Books, 1968), p. 106.

do as well to describe it, or maybe a number of them. But the quality this "stuffing" has, that the other parts of verbality do not have, is two-parted, perhaps: (1) an "endless" quality and (2) a "sludge" quality. Of course that is possibly two qualities but I prefer to think of them as aspects of a single quality, if you can think that way. The "endless" aspect of "stuffing" is that it goes on and on, in many different forms, and in fact our exchanges are in large measure composed of it, in larger measure even, perhaps, than they are composed of that which is not "stuffing". The sludge quality is the heaviness that this "stuff" has, similar to the heavier motor oils, a kind of downward pull, but still fluid, if you follow me, and I can't help thinking that this downwardness is valuable, although it's hard to say how right at the moment. So, summing up, there is a relation between what I have been saying and what we are doing here at the plant with these plastic buffalo humps. Now you're probably familiar with the fact that the per-capita production of trash in this country is up from 2.75 pounds per day in 1920 to 4.5 pounds per day in 1965, the last year for which we have figures, and is increasing at the rate of about four percent per year. Now that rate will probably go up, because it's *been* going up, and I hazard that we may very well soon reach a point where it's 100 percent. Now at such a point, you will agree, the question turns from a question of disposing of this "trash" to a question of appreciating its qualities, because, after all, it's 100 percent, right? And there can no longer be any question of "disposing" of it, because it's all there is, and we will simply have to learn how to "dig" it – that's slang, but peculiarly appropriate here. So that's why we're in humps, right now, more really from a philosophical point of view than because we find them a great moneymaker. They are "trash", and what in fact could be more useless or trashlike? It's that we want to be on the leading edge of this trash phenomenon, the everted sphere of the future, and that's why we pay particular attention, too, to those aspects of language that may be seen as a model of the trash phenomenon. And it's certainly been a pleasure showing you around the plant this afternoon, and meeting you, and talking to you about these things, which are really more important, I believe, than people tend to think. Would you like a cold Coke from the Coke machine now, before you go?'[8]

Twenty years after *Snow White*, the United States cannot dispose of its mounting production of trash and must indeed learn to 'dig it'. This seems an allegory of postmodernism and of its success, which *Snow White* itself exemplifies, in converting rubbish to durables. But this story – that in a world of rubbish, art has learned to exploit rubbish – may well be too easy. Dan's other theme in this passage, language as stuffing or endless sludge, suggests in fact quite a different account: not that the economic system has brought the postmodern world an increase of rubbish, and that art has participated in this,[9] but that the

[8] Ibid., pp. 96–8.
[9] See Fredric Jameson, 'Postmodernism, or The Logic of Late Capitalism', *New Left Review* 146 (July/August 1984).

element of rubbish, 'aspects of language that may be seen as a model of the trash phenomenon', have been part of sign systems and systems of value all along. The stuffing, the sludge, the non-significative materiality of language is what has enabled sign systems to function. If this is so – and Thompson's model gives us every reason to imagine that it is – then we cannot dispose of rubbish with a narrative about its emergence or new role in the postmodern world but must reflect on the structure that locates this sludge or dross within or at the heart of systems of value or language. Thompson remarks that rubbish theory 'seems always to lead straight into illogicality, anomaly, and paradox. Regrettably, there are many who find these qualities not so much charming as monstrous, and there are some who would go so far as to maintain that the proper aim and object of serious thought should be the exclusion of such monsters' (RT, p. 131). In resisting this exclusion, which can also be effected by apparently inclusive narratives, we can look to literature, which will not only engage in what Thompson calls 'monster conservation' but also give birth to new monsters, like the modern *Snow White*, which dramatize the semiotic functioning of value and its irremediable complications.

PART IV

Framing Language

11

Habermas and Norms of Language

One of the signal virtues of Jürgen Habermas's work is his insistence that inquiry in the social sciences must focus on language, and that social sciences must be based on a theory of linguistic activity or communication. Habermas treats linguistic communication as a constitutive feature of the object domain of the social sciences and has worked to develop a theory of communicative action which, he writes, 'is not a metatheory but the beginning of a social theory concerned to validate its own critical standards'.[1] Ultimately, a theory of communicative action, an analysis of communicative competence, would integrate a great many investigations in an enterprise modeled on the reconstruction of linguistic competence in generative grammar. The attempt to link social theory with a wide-ranging theoretical investigation of language games and the competencies they require is in itself extremely valuable, a source of considerable potential for a group of disciplines that seem to have turned aside from all the most powerful theoretical work that has been done in their domains. But since psychology has rejected Freud to work with rats in mazes, it should not surprise us if sociology rejects Habermas.

A second important feature of Habermas's work is the turn to communicative action and communicative competence in an attempt to deal with the problem of the normative force of discourses, particularly of social theory. Once a solid connection is established between knowledge and human interests, critical reflection cannot establish itself as a disinterested pursuit of truth and must find some other way of justifying the normative force it seeks. A universal theory of pragmatics, Habermas suggests, would be a suitable foundation for social theory.

---

[1] Jürgen Habermas, *The Theory of Communicative Action*, vol. 1, trans. Thomas McCarthy (Boston: Beacon Press, 1984), p. xxxiv. Henceforth cited in the text as CA.

To develop a universal pragmatics, an account of the conditions of possible understanding and the norms presupposed by acts of communication, Habermas investigates communicative competence, the implicit knowledge possessed by competent speaking and acting subjects. As opposed to 'purposive-rational action', communicative action obeys binding prevailing norms that define reciprocal expectations about behavior. Instead of adducing values claimed to stand beyond argument and ground the normative claims of a discourse, Habermas wants to show that certain values are inescapable, and hence available as grounding principles, because they are presupposed by the process of discussion itself. Just as the Cartesian *cogito* purports to show that the self cannot be doubted or questioned but is presupposed by any act of doubting or questioning, so Habermas argues that certain ideals correlated with a way of life we ought to be striving to bring about – such as truth, sincerity, rationality, freedom, the pursuit of understanding and agreement in a context devoid of coercion – are presupposed by the exercise of language itself. In 'What is Universal Pragmatics' he writes,

I shall develop the thesis that anyone acting communicatively must, in performing any speech action, raise universal validity claims and suppose that they can be vindicated [or redeemed: *einlösen*]. Insofar as he wants to participate in a process of reaching understanding, he cannot avoid raising the following – and indeed precisely the following – validity claims. He claims to be:

(a)   *Uttering* something understandably;
(b)   Giving [the hearer] *something* to understand;
(c)   Making *himself* thereby understandable; and
(d)   Coming to an understanding *with another person.*

The speaker must choose a comprehensible [*verständlich*] expression so that speaker and hearer can understand one another. The speaker must have the intention of communicating a true [*wahr*] proposition (or a propositional content, the existential presuppositions of which are satisfied) so that the hearer can share the knowledge of the speaker. The speaker must want to express his intentions truthfully [*wahrhaftig*] so that the hearer can believe the utterance of the speaker (can trust him). Finally, the speaker must choose an utterance that is right [*richtig*] so that the hearer can accept the utterance and speaker and hearer can agree with one another in the utterance with respect to a recognized normative background. Moreover, communicative action can continue undisturbed only as long as participants suppose that the validity claims they reciprocally raise are justified.[2]

---

[2]   Habermas, 'What is Universal Pragmatics?', in *Communication and the Evolution of Society,* trans. Thomas McCarthy (Boston: Beacon Press, 1979), pp. 2–3. Henceforth cited in the text as UP.

Here Habermas's claims seem to apply only to communication animated by a particular intention: 'Insofar as he wants to participate in a process of reaching understanding' is his phrase. But Habermas wishes to take this particular sort of communication, which will be the source of norms, as the norm. 'Reaching understanding', he writes in the *Theory of Communicative Action*, 'is the inherent telos of human speech' (CA, p. 287). To explore this argument one needs to know what types of speech or linguistic activity are recognized by this account of communicative competence – what possibilities are there in addition to what Habermas calls 'consensual speech actions' and regards as normal speech.

The answer appears to be that Habermas contrasts communicative action with symbolic action and strategic action. Symbolic action he calls 'still insufficiently analysed . . . (e.g. a concert, a dance – in general modes of action that are bound to non-propositional systems of symbolic expression)' (UP, p. 41). Symbolic action would seem to be non-linguistic as well as non-propositional, since elsewhere Habermas puts 'dramaturgical action' under the heading of communicative action rather than symbolic action, on the grounds that it too is oriented toward reaching understanding (CA, p. 329). Strategic action is 'oriented to success' rather than understanding. It treats others as objects to be manipulated rather than as subjects. 'By contrast, I shall speak of communicative action', he writes, 'whenever the actions of the agents involved are coordinated not through egocentric calculation of success but through acts of reaching understanding' (CA, pp. 285–6).

Clearly the distinction between communicative action and strategic action is crucial to a pragmatics which would ground the normative force of discourse. Habermas writes,

In identifying strategic action and communicative action as types, I am assuming that concrete actions can be classified from these points of view. I do not want to use the terms 'strategic' and 'communicative' only to designate two analytic aspects under which the same action could be described – on the one hand as a reciprocal influencing of one another by opponents acting in a purposive-rational manner and, on the other hand, as a process of reaching understanding among members of a life-world. Rather, social actions can be distinguished according to whether the participants adopt either a success-oriented attitude or one oriented to reaching understanding. And, under suitable conditions, these attitudes should be identifiable on the basis of the intuitive knowledge of the participants themselves. (CA, p. 286)

This is an important claim: that we are dealing not with two analytical perspectives but two quite different types of action. The distinction, he emphasizes, is not a psychological one but does involve 'the pretheoretical knowledge of competent speakers, who can themselves distinguish situations in which they are causally exerting an influence *upon* others from those in which they are coming to an understanding *with* them, and who know when their attempts have failed' (CA, p. 286). Two immediate questions are whether this is a possible and pertinent distinction for a wide range of cases and what are the ideological presuppositions of the attempt to make this distinction central. Habermas seems to have in mind the situation of one-to-one discussion between equals, but even there the attempt to come to an understanding frequently involves the attempt to persuade, to exert influence. In any event, relatively little language use occurs in wholly non-hierarchical situations: much one-to-one linguistic exchange occurs between people who are differently situated, so that reaching an understanding involves precisely influence and accommodation. Mary Louise Pratt, in a telling critique of speech act theory, argues that 'only some speech situations are characterized by shared objectives among participants. Clearly it is at least as common for speakers to have divergent goals and interests in a situation. . . . There may be no good reason to think of shared goals as representing any kind of natural norm in verbal interaction'.[3] Moreover, a great deal of communication involves more than two people, with consequent complications for distinguishing a pure communicative use of language from the strategic. Some readers of this chapter may feel engaged in an attempt to reach an understanding, but others will doubtless feel that the author is seeking to exert influence upon them – albeit by bringing them to a certain understanding of the matters under discussion. The more one thinks about a range of cases, the more difficult it is to feel that the distinction between communicative and strategic is central to the linguistic activity itself; it seems rather a moral distinction of considerable pertinence elsewhere, which can certainly be applied to linguistic exchange but scarcely derived from it.

Habermas admits that a good deal of linguistic exchange would probably have to count as strategic action – inducing someone to adopt a particular view or behave in a desired way by employing linguistic means. 'Such examples of the use of language with an orientation to consequences seem to decrease the value of speech acts as a model for action oriented to reaching understanding' (CA, p. 288). 'This will turn out not to be the case', he continues, 'only if it can be shown that the use of language with an orientation to reaching

---

[3] Mary Louise Pratt, 'Ideology and Speech Act Theory', *Poetics Today* 7:1 (1986), pp. 66–7.

understanding is the *original mode* of language use' and that the instrumental use of language is 'parasitic' upon this.

This is a classic problem: the attempt to show that supposed misuse is secondary and derivative. It is more difficult than usual in this case, for stories of the origin of language tend to evoke primitive man's practical or instrumental use of noises. It is hard to imagine how one could show that language was used to reach understanding before it was used 'with an orientation to consequences'. Indeed, several studies criticize the ethnocentrism of speech act theory's emphasis on sincerity, intentionality, and perspicuousness in language use. In other societies it may be clearer than in our own that disinterested exchange of information is a very minor aspect of linguistic activity.[4] Habermas, in fact, does not attempt to show that the use of language to achieve understanding is the original mode of language use but takes another tack. He tries to show the derivative character of the strategic use of speech by appealing to J. L. Austin's distinction between illocutionary and perlocutionary acts. This proves to be an unconvincing move, with little bearing on the point at issue, which fails in several ways: first because the distinction between the illocutionary and perlocutionary is not a distinction between communicative and strategic actions. Many illocutionary acts seem primarily designed to produce certain effects rather than to bring about understanding: think, for example, of commanding someone to get out, warning them to look out, or calling them out, not to mention pronouncing them man and wife or appointing them to a committee. Since the distinction between illocutionary and perlocutionary acts is not a distinction between communicative and strategic action, even if one could show the dependency of the perlocutionary on the illocutionary, it would not advance Habermas's argument.

Second, since it is difficult to show dependency, Habermas claims that understanding utterances is prior to and independent of understanding purposive activity. He writes

what we initially designated as 'the use of language with an orientation to consequences' is not an original use of language but the subsumption of speech acts that serve illocutionary aims under conditions of action oriented to success. As speech acts by no means always function in this way, however, it must also be possible to clarify the structure of linguistic communication without reference to structures of purposive activity. (CA, p. 293)

[4]   See, for example, Michelle Zimbalist Rosaldo, 'The Things We Do with Words', *Language in Society* 11 (1982), and Elinor Keenan, 'The Universality of Conversational Postulates', *Language in Society* 5 (1976).

Now it is difficult to derive this conclusion from speech act theory, which has generally worked to demonstrate precisely the opposite: that understanding utterances depends upon understanding purposive activity – what speakers are doing – and that understanding sentences is not prior to and independent of understanding sentences in action, as linguistics generally would have it, but rather dependent, in that to understand sentences is just to understand how they might function in purposive activity. To understand 'Could you close the window' is to grasp that it could be used to get someone to close the window as well as to inquire about their ability to achieve this result. Habermas gets no help from speech act theory and in effect must simply presuppose what he needs to show: that there is something called understanding an utterance that can be described without reference to any purposive activity.

But my concern is not whether and why this argument fails – though it seems one of the weaker versions of the classic metaphysical attempt to separate intrinsic from extrinsic or pure from corrupt and deem the latter irrelevant.[5] It is clear why Habermas seeks to make an argument of this sort: if he cannot show that language in strategic action is somehow derivative from and dependent on language in communicative action that presupposes an ideal communicative situation, he would be left with two sorts of linguistic communication, that which presupposes these norms and that which works differently; and if he were left with two separate uses of language, appeal to the norms that subtend consensual speech situations would just be a case of choosing values that one preferred rather than relying on values inevitably implied by linguistic communication. To give the norms implied by communicative action a foundational character, Habermas wishes to show that communicative action is original and strategic action derivative and dependent, unworthy of separate consideration, but the plausibility of this argument is likely to depend in good measure on our preference for the norms of communicative action, our feeling that they are better, more basic – which is what was to be proven. I shall return to this question of the relation between communicative and strategic action, but I want first to ask what would happen if one accepted Habermas's argument about the primacy of communicative action for thinking about discourse and considered various non-strategic communicative practices as the source of communicative norms. What is at stake here and what is involved in Habermas's theorization of non-strategic language use?

---

[5] For further discussion of this problem, see my *On Deconstruction* (Ithaca: Cornell University Press, 1982), pp. 92–5, 100–25, 160–2, 175–7.

The question is central since Habermas's project is to substitute for the subject-centered rationality of the philosophical tradition, with its emphasis on the transcendental character of reason and the autonomy of the rational subject, a communicative rationality drawn from the norms inherent in language use and to defend this rationality against what he calls the 'philosophical discourse of modernity'. At Cornell University in September 1984, when delivering six of the lectures that were soon to form the book entitled *Der philosophische Diskurs der Moderne*, Habermas seemed uncomfortable or impatient with questions that focused on the use of language, specifically the rhetorical or literary dimensions of the philosophical and modernist texts he was discussing. He may have felt a certain understandable perplexity at the odd situation in the United States, where much of what is regarded as belonging to the realm of philosophy and social theory in Europe has entered our intellectual life through departments of literature, and where the European philosopher finds himself facing an audience for whom questions about language and meaning are tied in with questions about rhetorical structures in literary and non-literary texts. An unwillingness to address questions about what he regarded as the literary style of philosophical texts – Heidegger's or Nietzsche's mode of writing – might be explained as a consequence of *depaysement* or a desire not to be distracted from his main points, but it also sheds light on what he regards as inherent in the use of language. The reluctance to consider his texts as texts may seem strange in a philosopher who has brought to the social sciences a hitherto unparalleled concern with language and its constitutive force, but it may also prove to have a decisive structural role in his account of language and rationality.

How does the rhetoricity or literariness of language relate to communicative action and to the attempt to ground critical reflection in the norms intrinsic to communicative competence? Where does the literary fit in? On the one hand, literary discourse seems to belong to communicative rather than strategic or symbolic action. The traditional view of works of art as purposive wholes without purpose provides a prima facie reason for seeing literature as communication rather than strategic action. Symbolic action may seem a more promising category, but if the test is reliance on non-propositional systems of expression, then literature, like 'dramaturgical action', which Habermas sees as oriented towards understanding, belongs to communicative action. Indeed, given the amount of hermeneutical attention devoted to literary classics, it would be difficult to exclude literature from uses of language where understanding is central. But if literature is indeed communicative action, it is not evident that literary discourse entails the inevitable presuppositions Habermas ascribes to this mode. Must the reader of literature necessarily presume that the speaker has the intention of communicating a true proposition or propositional content whose existential presuppositions are satisfied? Is the reader in fact compelled to assume that the speaker must want to express his intentions truthfully so that the hearer can believe his utterance and trust him? Do we necessarily presume a speaker, or is not this presumption a move in a particular set of language games? Do Habermas's norms in fact form part of the communicative competence that makes possible the production and interpretation of literary texts, among other discourses? They are not entirely irrelevant, certainly, but they are displaced and complicated in ways that might have a bearing on universal pragmatics.

Consider the briefest of examples, Guillaume Apollinaire's famous one line poem, 'Chantre' (Bard):

> Et l'unique cordeau des trompettes marines.
> (And the single string of the marine trumpets)

What are the most basic conditions of understanding that can be identified through examples of this sort? The primary norm seems to be the assumption of significance: not that something true is being said or that some speaker could provide evidence for what is asserted, but that there is something worth attending to here. It is this presumption that sets in motion the process of understanding and makes possible the exploration of meaning. Mary Louise Pratt, in a discussion drawing on Grice's account of conversational implicature, speaks of the 'hyper-protected cooperative principle': the presumption of all interpretive activity, that there is some point to what seems to need interpretation, even if the point is an absence of point.[6] Recognition of this powerful norm, the presumption of significance, ought to suit the author of *Knowledge and Human Interests*.

The second decisive norm here seems to be the presumption of unity, which encourages investigation of relations between elements: between the two halves of the alexandrine (a *cor d'eau* is a *trompette marine*), between the title and the line (bard and instrument), and between form and statement (the poem has but a single line, as the marine trumpet has but one string). Note that we do not seem required to make any presumptions about speakers, or about speaker's intentions and relations to hearers, but only about an underlying intentionality. Presumptions about speakers seem to arise in particular

---

[6] Mary Louise Pratt, *Towards a Speech Act Theory of Literary Discourse* (Bloomington: Indiana University Press, 1977), pp. 132–223.

cases, where pronouns or other linguistic features lead readers to posit a speaking voice, but these presumptions are still not exactly those elucidated by Habermas. Consider Herrick's brief lyric,

> Whenas in silks my Julia goes,
> Then, then, methinks, how sweetly flows
> The liquefaction of her clothes.
>
> Next, when I cast mine eyes and see
> That brave vibration, each way free,
> O how that glittering taketh me!

Here one does not need to presume that a speaker is making a true statement (Julia is a conventional literary name), nor presume that his values are right so that the hearer can accept the utterance, but one does presume the possibility of positing on the one hand a speaking voice and on the other an authorial consciousness, whose relation is a subject for interpretive explanation. Interpretation may frequently take the form of accentuating the distance between values and implicit claims of the posited speaking voice and those of the posited authorial attitude – between, shall we say, the male appreciation of an undulating walk and another attitude emerging from the articulation of this scene by two latinate terms, 'liquefaction' and 'vibration', which, elegantly naming, create the two distinct moments, 'then' and 'next', by which the speaker claims himself taken. Understanding does not presume, as Habermas claims, 'speaker and hearer agreeing with one another in the utterance' – a special presumption – but works rather on the frequently counterfactual assumption of the possibility that the reader can see and grasp what the speaker failed to see and even what the author failed to see. Tragedy, for instance, makes this the very model of understanding: to grasp both what Oedipus sees and what he does not see but which works powerfully in his utterance. Communication, one might say, is structurally asymmetrical, and symmetry is an accident and a myth of moralists, not a norm.

To address the question of the literary would be to raise problems of how far Habermas's norms are really presupposed in all communicative discourse – something that is far from clear – and whether other presumptions, such as those of unity and significance, do not in fact play just as crucial a role in the interpretation of linguistic activity. One could raise such questions with other non-literary examples, which might suggest, for instance, that the presupposition of sincerity is a special feature of particular situations rather than a universal norm: when I am reading the instructions for my word-processing program, I assume that statements are correct descriptions of the system's capabilities and that the manual has been checked for errors, but there seems no interesting sense in which I presuppose the sincerity of any individual communicator. However, one suspects that whenever one cited examples of language that raised difficulties about the universality of Habermas's norms, he would relegate them to strategic action not aimed at proper understanding but seeking some end (e.g. enabling you to make the program work). The repeated exclusion of interesting examples would strengthen one's conviction that while Habermas claims not to choose norms but to find them inescapably implied in communicative action, he in effect chooses these norms by setting aside as derivative and irrelevant those sorts of language that might be said not to imply them. Since most interesting linguistic exchange can be said to seek some end, one cannot convincingly contest its relegation to strategic action. Therefore literary discourse, since it resists being set aside as instrumental, becomes particularly germane to the project of describing the communicative competence that makes possible communicative action, especially given its propensity to foreground and thematize questions of communication and interpretation.

Habermas proposes one further distinction I have not mentioned: a distinction within communicative action between ordinary communication in which the validity claims unavoidably raised (truth, truthfulness, and rightness) are naively presumed and what he calls 'discourse' in which the validity claims are treated as hypothetical and subject to discussion. Literary discourse might seem to belong to discourse – language which raises questions about its own truth, sincerity, and rightness. It might indeed seem in some ways the best case of communication whose presumed relations to states of affairs, values, and intentions are suspended, but Habermas cannot allow this, for discourse is to be the pure case of communication, where everything is suspended except the aim of reaching a rational consensus, an agreement based on understanding and involving absolutely no forces except those of rational argument. Discourse presumes the ideal speech situation. 'The ideal speech situation', Habermas writes, 'is neither an empirical phenomenon nor a mere construct but rather an unavoidable supposition reciprocally made in discourse'.[7]

The more one reads Habermas, the more circular his foundational project appears. The ideal speech situation, the model for an ideal

[7]   Habermas, 'Wahrheitstheorien', in *Wirklichkeit und Reflexion: Festschrift für Walter Schulz*, ed. H. Fahrenbach (Pfullingen, 1973), p. 258. Quoted in Thomas McCarthy's invaluable *The Critical Theory of Jürgen Habermas* (Cambridge, Mass.: MIT Press, 1978), p. 310.

society said to be inescapably presupposed in communicative action itself, emerges as the result of a series of exclusions of those communicative activities that do not seem to presuppose these norms – so that what we have is, on the one hand, Habermas's impressive synthesizing labors disguising a choice of norms that we all would admire and, on the other hand, an account of communicative competence whose interest is greatly restricted by the exclusions the normative project required.

I have emphasized literary discourse, which is hard to exclude by the criteria Habermas gives. In his discussions of communicative action he does not bother to define criteria that exclude it, I imagine, because he thought it so obviously marginal – a case of communicative action in which the inescapable presumptions of truth and truthfulness were not fulfilled.[8] His American encounters, however, and his engagement with a tradition of thought which takes literature seriously, from Nietzsche to Heidegger, Bataille, Foucault, and Derrida, have led him to address the problem of the relationship between philosophical and literary language or between logic and rhetoric. In a chapter of *The Philosophical Discourse of Modernity* entitled 'Excursus on Leveling the Genre Distinction between Philosophy and Literature' he takes the key move of deconstruction to be the questioning of the well-foundedness of this distinction in a reversal of the hierarchical relation between logic and rhetoric. The move from a Heideggerian '"destruction" into the "deconstruction" of the philosophical tradition transposes the radical critique of reason into the domain of rhetoric and thereby shows it a way out of the aporia of self-referentiality'.[9] That is, the deconstructive critique of philosophy would escape what he regards as the debilitating paradox of relying on what it criticizes to the extent that it grounds itself not on philosophy or on reason but in a larger domain of rhetoric. 'Derrida can only attain Heidegger's goal of bursting metaphysical thought-forms from the inside by means of his essentially rhetorical procedure if the philosophical text is *in truth* a literary one – if one can *demonstrate* that the genre distinction between philosophy and literature dissolves upon

[8]   The determination of philosophers to relegate literary language to a derivative status where it can be claimed to have no bearing on questions about the nature of language and models for its description suggests that any attempt to take into consideration literary discourse and its interpretation would have significant effects on normative accounts. The arguments used to set literature aside are often so conspicuously weak as to indicate that its exclusion is not a defensible move *within* the discourse of philosophy but a prior exclusion which makes traditional philosophical discourse possible.

[9]   Jürgen Habermas, *The Philosphical Discourse of Modernity,* trans. Thomas McCarthy (Cambridge: MIT Press, 1987), p. 190. Henceforth cited in the text as PM.

closer examination' (PM, p. 189). The practice of deconstruction demonstrates the frailty of the distinction, as philosphical texts are shown to depend on precisely those rhetorical operations or metaphorical totalizations from which they seek to distinguish themselves. 'This is the ground of the primacy of rhetoric, which is concerned with the qualities of texts in general, over logic, as a system of rules to which only certain types of discourse are subjected in an exclusive manner – those bound to argumentation' (PM, p. 190). Habermas identifies as 'the thesis on which everything depends – both the self-understanding of a literary criticism upgraded to the critique of metaphysics and the deconstructionist dissolution of the performative contradiction of a self-referential critique of reason' – a statement from *On Deconstruction*: 'if serious language is a special case of the non-serious, if truths are fictions whose fictionality has been forgotten, then literature is not a deviant, parasitical instance of language. On the contrary, other discourses can be seen as cases of a generalized literature, or archi-literature'.[10]

Taking up the question of whether serious language can be seen as a special case of the non-serious, Habermas does concede that serious discourse is based on iterable formulae or conventions but defends the possibility of separating normal speech from derivative forms in terms of idealizing assumptions in the former: 'the constraints under which illocutionary acts develop a force for coordinating action and have consequences relevant to action define the domain of "normal" language. They can be analysed as the kind of idealizing assumptions we have to make in communicative action' (PM, p. 196). But since he relies on claims by literary critics such as Richard Ohmann that literary works involve 'impaired and incomplete speech acts ... whose sentences lack the illocutionary forces that would normally attach to them' (PM, p. 201) – a claim we shall consider in chapter twelve – he begs the question at issue, which is whether the illocutionary force of assertions is not a special case of a generalized rhetorical function of language. However, the main issue for Habermas becomes the contrast between the poetic, world-disclosing function of literary discourse and the function of 'carrying on the world's business'. He accuses Derrida of permitting 'the capacity to solve problems to vanish behind the world-creating capacity of language' (PM, p. 205). Emphasizing this distinction between world-disclosing and problem-solving, he writes, 'The polar tension between world-disclosure and problem-solving is held together within the functional matrix of ordinary language; but art and literature on the

---

[10]   Culler, *On Deconstruction*, p. 181. Quoted by Habermas, PM, p. 193.

one side, and science, morality, and law on the other, are specialized for experiences and modes of knowledge that can be shaped and worked out within the compass of *one* linguistic function and *one* dimension of validity at a time' (PM, p. 207). Although he now recognizes the fundamental rhetoricity of language, he wishes to maintain, relying on this distinction between two functions of language, that in the two cases

the rhetorical elements of language assume *entirely different* roles. The rhetorical element occurs in its *pure form* only in the self-referentiality of the poetic expression, that is in the language of fiction specialized for world-disclosure. Even the normal language of everyday life is ineradicably rhetorical; but within the matrix of different linguistic functions, the rhetorical elements recede here. The world-disclosive linguistic framework is almost at a standstill in the routines of everyday practice. The same holds true of the specialized languages of science and technology, law and morality, economics, political science, etc. They, too, live off the illuminating power of metaphorical tropes; but the rhetorical elements, which are by no means expunged, are tamed, as it were, and enlisted for the special purposes of problem-solving. (PM, p. 209)

Now in one sense this is perfectly true. Rhetorical elements conventionally, practically, have a different function and importance in fiction, in everyday conversation, and in the discourse of philosophy, or law or economics. The question is the status of that function. The distinction between problem-solving and world-disclosing has a certain practical relevance but once again seems derived rather than primary, in that one can certainly show that the problem-solving capacity of language may be based precisely on the redescriptions of a particular vocabulary which puts a situation in a new light, eliminating what were thought to be problems and bringing new ones to attention. Moreover, deconstructive readings have suggested that the supposed problem-solving function of discourse may rely precisely on the constitutive rhetoricity from which it would distinguish itself. Here Habermas, in taking up the problem of the rhetorical status of language and the role of the literary in any account of the conditions of communicative rationality, simply reaffirms the basic distinction between a normal language, now called 'problem-solving', and an abnormal one, called 'world-disclosing'. But this shift in appellations is already a considerable improvement: the theory of communicative action now seems restricted to problem-solving language, which is a step towards seeing so-called problem-solving as a special case of language rather than its norm and model. On the other hand, the recognition of the special character of different discourses – the languages of literature, science, morality, law and 'everyday' – represents a potential enrichment of the theory, though an attenuation of its foundational possibilities.

Habermas thus recognizes the importance and even pervasiveness of the rhetorical, constitutive (world-disclosing) function of language, but he continues to insist on the abnormality of this literary quality. Literature has long served philosophy in this way, as a margin close at hand, into which problematical aspects of language could be shunted so as not to complicate normative accounts; as the name for every-thing non-serious or abnormal which permits accounts of language to focus on so-called normal, serious communicative action. But that very relationship indicates a dependency I have asserted in claiming that literature would provide evidence about the norms of a generalized communicative competence, within which the norms Habermas defines would belong to restricted discursive practices (where one does not just assume significance but posits speakers and, further, presumes their sincerity and the truth of their assertions). I mentioned the presumption of significance, which underlies inter-pretive activity, a principle of pragmatics whose writ runs at least as far as principles of truth, sincerity, and rightness, which are special norms for particular types of language games. I have also suggested that the symmetry Habermas presumes – understanding as a coincidence of the thoughts of interlocutors – would emerge, if a range of communicative action were considered, as a special case of the generalized asymmetry of linguistic and interpretive activity. In fact, Habermas is elucidating a highly restricted ideological notion of understanding. If he were correct, we would be compelled to say that we had misunderstood when, by virtue of our temporal or spatial position, we see a speech act in a context that its perpetrator could not see. Indeed, Wayne Booth, in a similar normative project which owes nothing to Habermas, calls such understanding 'overstanding'.[11] But the more comprehensive perspective created by the temporality of the interpretive situation is not thought to produce misunderstanding, except in special cases (which Habermas seems to take as the norm) where we take the goal to be agreement with the producer of the language in question. This is not the goal of most communicative activity.

Although Habermas believes that he is taking seriously Wittgen-stein's notion that language-games are forms of life and attempting a theoretical investigation of the competencies that make language

[11]   Wayne Booth, *Critical Understanding* (Chicago: University of Chicago Press, 1979).

games possible, he lacks the understanding of language as an uncanny, rhetorical, inhuman force that emerges here and there in Wittgenstein: for instance, in the famous remark that 'Philosophy is a battle against the bewitchment of our intelligence by means of language', which credits words with a power to bewitch; or in the enigmatical passage where Wittgenstein discusses his strong inclination to call Wednesday fat and Tuesday lean. 'Would you be rather inclined to say that Wednesday is fat and Tuesday lean or vice versa?' asks a voice in the *Philosophical Investigations.*

(I incline decisively toward the former). Now have 'fat' and 'lean' some different meaning here from their usual one? – They have a different use. – So ought I really to have used different words? Certainly not that. – I want to use *these* words (with their familiar meanings) *here.* – Now I say nothing about the causes of this phenomenon ... Whatever the explanation, – the inclination is there. [Wittgenstein's ellipsis][12]

Discussion of these matters does not belong in an account of presupposed norms, as Habermas conceives it, but perhaps to say this is to indicate that what he is analysing is not language so much as ideologically restricted notions of understanding, communication, rationality, or, more generously, a philosophical conception of communication that goes with the value choices he wishes to make normative. This does not tell us much about language generally or about the communicative competence exercised in our dealings with language – we would not be very competent if we invariably approached language with the presumption that it is true, truthful, right and serious.[13]

Habermas does not succeed in grounding rationality, but there is one interesting and illuminating aspect of his project which should not be ignored. Habermas takes up the difficult question of where discourses might get their normative force and provides an answer: from norms that are presupposed by the relevant communicative activity itself and lodged in the communicative competence of members of the culture. Any other kind of norm would be in effect chosen and, since this choice would need to be justified in turn, could not be appealed to for justification. Though I have questioned Habermas's procedure and the status of the norms he discovers, this argument sheds light upon the case where critical discourses appeal to

[12] Ludwig Wittgenstein, *Philosophical Investigations,* trans. G.E.M. Anscombe (New York: Macmillan, 1958), p. 216.
[13] Quarreling, for example, is a common linguistic activity with different and quite interesting rules.

norms they wish to contest, as when proponents of the pragmatist concept of truth as warrantable assertion maintain that this is simply what truth is, or when a deconstructive critique of logocentrism conducts its argument in terms drawn from the system of concepts it wishes to displace. This reliance upon fundamental concepts that are contested is frequently seen as a failing – a crucial and disabling inconsistency – but Habermas's linking of normative force with communicative competence suggests that perhaps this is inevitable in discourse, that the crucial concepts do not form some separate system of beliefs which one might be faulted for inconsistently adhering to, but are part of our communicative competence and will be presupposed in arguments that contest them. This important conclusion suggests that the frequent demands for argumentative discourse to instantiate the principles it wishes to promote and not rely on those it rejects seek an impossible purity; that the self-reflexivity of discourse is a self-division rather than self-possession. But, one wonders, is this inevitable, inescapable appeal to norms that one is seeking to change communicative action or strategic action? Might it be 'blind tactics', in Derrida's phrase? This is a question Habermas's work might help one to address.

12

Problems in the Theory of Fiction

'Fiction' is a somewhat problematical notion, more heavily used, it would seem, in the publishing trade and in public libraries than in literary criticism. It suggests that for readers and editors the most important distinction, when confronted with a piece of writing, is whether it speaks of real situations and events or imagined ones. When one asks for a title in a bookstore, the clerk is likely to ask whether it is fiction or non-fiction, and bestseller lists have, for reasons that remain obscure, chosen 'fiction' and 'non-fiction' as the appropriate way of dividing the multifarious corpus of publications. But when we turn from the organizing principles of bookstores, libraries and bestseller lists to the books themselves, it is not clear how important this distinction is. If one compares books on the fiction bestseller list with those on the non-fiction bestseller list, one finds that many of the latter seem much more fantastically fictional than the former: *Thin Thighs in Thirty Days* – a seductive fiction; *How to Make a Fortune in Real Estate* – an improbable narrative; *No Bad Dogs* – obviously about a fictional world. Certainly, there are many weeks when the non-fiction bestseller list seems more resolutely fictional – more imaginatively devoted to fantasies designed to gratify the reading public – than the so-called fiction list.

But, of course, the term 'fiction' when used by publishers, booksellers, and most readers except some theoretically-inclined specialists, designates imaginative prose narratives (novels and short stories) – as opposed to poetry, on the one hand, which will not be found in the fiction section, nor on the fiction bestseller list, and to non-fiction on the other. Non-fiction seems to comprise works which either are not narratives, or, if they are narratives, claim to recount historical events of some sort. This terminological situation is somewhat strange: we speak of 'fiction-writers', for example, and famous books bear titles such as *The Craft of Fiction* and *The Rhetoric of Fiction*. The most general problem of the theory of fiction might therefore be, what is the relationship of the notion of fiction to the qualities of the writings discussed under this heading? What is the role of the notion of fiction in the theory of fiction? Surprisingly, most of the advances in the theory of fiction of the past twenty-five years come from the study not of fiction as a mode, nor even of the novel as a genre, but of something else. For example, René Girard's pioneering *Deceit, Desire and the Novel* studied major European novels as dramas based on the mimetic mechanisms of desire, 'triangular desire', in which the subject's desire is constituted as imitation of another desire. But mimetic desire turned out to be neither restricted to the novel nor able to define a distinctive generic structure but a phenomenon of pervasive importance, as Girard's later work has shown. His book might stand as an illustration of the way the most pertinent and productive investigations in our field seem to bear in the end not on the canon of masterpieces of fiction but on some different and larger class of phenomena.

Most advances in the theory of fiction, though, have focused on narrative and can be grouped under the heading of narratology, study of the structure of narrative and the functioning of its major constituents. First, recent criticism has enormously refined the Russian Formalists' distinction between *fabula* and *sjuzhet*, as in Gérard Genette's *Narrative Discourse*, Meir Sternberg's *Expositional Modes and Temporal Ordering in Fiction*, and Mieke Bal's *Narratology*, which investigate the potential of a great many different relations between narrative presentation or narrative order and plot order or story time. But there is a sense in which these subtle and exhaustive studies of the relations between the level of event and the level of narrative in fictional narratives do not go far enough; they miss the kind of insight afforded by studies which look at the relations between *fabula* and *sjuzhet* in non-literary cases. For example, a number of analyses have pursued the productive enterprise of reading Freud's case histories as narratives, where relations between the *fabula* and *sjuzhet* prove quite complicated. The operation of deferred action (*Nachträglichkeit*), for instance, makes it difficult to establish a bedrock of events which then get reordered by narrative, for narrative ordering may be what constitutes key events as events. In the case of the Wolfman, whose neurosis is traced to a traumatic primal scene – the sight at age one and a half of his parents copulating – Freud notes that this decisive, originary moment might in fact be a fantasy, concocted from later observation of animals copulating and transferred to the parents: a fantasy operating as primal event through deferred action. The situating of the fantasy at the age of one and a half, which is what gives it primacy in the fabula of this narrative, would then be the product of narrative requirements. Freud writes, 'The scene which was to be made up had to fulfill certain conditions, which, in consequence of the circumstances of the dreamer's life, could only be found in this early period; such, for instance, was the condition that he should be in bed in his parent's bedroom'.[1] Here, as Peter Brooks puts it, 'A narrative explanation which surely foresaw that much of its celebrity would come from its recovery of so spectacular a moment of origin doubles back on itself . . . to suggest another kind of referentiality'. With the constitution of events by fundamental fantasies, 'tales may lead back not so much to events as to other tales, to man as a structure of the fictions he tells about himself'.[2] By pursuing a narratological problem into non-literary realms, we discover to what extent the case history – a non-fictional scientific genre concerning real people, their circumstances and their suffering, etc. – is ultimately allied to the fictional. This shows the scope and functioning of the fictional in ways relevant to literary study itself. It also indicates a problem in the theory of fiction: when you leave fiction you rediscover fictions.

The second development has been reflection on the narrative audience, in all its guises: narratees, actual readers, ideal readers, intended readers, superreaders, authorial audiences, implied readers.[3] The most useful scheme may be that offered by Peter Rabinowitz in 'Truth in Fiction: A Reexamination of Audiences', which distinguishes the actual audience, the authorial audience (which takes the work as a fictional communication from the author), the narrative audience (which takes the work as a communication from the narrator), and the ideal narrative audience (perhaps unfortunately named) which interprets the narrator's communication as the narrator appears to wish.[4] The greater the refinements in the study of narratees, of various sorts of implied and real readers, though, the more apparent it becomes that this is an exercise in fiction-making. This is relatively clear in the case of the implied reader, which in Wolfgang Iser's account, for example, functions to enable him to cast his interpretation in the form of a narrative, a story of what the implied reader grasps and does not grasp, where she encounters gaps and how she fills them in. The implied reader functions as a fictional character in a story of reading.

[1] Muriel Gardner (ed.), *The Wolfman and Sigmund Freud* (Harmondsworth: Penguin, 1973), p. 223.

[2] Peter Brooks, 'Fictions of the Wolfman', *Diacritics* 9:1 (Spring 1979), p. 78.

[3] For all the matters discussed in this paragraph, see my 'Readers and Reading', chapter 1 of *On Deconstruction* (Ithaca: Cornell University Press, 1982).

[4] Peter Rabinowitz, 'Truth in Fiction: A Reexamination of Audiences', *Critical Inquiry* 4 (1977).

In many cases, reference to the reader is an attempt to ground interpretations upon a supposed experience. Stanley Fish's reader never learns anything from his reading, but repeatedly expects a line-ending to close a syntactic unit, and is repeatedly astonished or discomfited when the next line brings a change in the hypothesized construction. I have also argued that certain modes of feminist criticism are best regarded, not as records of the experience of women readers but, in Elaine Showalter's words, as exploration of 'the way in which the *hypothesis* of a female reader changes our apprehension of a given text, awakening us to the significance of its sexual codes'.[5] A well-known article by Walter Ong is entitled 'The Writer's Audience is Always a Fiction', to which one might add that the reader's experience – at least in interpretations – is always a fiction: a narrative construction in a story of reading. Study of readers of various sorts has resulted in a wide range of stories of reading, narratives of what happens to the reader as he or she encounters the sequence of words. When students write papers about novels they frequently proceed by imagining a reader – what it would be like to be a reader – and cast their papers as fictional narratives of what 'the reader' feels, perceives, realizes. The fiction of a reader is absolutely central to the reading of fiction. What we discover when we try to explain fiction by reference to the reader is this central role of fictions of reading. There is a certain circularity here that seems to me crucial to the theory of fiction.

The third development in the field of narratology has been the expansion of work on the discrimination of narrators and narrative perspectives – the tradition of Henry James and Percy Lubbock. The notion of narrative point of view in fiction has itself been made more coherent by the concept of focalization proposed by Genette and clarified by Mieke Bal, which emphasizes a distinction between who sees and who speaks, a distinction often elided by the association of point of view with narrative consciousness. The discrimination of narrators has reached a stage of immense sophistication. This whole aspect of the poetics of fiction is ably synthesized in Susan Lanser's *The Narrative Act: Point of View in Prose Fiction*, which comprehensively identifies a great range of variables affecting narrative point of view and locates them on a series of scales (rather than as features which are simply present or absent.) In the course of this she raises one problem which previous theorists have neglected, the sex of narrators. 'Sex differences permeate the uses of language and condition the

    [5] Elaine Showalter, 'Towards a Feminist Poetics', in *Women Writing and Writing about Women*, ed. Mary Jacobus (London: Croom Helm, 1979), p. 25. See *On Deconstruction*, pp. 43–64.

reception of discourse', she argues; 'along with other social identifiers marking the relationship of a textual personage to the dominant social class, sex is important to the encoding and decoding of narrative voice'.[6]

This is an interesting line of investigation, but instead of looking for discursive features that might identify a female narrative voice, Lanser suggests that the 'presence of a female name on the title page signals a female narrative voice, in the absence of markings to the contrary'. Later this is treated as a convention to appeal to: 'By virtue of the conventions linking the author's social identity with that of the heterodiegetic [third person] narrative voice, the narrator [in this particular case] is female'.[7] The question is, first, whether this is really so. Do we construct narrators on this principle – invariably giving them a sex (the same sex as the author unless there are contrary indications)? Do readers in fact assume that it is a woman who says, 'It is a truth universally acknowledged that a single man in possession of a good fortune must be in want of a wife' because *Pride and Prejudice* is signed 'Jane Austen'? Lanser's argument that prior critics have neglected the question of the sex of narrators and have treated narrators as male suggests that readers have not in fact worked on the assumptions she claims to identify. One might note that Mary Louise Pratt, whom Lanser generally admires, in *Towards a Speech Act Theory of Literary Discourse* repeatedly refers to the fictional speaker of this opening sentence as 'he'.

This question of the sex of narrative voices is in fact a significant problem in the theory of fiction which focuses a number of important issues. First, there is the problem of what to appeal to in discussion of texts and reading. Lanser appeals here to convention, but if one is interested in changing our procedures of reading, as she seems to be, this will not suffice. If she wants us to recognize that aspects of the vision or discourse of narrators which we value belong to women, she must proceed differently. Not that one can avoid the reference to convention altogether, since narrators are constructed by conventional procedures of reading, but one must at some point appeal to the way in which following or not following a given convention will affect the significance of the works being read.

This brings us to the second point, a question about the politics of reading. No doubt critics have generally assumed that the voice of authority is male, albeit a comprehensive male voice in which sexual

[6] Susan Lanser, *The Narrative Act: Point of View in Prose Fiction* (Princeton: Princeton University Press, 1981), p. 166.
[7] Ibid., pp. 167 and 250.

distinctiveness is to some extent neutralized. One might imagine that one was being scrupulous and scientific in speaking of the narrator of a Jane Austen or George Eliot novel as 'he' – which only confirms a link between patriarchy and systematic thought that we ought to be working to change. Yet what is the best way to change? To call the narrators of all novels by women 'she' (unless instructed otherwise) begs important questions about gender and genre by presuming that a feminine voice is what women writers naturally produce. If, however, one stipulates instead that critics should try to infer the sex of *individual* narrators from the character of their reflections and judgments, this risks conferring authority on the most tendentious stereotypes, which would come to serve as standards (this observation sounds feminine, this one masculine . . .). Might it not be better to call *all* narrators of all novels 'she', unless otherwise instructed? The question seems to me at the very least an open one. If Lanser is right that we do identify narrators of novels by women as female, then the question is whether there might be better strategies.

Third, the issue of the sex of narrators illustrates the compulsion, endemic to the recent study of narrative, to explain textual details by relating them to qualities of persons. This has been our most powerful strategy of naturalization for dealing with refractory modern fictions: the most bizarre formulations and juxtapositions are recuperated as the discourse of an obsessional, neurotic, or otherwise deranged narrator. The more sophisticated we become in treating discursive details as reflections of the attitudes and assumptions of narrators, the more we encourage the notion that to interpret fiction is above all to identify in all detail the person who speaks it. The argument would be, though this is not how Lanser presents it, that since every person has a sex, and narrators are people, every narrator must have a sex, and to omit discussion of the sex of narrators is to miss important aspects of novels. This argument is plausible only, it seems to me, because we have come to take for granted that we explain textual details by adducing narrators and explain narrators by adducing qualities of real people.

Now fictions have their source in persons in that authors construct them, but this is a far cry from the notion that the meaning of elements is what they reveal about the personalities and attitudes of people who function as narrators. I think here lies a major problem for the theory of fiction today, when narrative analysis has become so resourceful and, in dubious collusion with speech act theory, is attempting to convince us that a narrative is an act of a person. The theory of fiction needs to be alert to the inadequacies of this orientation, which strives to convert everything in language to a mark of human personalities.

There is, of course, a great deal of patterning in texts that is not a sign of personality. Much of literature is interesting and compelling precisely because it does something other than illustrate the personality of a narrator. For the moment I want to suggest that this strategy of naturalization and anthropomorphism should be recognized not as an analytical perspective on fiction but as part of the fiction-making process. That is to say, making narrators is not an analytical operation that lies outside the domain of fiction but very much a continuation of fiction-making: dealing with details by imagining a narrator; telling a story about a narrator and his/her responses so as to make sense of them.

To explore the nature and problems of this naturalizing presumption we should first return to the notion of fiction. Generally, fiction is conceived in opposition to non-fiction: non-fiction treats real characters and events while fiction treats imaginary ones, makes assertions about characters who do not exist, events that never occurred, or in short, about fictional worlds. But a number of critics who have addressed the theory of fiction recently have argued that novels are not real assertions about fictional characters but fictional assertions – or rather, fictional imitations of assertions. Barbara Herrnstein Smith argues that literary artworks should be considered as depictions or imitations of natural discourse. 'The various genres of literary art . . . can to some extent be distinguished according to what types of discourse . . . they characteristically represent'. A novel 'is a depiction of – a fictive instance of – a kind of book'. Novels 'have typically been representations of chronicles, journals, letters, memoirs, and biographies'.[8]

For Smith, the essential contrast is between natural discourse and fictive discourse. Natural discourse is 'the verbal acts of real persons on particular occasions in response to particular sets of circumstances'. Fictive discourse imitates or represents real discourse. Of course, the characters, events and the narrator of a novel are all fictional. 'The essential fictiveness of novels, however, is not to be discovered in the unreality of the characters, objects, and events alluded to, but in the unreality of the alludings themselves. In other words, in a novel or tale, it is the act of reporting events, the act of describing persons and referring to places that is fictive. The novel represents the verbal action of a man reporting, describing, and

[8] Barbara Herrnstein Smith, *On the Margins of Discourse* (Chicago: University of Chicago Press, 1979), pp. 8, 31 and 30.

Framing Language

referring'. The writer of fiction, for example, is 'pretending to be *writing* a biography while actually *fabricating* one'. Although a literary work 'is a representation of discourse, we can understand it, infer meanings from it, only through our prior experiences with the sort of things it does represent, namely natural utterances in historical contexts'.[9] To understand fictive discourse, then, is to treat it as if it were a representation of a real person performing a natural discursive act.

The distinction comes to be one between utterances that are really *said* by speakers or writers and those that are not said but constructed, fabricated, and so on. Felix Martinez-Bonati in *Fictive Discourse and the Structures of Literature* puts it slightly differently but more dramatically: a literary work consists of non-linguistic signs that imitate linguistic signs, pseudo-sentences which 'make present an authentic sentence from another communicative situation' (and to comprehend the sentence is to imagine its communicative situation). 'The author communicates to us not a particular situation by means of real linguistic signs, but, rather, imaginary linguistic signs by means of non-linguistic ones. In other words, the author himself does not communicate with us by means of language; instead he communicates language to us'.[10]

For both these theorists, fiction is an imitation of real historical utterance and is understood by taking real world utterances as a model for the relations between fictional utterance, fictional speaker and fictional world. But when in order to elucidate the model we inquire about the structure and properties of the real-world, historical discourses of which literature is a fictional imitation, we come upon a fertile branch of narratology which in its recent investigations of narrative as a fundamental category of understanding or scheme of intelligibility has come to assert the fictional character of this supposedly natural or real substratum. If a novel is a fictional imitation of real historical-interpretive discourse, what if history-writing is a form of fiction-making? I cite Hayden White, who urges that we overcome our 'reluctance to consider historical narratives as what they most manifestly are, verbal fictions, the contents of which are as much *invented* as *found* and the forms of which have more in common with their counterparts in literature than they have with those in the sciences'. Histories achieve explanatory effect by operations of 'emplotment': 'by emplotment I mean simply the

---

[9]   Ibid., pp. 15, 29, 30 and 37.
[10]   Felix Martinez-Bonati, *Fictive Discourse and the Structures of Literature* (Ithaca: Cornell University Press, 1981), pp. 79 and 81.

encodation of facts contained in chronicle as components of specific kinds of plot structure, in precisely the way [Northrop] Frye has suggested is the case with "fictions" in general'. For White, 'understanding historical narratives involves coming to realize that the story is of one kind rather than another, romance, tragedy, comedy, satire, epic' and so on.[11] In other words, intelligibility depends on their emplotment according to literary models, which they could be said to imitate.

Nor is White's argument an isolated case. W. B. Gallie, working out of a quite different English tradition, explains real-world historical narrative on the model of the very sorts of stories which the theoreticians of fiction tell us are imitation histories. Taking literature as the model for describing historical intelligibility, Gallie argues that historical understanding is a special case of what is involved in following a story and appeals to 'the familiar unquestionable facts of the experience of following a story. We follow a story through or across contingencies – accidents, coincidences, unpredictable events of all kinds; yet the story's general direction and continuous advance towards its final conclusion somehow succeed in rendering these contingencies acceptable'.[12] 'To make sense of their span', writes Frank Kermode, 'men need fictive concords with origins and ends, such as give meaning to lives and to poems'.[13] The repetition of a clock's ticking is mastered, ordered, by the fiction which articulates identical sounds as *tick, tock*, with a beginning and end – the elementary model, Kermode avers, of what we call a plot.

When we consult this branch of narratology – the study of narrative as a fundamental system of intelligibility – we find once again that non-literary discourses prove to function according to principles and processes most dramatically and explicitly manifested in literature, so that literature serves as the model for what is involved in the intelligibility they confer. Moreover, this sort of analysis, which reverses the usual hierarchical relation of dependency between the literary and the non-literary, alters one's conception of these fictive structures, suggesting, as in Kermode's *The Sense of an Ending*, the possibility of taking literature as the point of departure for a general theory of fictions. 'That there is a simple relation between literary and other fictions seems, if one attends to it, more obvious than has

[11] Hayden White, *Tropics of Discourse* (Baltimore: Johns Hopkins Press, 1978), pp. 82, 83 and 86.
[12] W.B. Gallie, *Philosophy and Historical Understanding* (London: Chatto, 1964), p. 30.
[13] Frank Kermode, *The Sense of an Ending* (New York: Oxford University Press, 1967), p. 36.

appeared', Kermode writes, noting that literary fictions are models that enable us to make sense of the world.[14] In describing how theorists of fiction treat literary narratives as imitations of real-world historical accounts, and how analysts of historical narrative in turn present historical discourse as constructed according to literary models – White speaks of 'the essentially literary nature of the historical classics'[15] – I am identifying a certain circularity into which these concepts seem to entrap us. But in fact this process of reversal is not fully circular, because the fictions of the historian are not the same as the fictions of these literary theorists. The former are fictions that order and interpret – *constructs*, shall we say – a vital and primary sense of fiction, one which is even more central to the functioning of literary fictions than other senses. ('What can be thought must certainly be a fiction', says Nietzsche). The theorists of fiction who are drawing upon speech act theory have placed the emphasis on a different sense of fiction – fiction as imitation speech act; and what this does, oddly enough, is to give a central role to the narrator – the perpetrator of this represented act – and to disguise the more fundamental fictionality of literary artifice or literary ordering by positing that the work fictively represents what must be interpreted as if it were a real person uttering the discourse of the work.

In order to see what is at stake here and the problems that arise in the relations between the orientation of speech act theory, the emphasis on narrators, and the concept of fiction as applied to the novel, let me turn to one of the most pertinent critical books of recent years, Mary Louise Pratt's *Towards a Speech Act Theory of Literary Discourse*. Unlike Barbara Herrnstein Smith and Richard Ohmann, who from the outset treat literary works as fictional imitations of other sorts of non-fictional discourse, Pratt, once she gets past a misguided polemic that tries to oppose speech act theory and structuralism, is interested in showing that literary narratives are members of a large class of 'narrative display texts' – stories 'representing states of affairs and experiences which are held to be unusual or problematic in such a way that the addressee will respond affectively in the intended way, adopt the intended evaluation and interpretation, take pleasure in doing so, and generally find the whole undertaking worth it'. Her favorite examples, designed to show that supposedly literary qualities are found in discourse not regarded as literature, are stories the socio-linguist William Labov collected in his work on speech patterns and which he somewhat tendentiously calls

[14] Ibid, p. 36.
[15] White, *Tropics*, p. 89.

'natural narrative'. Evoking Labov's analyses, Pratt argues that 'literary and natural narrative are formally and functionally very much alike. Put another way, all the problems of coherence, chronology, causality, foregrounding, plausibility, selection of detail, tense, point of view, and emotional intensity exist for the natural narrator just as much as they do for the novelist, and they are confronted and solved by speakers of the language every day'. She concludes, 'Unless we are foolish enough to claim that people organize their oral anecdotes around patterns they learn from reading literature' – not quite so absurd an idea as she seems to think – 'we are obliged to draw the obvious conclusion that the formal similarities between natural narrative and literary narrative derive from the fact that at some level of analysis they are utterances of the same type'. Most of the features which poeticians have believed constituted the literariness of novels are not literary at all. 'They occur in novels not because they are novels but because they are members of some other more general category of speech acts': narrative display texts, i.e. utterances whose relevance is tellability.[16]

The claim is that novels are not fictional imitations of real speech acts, such as writing an autobiography, but real instances of the speech act of articulating a narrative display text. For Pratt, what is distinctive about literary works within this genre is that they are published. They have undergone a process of selection (and may have become part of a formal canon), so that we can assume they are deliberately constructed as they are (free of gross errors) and have been thought well-constructed and 'worth it' by other people. Most important, the literary work is distinguished by what Pratt calls a 'hyper-protected cooperative principle': we can assume that digressions, apparent irrelevancies, and obscurities have a communicative purpose and, instead of imagining that the speaker is being uncooperative, as we would in other speech contexts, we struggle to interpret the elements that flout principles of efficient communication, in the interests of some further communicative goal.

This is a powerful and perspicacious discussion of fiction. Pratt uses H. L. Grice's account of conversational implicature to describe, explicitly, how a wide range of literary effects are made possible by the assumption of purposiveness (the hyper-protected cooperative principle). Novels are treated not as non-serious or fictional speech acts, or as conglomerations of pseudo-sentences or non-linguistic signs, but as real instances of a broad class of discourses: narrative display texts.

---

[16] Mary Louise Pratt, *Towards a Speech Act Theory of Literary Discourse* (Bloomington: Indiana University Press, 1977), pp. 66, 69 and 148.

In the course of this analysis, Pratt maintains that fictionality is a relatively unimportant feature of narrative display texts. Countering Richard Ohmann's suggestion that literature is a series of quasi-speech-acts (fictional imitations of real-world speech acts), she argues that fictionality is not centrally functional. A supposedly non-fictional narrative display text, such as Truman Capote's *In Cold Blood*, requires the same kind of interpretive moves as, say, *Emma*. 'Pragmatically speaking, I have no more knowledge of the situations reported and the reporting circumstances in the former case than I do in the latter. Unless I am otherwise acquainted with Capote or his characters, the events and the speakers of *In Cold Blood*, like those of *Emma*, do not exist for me outside the text'. Non-fictional narrative accounts, that is to say, are world-creating in the same sense as are works of literature. 'The only difference for me between the two speech situations is my knowledge that Capote intends me to believe his story really happened, and the only effect this has on my reading experience is perhaps an intensification of certain perlocutionary effects – the same perlocutionary effects Conrad tries to capture by having Marlow tell us *Lord Jim*'.[17] Moreover, she notes that natural narratives do not become infelicitous when they concern people and places the audience has never heard of (or which perhaps even do not exist); Labov's natural narratives contain a good portion of hyperbole which might well be regarded as fictional. Often the line between fiction and non-fiction is extremely unclear, and in many cases it is entirely appropriate for the issue to remain undecided. If a lecturer begins a talk with a joke about what happened on the way to the lecture room, the audience is not supposed to decide whether this incident really occurred or not. Fictionality, Pratt claims, is not an important criterion for setting off a major class of narrative display texts.

This seems a very promising line of argument, but, alas, the notion of fictionality reappears, and the reasons why it does are quite instructive. It is reintroduced not because Pratt decides that it matters after all whether the events recounted in narrative display texts really occurred or whether the characters described actually exist. It reappears in connection with narrators, because of the need to make a distinction between the author of a narrative display text and the fictional speaker or narrator. We have been regarding novels as real-world narrative display texts: Labov's narrative display texts are presented by their authors to an audience, and so are novels. But in discussing *Tristram Shandy* Pratt must distinguish what Sterne, the

---

[17] Ibid., p. 94.

author, does from what 'Shandy, the fictional speaker', does. Pratt recognizes that she is here doing something at odds with her previous position: 'In distinguishing between the fictional speaker of a work of literature and its real-world speaker, the author, I have tacitly adopted the view that many literary works are, as Ohmann puts it, "imitation speech acts". Though I disagree with Ohmann on the consequences of that view, I think such an analysis is in itself correct and necessary if we are to describe the reader's role in the literary speech situation'.[18]

In books with first person narrators, some move of this sort is clearly necessary. The author is producing a display text in which a fictional speaker in a fictional speech situation addresses an audience of some sort. The fictional speakers may fail to fulfill numerous communicative maxims. The author always (by virtue of the hyper-protected cooperative principle) exploits these principles by flouting them. 'Authors, in other words, can mimetically represent all kinds of nonfulfillment, for what counts as a lie, a clash, an opting out, or an unintentional failure on the part of the fictional speaker or writer counts as a flouting on the part of the real-world author and involves an implicature that the nonfulfillment is in accord with the purpose of the exchange in which the reader and the author are engaged'.[19] But once having treated novels as fictional speech acts, Pratt, following the precepts inculcated by narrative analysis, extends this principle to all novels. She writes of *Pride and Prejudice*, *The Mayor of Casterbridge*, and *Père Goriot* for example, all of which by her earlier arguments might be regarded as real-world narrative display texts, 'We are intended to treat these novels as (imitation) written narrative display texts and to decode them according to generic norms alone . . . We execute *In Cold Blood* in the same way we execute a novel, because we execute novels in the same way we execute *In Cold Blood* – as if they were real-world narrative display texts'.[20] Although Jane Austen and Truman Capote both wrote narratives for display in the real world, his is said to be a real-world written narrative display text and hers an imitation of a written narrative display text.

Pratt reintroduces the notion of novels as fictional speech acts in order to account for cases where, as in first person narratives, readers need to treat the speaker as a character engaging in certain discursive actions: explaining his past, wondering about his future, failing to make sense of things, contradicting himself, and so on. But she then assumes, against her own arguments, that all novels are fictional

---

[18] Ibid., p. 173.
[19] Ibid., p. 174.
[20] Ibid., p. 207.

speech acts – doubtless because we have been trained to think that all novels have narrators. Perhaps one should have known that someone who accepts the term 'natural narrative' for Labov's examples would end by finding a way to make novels unnatural.

The consequence of this definition of novels as imitation speech acts is to focus attention on narrators – who is the narrator? what act is he or she performing? – and to urge us to seek in all novels something that resembles a real act by a real person. This is a powerful recuperative move: a reader of Robbe-Grillet's *La Jalousie* can make sense of this strange work by finding a person performing some plausible discursive act. Pratt writes, 'obsessive jealousy . . . in the fictional speaker of Alain Robbe-Grillet's *Jealousy* brings about complete narrative and evaluative paralysis'. A very peculiar, geometrical descriptive discourse is recuperated by imagining, on the slimmest of pretexts, that it is the speech of a husband so obsessed with jealousy that he cannot talk straight and cannot make sense of things.

There is real potential for banalization here, in the assumption fostered by the theory of fiction that the strangest textual patterns can be interpreted as signs of some familiar discursive act. There are, however, points at which this powerful strategy breaks down and reveals the dubiousness of the assumptions on which it is based. For example, in the case of novels with distinctive first person narrators – the case for which the theory is explicitly designed – one often finds not an imitation of a real world speech act but a quite fantastic speech situation and mode of utterance. Martinez-Bonati, who is critical of Pratt on this point, cites the beginnings of Ken Kesey's *One Flew Over the Cuckoo's Nest*, which portrays a world we find quite realistic but through an impossible speech situation. The first person narrator is not telling his life story – the narrative, in the present tense, offers an ongoing account of what happens, or what is happening now. It is not interior monologue, in that much of the information is not what one would impart or represent to oneself; yet it is not speech spoken to any audience. As Martinez-Bonati notes, 'It is precisely in modern *realistic* literature that we find the most *unrealistic* types of discourse and of speech-situations'.[21]

They're out there.
Black boys in white suits up before me to commit sex acts in the hall and get it mopped up before I can catch them.
They're mopping when I come out of the dorm, all three of them sulky and hating everything, the time of day, the place they're at here, the people they got to work around . . . I creep along the wall quiet as dust in my canvas shoes, but they got special sensitive equipment detects my fear and they all look up . . .

21 Martinez-Bonati, *Fictive Discourse*, p. 104.

The effect of this kind of discourse is the vivid portrayal of a speaker – his world, his language and his thought processes. The one thing we *cannot* say about it is that it is a fictional imitation of a real-world speech act, for if we ask what real-world speech act it is fictionally imitating, the one we are likely to think of is that of someone articulating a dream or a fantasy or telling an imagined story, which is not at all what the narrative claims itself to be. In short, the theory breaks down for some of the very cases for which it was designed: narrative discourses which are most vividly the language of a fictional speaker.

A second difficulty bears on the distinction between real and imitation speech acts. Pratt's definition makes third person narratives such as *Le Père Goriot* and *Pride and Prejudice* imitation narrative display texts, while Labov's anecdotes are real narrative display texts. In the latter a real speaker tells a story; in the former a fictional speaker tells a story, and we can discuss the qualities of this implied speaker, as opposed to those of the author. But of course we can also identify just as readily the assumptions, the authority, and other qualities of the speakers in Labov's narratives. We have no knowledge of the real speakers but only of the narrative personae projected by the stories. The two do not necessarily correspond – part of the point of telling a story in the real world is to project oneself as a person who is not entirely one's everyday self – and, of course, two different stories by the same speaker may project quite different narrators, especially if the speaker is a skillful storyteller.

If the possibility of identifying a narrator is what justifies treating third person novels as imitation speech acts, then natural narratives, which also have narrative personae, are also imitation speech acts – in which a projected or created speaker recounts a story. Indeed, there is a sense in which all speech acts are imitation speech acts. To perform a speech act is to imitate a model, to take on the role of someone performing this particular speech act. The self-consciousness with which introducers perform their introductions, or with which a chairperson says 'I hereby call this meeting to order', testifies to the fact that to perform a speech act is to adopt a persona. The more formal the act, the more vivid our sense of this fundamental truth.

Thus the definition of fiction as fictional speech acts is inexact: at once too broad and too narrow. Many literary narratives, especially first person narratives, are representations of speech acts by fictional speakers (but even here the idea that they are imitations of real-world speech acts may be wrong); but to assimilate all novels to this model is misleading and banalizing. Moreover, the notion of fictional speech acts does not distinguish novels from anecdotes, for in the second, broader sense, all contain narrative personae, as do all speech acts.

The theory I am contesting emerges from the convergence of point of view studies and speech act theory. It promotes the notion that a literary work is above all a narrative act and that to analyse a narrative act is above all to relate textual details to the attitude of a speaker, who acts like a real person. Susan Lanser writes, 'Speech act theory reminds us that every speech act is produced by someone (or some group)'.[22] Certainly discourses are written by someone, but this is not what the proponents of these theories have in mind, for they want us to ask not what Henry James or Jane Austen is doing (the answer would be, articulating a narrative display text); they want us to investigate the speaker or narrator as, in Lanser's phrase, 'an originating subject'. This orientation in the theory of fiction carries an ideology that needs to be investigated. At the very least, it seems to be dedicated to eradicating the possibility that language might prove to be in some way inhuman.

These remarks on the theory of fiction have focused on two problems. First, there is the question of the role of the notion of fiction in the theory of fiction. It seems as though attempts to explain fiction and fictions end up either constructing fictions – imagined readers, stories of reading, imagined speakers – or appealing to structures which themselves turn out to rely on fiction, as in the case of the fictional emplotting that organizes the real-world discourses fiction is said to imitate. Second, there is the problem of the convergence of narrative studies and speech act theory, where the new emphasis on fictionality – the claim that literary works are fictional speech acts – paradoxically urges us to treat narrators as if they were real people, with all that that entails. There is a powerful humanistic ideology behind this claim. The theory of fiction needs to challenge this orientation and explore the possibility that literary narratives are, as in Pratt's first account, real-world narrative display texts: not fictional speech acts but, if they must be acts at all, real acts of narration.

[22]   Lanser, *Narrative Act*, p. 81.

13

Towards a Linguistics of Writing

Since so much language comes to us as writing, it seems obvious that we need to develop a linguistics of writing: a linguistics that would attend seriously to the structures, strategies, and effects of writing. To do this would challenge the assumptions, even the imperatives of linguistic science, which designate writing as a way of recording speech, a sign of a sign, which is irrelevant to the nature of language in general. Most readers interested in language will have encountered some of the more intemperate statements by which linguists or theorists of language set writing aside as a corruption of speech: writing is a mode of representation that can erroneously affect or infect conceptions of language, which ought to be based solely on the proper and natural form of language, speech, whose priority to writing is at once phylogenetic, ontogenetic, functional, and structural.[1] The use of linguistics as a model for the semiological analysis of cultural artifacts of all sorts has consisted, it would be argued, of applying to other domains, including the study of written texts, models based on the assumed primacy of speech. To produce a pertinent linguistics of writing, then, would not be simply to take account of the special effects of the written character and of any supplementary conventions it might involve or structures on which it might depend; one would need to challenge the governing assumptions and rethink the study of language *ab initio*, so as not to prejudge issues by relying on a model of language based on an idealized conception of speech.

There is, it seems to me, much truth to this view. However, to conceive of the development of a linguistics of writing in precisely this way, on the presumption that linguistics has in fact been based on speech, risks mistaking the situation in which one finds oneself and

---

[1] See John Lyons, 'Human Language', in *Non-Verbal Communication,* ed. R. A. Hinde (Cambridge: Cambridge University Press, 1972), pp. 49–85.

thus misjudging what is at issue. One can argue that linguists' commands to ignore writing and concentrate only on speech are provoked by a silent suspicion that what we have had all along is in some respects a linguistics of writing – namely, a linguistics which, despite its pretenses to the contrary, focuses on units more easily identified in writing than in speech. There are various aspects of the dependence of modern linguistics on writing, which Roy Harris wittily sums up in *The Language-Makers*, a book that deserves wider attention than it has received, in suggesting that the 'real discovery procedure' of modern linguistics is 'Assume that standard orthography identifies all the relevant distinctions, until you are forced to assume otherwise'.[2] Let me swiftly mention three indications of this dependence.

1   Ferdinand de Saussure, despite his denunciation of the 'dangers' of writing, which 'disguises' language and whose 'tyranny' leads to errors of pronunciation that are 'pathological', nevertheless has recourse to the example of writing to explain the notion of the relational identity of linguistic units: the written character proves the best example of the linguistic unit.

2   The idea of an ambiguous sentence – *Flying planes can be dangerous* – seems to owe something to the model of writing: the idea of a sentence as a sequence of words stipulated outside any context and stripped of any intonation contours. For if one were working solely with speech, one would have no reason to treat *George bought the picture* (an answer to 'Who bought the picture?') as the same as *George bought the picture?* (an expression of astonishment at his choice). The differences between the physical signals and the import of those two sequences are arguably greater than between *George bought the picture* and *George bought the painting*; and the inclination to treat the former pair as variant articulations of a single ambiguous object and the latter pair as two quite distinct objects seems more easily explained as an effect of the apparent self-evidence of writing than of the various factors purported to determine the identification of linguistic units. Ambiguities, which linguistics sets out to account for, frequently seem to be ambiguities of a written sentence presented as examples in a paper on linguistics rather than ambiguities in utterances, where the differences in intonation patterns and import would prevent listeners from confusing what seem quite distinct sequences.

3   Finally, transformational-generative grammar seems to make more sense as a linguistics of writing than as a linguistics of speech.

2   Roy Harris, *The Language-Makers* (Ithaca: Cornell University Press, 1980), p. 9.

Not only is phonological form assigned at a late stage of derivation by an 'interpretive' component and thus not central to the conception of a linguistic sequence, but a vast array of features of ordinary speech – hesitations, interruptions, false starts, changes of construction – are all relegated to 'performance' and set aside as irrelevant to an account of the language. What is relevant, linguistic competence, is an ability to produce an infinite set of complete, well-formed sentences, with none of the imperfections of actual speech. As Roy Harris asks,

suppose we strip away this superficial phonetic garb of the sentence, what lies beneath it? Something which must have all its words in place, their order determined, their grammatical relationships established, and their meanings assigned – but which simply lacks a phonetic embodiment: a string of words with the sound turned off. In short, a linguistic abstraction for which there is only one conceivable archetype so far in human history: the sentence of writing.[3]

I am arguing, then, that we are likely to go astray if we assume, as some interpretations of deconstruction might incline us to, that the linguistics we have is a linguistics of speech and that the corrective to it would be a linguistics that took writing seriously. Certain aspects of writing – specifically writing as manifestation of an ideal, iterable linguistic object – have determined the linguistics which presents itself as a linguistics of speech; in relation to this linguistics, attention to the materiality of speech itself could be quite disruptive. A linguistics which sought to address all the contours of hesitation and of emphasis, the tones of voice that function as modal operators to indicate degrees of assurance, aggressiveness, modesty, and so on, as well as all the dialectal variations of speech that carry social information, would be distinctly more complicated than one which sought above all to assign the correct grammatical descriptions to sentences regarded as ideal objects. Such a linguistics, attending to potentially signifying qualities of speech – speech as gesture, shall we say – would in fact be confronting a certain textuality of voice: potentially signifying differences not easily reducible to systems of convention.

A particularly interesting evocation of these problems is Dennis Tedlock's work on oral narrative, *The Spoken Word and the Work of Interpretation*, which argues that our logocentric or phonocentric linguistics is inadequate to oral narration. The distinction by which linguistics separates phonetics from phonology, defining phonetics as the realm of physical signals only and assigning questions of how

---

[3] Ibid., p. 18.

physical features are put to use by language to the realm of phonology, leaves phonetics outside of linguistics, and with it numerous physical features of vocal signals which may be crucial to the effect of oral narratives. When the relevance of these phonetic features to differences of meaning is demonstrated, they are let back into linguistics in supplementary fashion, designated as 'paralinguistic features', 'suprasegmentals', etc. When they are recognized as signals to be deciphered, the code and the domain of codes are extended a little further. But, as Tedlock writes,

It is not just that the phenomena of contouring, timing, and amplitude have somehow been overlooked and present a new domain for decipherment, but that they have always resisted reduction to particulate units of the kind that can be ordered within a closed code. The pitch contours of an audible sentence mark it with a *degree* of incompleteness or finality; a range of possible lengths for an audible line or a silence occupies a *continuum*, and so does the range of possible loudness or softness within a line. Such phenomena have both obvious and subtle effects on the meaning of what the storyteller says, but the possible *shades* of meaning are infinite, whereas the deciphering eye allows no shadings.[4]

Continuous rather than discrete phenomena take us outside the principles of phonology and outside a phonologically based linguistics – a code of discreteness – though one can seek to bring these phenomena within its perspective by working to identify contrasts on which physically continuous phenomena can be said to depend for their significance, their production of shades of meaning.

To break out of this perspective one might, for instance, take the heuristic step of treating a storyteller's narrative initially as a purely acoustic signal to be measured rather than as a code to be deciphered, working with devices for physical measurement that reveal regularities and discontinuities – striking physical variations in the signal. A machine that records variations of pitch and amplitude on a moving scroll produces a transcription of the narrative, a kind of writing that could provide various clues and stimuli for a new linguistics of writing. As Tedlock notes, 'Aspects of the speaking voice that our mechanical transcription graphs so clearly, – including vast amounts of silence, utterances that vary greatly in length and often correspond neither with breath groups nor with intonational contours, hypertrophied syllables, and other features we will leave aside for now – go under the heading of "paralinguistic" features' (SW, p. 202). Silence,

    [4] Dennis Tedlock, *The Spoken Word and the Work of Interpretation* (Philadelphia: University of Pennsylvania Press, 1983), p. 9. Hereafter cited in the text as SW.

which looks very important in a mechanical transcription of a performance, is granted a tiny role by phonology: pause junctures are allowed as gaps that make a semantic difference, but they are boundaries without duration, present or absent rather than signifying by their length. The timing crucial to a successful comedian, for example, lies outside phonology, although the length of a pause may determine whether an utterance plays as a joke or falls flat.

Tedlock notes that 'pause junctures, intonational markers, stresses, and vowel quantities lie at the borders of proper phonology. Each one can be and often is treated as supersegmental rather than segmental, prosodic rather than phonemic. . . . The one problem all these features pose in common is that of temporality, and a given feature will be accepted phonologically to precisely the degree that a way may be found to reduce its temporality to instantaneity'. 'What is left out when the acoustical signal of the speaking voice is transformed . . . by means of phonological reduction', he continues, is the temporal dimension, as if a musical score had 'no indication of total performance time, no time signature, no marks of sustained tempo, no marks of changing tempo, no indications of differential time value among the notes, no rests, and no ties' (SW, p. 204) A good deal is missing. What mechanical transcription of narrative performance on a moving scroll does is to mark through this special writing the temporal dimensions elided by a phonology attuned to alphabetic writing.

The question is whether to attempt to integrate such features with a linguistics of the sign by drawing up supplementary rules, subcodes, etc. or to reconsider the structure of the enterprise, to deny the demands of codification any claim to priority and finality, to place the supposedly borderline cases at the center and to consider the extent to which the supposedly discrete elements of linguistic codes are caught up in – are special cases of – the movement of signals. This is the basic structural question for a linguistics of writing: whether to extend linguistics to problematical but important domains, adding on descriptions in supplementary fashion, or whether to recast the enterprise by seeking to place the marginal at the center. 'Even phonology itself appears in a new light', writes Tedlock,

once we have made ourselves at home on its threshold rather than in its very midst . . . There are even cases where a phonemic distinction is important with respect to content in some words and melts into a continuum in others; that is to say, one might construct one set of evidence to support a phonemic discontinuity and another set of evidence to support treating two sounds as an allophonic variation of purely phonetic (as opposed to phonological) interest. (SW, p. 214)

In another instance he argues that 'the place occupied by the inversion of stress and pitch in the full spectrum of Zuni speech suggests that the kinds of concerns opened up by poetics and sociolinguistics do not lie outside or beyond or even on the boundary of proper linguistics, but may open up a breach that penetrates to the very core of linguistics' (SW, p. 191). This may be the strategy for a linguistics of writing to pursue; the project of reversal may be fruitful, even if the end is difficult to envisage.

Let me emphasize, though, the relevance of this prospect to a linguistics of writing. When discussions of language claim to focus on speech and set aside writing as unimportant, what they in fact do is set aside certain features of language or aspects of its functioning. If writing, which seems inescapably to involve mediation, impersonality, distance, the need for interpretation and the possibility of misunderstanding, and physical features that may exceed or escape codes, is treated as a mere technical device, then one can treat as if it were the norm of language an ideal associated with speech, namely the experience of hearing oneself speak, where hearing and understanding seem to be inseparable, where the expression seems bound to the meaning it arises to express, where signifier and signified seem immediately joined in a sign that seems both given to perception and immediately intelligible.[5] A linguistics of writing, by contrast, would be one that gives a central place to those aspects of language set aside by this model, whether they are associated with the written character or with features of speech neglected by linguistic idealization.

If Ferdinand de Saussure's conception of language as a system of signs can be seen as the basis of this first linguistics, the second linguistics will confront from the outset the problems that obsessed the 'other Saussure', as he has been called, the Saussure of the anagrams. Saussure believed that he had discovered anagrams of proper names in the writings of Latin poets. He amassed an impressive collection of examples and hypotheses about rules governing this patterning, but he left his speculations unpublished because he could find no references to the practice in classical texts and the advice he sought about the statistical probability of the anagrams he discovered was inconclusive. He confronted a paradoxical situation, as he wryly observed: if one finds few anagrams, then these can be dismissed as the results of chance; if one finds many, then that suggests that they are all too easy to find, a commonplace product of the repetition of twenty-six letters.[6] As he

[5] For discussion, see my *On Deconstruction,* (Ithaca: Cornell University Press, 1982), pp. 100–10.

[6] Jean Starobinski (ed)., *Words Upon Words* (New Haven: Yale University Press, 1979), p. 99.

wrote in a letter, 'I make no secret of the fact that I myself am perplexed – about the most important point: that is, how should one judge the reality or phantasmagoria of the whole question'.[7]

'Reality' versus 'phantasmagoria' is a version of a familiar problem: the dilemma about the signifying status of patterns identifiable in linguistic material. What has sometimes been seen as Saussure's chimerical obsession is his encounter with the problem of the relationship between the materiality of language and its signifying effects, the possibility that language functions in ways that bypass conventional linguistic codes and sign relations. Anagrams are a special case of a more general phenomenon, whose importance in the functioning of language needs to be assessed. In Saussure's account of language as system, *la langue* consists of signs which are the product of contrasts between elements that have no reality other than their differential function. These basic units are entirely defined by their ability to differentiate higher-level units, signs: the phoneme /b/ is the intersection of the contrasts that differentiate *bat* from *pat, cat, fat,* etc. If, when looking at a text, one begins to attend not to signs but to other patterns formed by their constituents and aspects of the materiality of those constituents, then a different perspective opens: the possibility of other signifying processes working beneath or alongside the manifest signs of the text.

Saussure himself was inclined to consider the repetition of letters important only when they could be seen as a dispersal or concealment of known signs relevant to the text's explicit statement. He thus insured, while identifying another level and mechanism of signification, that its textual energies reinforced meaning that was already present: anagrammatic repetition signified by reiterating key proper names. The idea of literary discourse as, to borrow a formulation from Derrida's discussion of Genet, 'the patient, stealthy, quasi-animal or vegetable, tireless, monumental, derisory transformation of one's name, a rebus, into a thing or name of a thing' lurks beyond the Saussurian horizon.[8] The project of looking at the constituents of signs for their role in anagrams establishes, though, two possibilities: (1) seeing discourse as motivated by a formal procedure tied to investments that might not be reflected in the text's apparent meaning, such as a proper name that did not overtly appear, and (2) finding patterns of repetition that are not easily resolvable into regular signs – as in 'kingfishers catch fire', 'proud as a peacock', or 'of a fresh and following folded rank'. Once one begins to think of letters or of

[7]   Ibid., pp. 105–6.
[8]   Jacques Derrida, *Glas* (Paris: Galilée, 1972), p. 11.

phonetic qualities as possible constituents of other patterns, one is approaching language in a new way.

From this perspective, language seems not so much a system of signs, each joining a signifier with its signified, as an infinite pattern of echoes and repetitions, where readers are confronted with the problem of determining which of numerous possible patterns to pursue, which to treat as endowed with significance. Signs are not simply given to perception: to perceive the signifier at all is to confer on some patterns and not on others the status of meaningful expressions.[9] It has been fashionable recently to speak of the play of the signifier or of the production of signifieds by the signifier, but this is something of a misnomer, for the question is precisely which identifiable features of a linguistic sequence belong to the signifier and which do not: whether patterns or relations are of the order of the signifier.

Saussure's work on anagrams has often been misconstrued as suggesting that meaning is the creation of readers, who find in language patterns they wish to find. Joe Gargery in Dickens's *Great Expectations* seems the satirical model of such a reader. He is, he tells Pip, 'oncommon fond of reading'.

'Are you, Joe?'
'Oncommon. Give me', said Joe, 'a good book, or a good newspaper and sit me down afore a good fire, and I ask no better. Lord!' he continued, after rubbing his knees a little, 'when you *do* come to a J and an O and says you, 'Here, at last, is a J-O, Joe', how interesting reading is!'[10]

Our judgment of readers so dedicated to finding anagrams of proper names may well agree with Pip's, who reports 'I derived from this last that Joe's education, like steam, was yet in its infancy'. But this example poses a genuine question, for the Js and the Os are undoubtedly there. What enables us to say that a text with a thick scattering of them, like a text with plethora of stop consonants, or nasals, or liquids is not affected by this? It is not a matter of statistical probability: questions about patterns may be posed in these terms if one is interested above all in whether they are to be counted as deliberate or accidental, but once the connection between the workings of language and the unconscious is admitted, this

---

[9] For discussion, see Paul de Man, 'Hypogram and Inscription', in *The Resistance to Theory* (Minneapolis: University of Minnesota Press, 1986), pp. 36–50, and Cynthia Chase, *Decomposing Figures: Rhetorical Readings in the Romantic Tradition* (Baltimore: Johns Hopkins University Press, 1986), pp. 96–107.

[10] Charles Dickens, *Great Expectations*, ch. vii.

becomes a matter of less urgency. It is easy to believe that many striking patterns are the result of what Lacan calls 'the insistence of the letter in the unconscious'.

Countering Roman Jakobson's discovery of myriad patterns, symmetries and asymmetries, in poetic texts, Michael Riffaterre proposed a 'law of perceptibility' which would rule irrelevant patterns that the reader could not perceive; but this manifestly fails as a principle of relevance, for any pattern in dispute has been perceived by at least one reader, and we can scarcely accept a model of language that eliminates in advance the possibility of discovering hitherto unnoticed patterns.[11] Not only are we unaware of most of the rules and regularities of our language, but we all have had the experience of seeing a text illuminated by patterns and echoes we had not previously noticed but which, once pointed out to us, seem thoroughly compelling. The problem highlighted by Saussure's pursuit of anagrams is the exclusion, by a linguistics of the sign and the code, of an array of potential patterns, about which it is difficult to determine whether they have meaning or signifying effects. Its problematic examples offer a glimpse of the possibility that what we call codes, discrete phenomena, and signs or sign systems are only special cases of an endless generalized iteration or patterning.

These cases present themselves under a double aspect. On the one hand, meaning seems to be produced by the reader, who pursues some leads and not others; but on the other hand, linguistic effects of various sorts may be produced by forces that do not seem to involve linguistic conventions at all, as in the sound patterning of advertising slogans or of poetry, which may do its work without a reader or listener explicitly becoming aware of it. Either way, the model of language as a system of signs seems under attack. The idea that prior linguistic conventions enable listeners or readers to identify signifiers and know their meaning seems to be undermined from both sides by the processes anagrams expose: there is patterning that seems to work without prior conventions or listeners' recognition, and there is patterning that seems willfully created by readers, who must determine what to count as a signifier.

This vision of language, which emerges as one follows Saussure's attempts to perceive key names anagrammatically dispersed in the text, tantalizingly confronts the idea that language is a system of signs by suggesting (1) that there are forces at work below the level of the sign, and (2) that signs are not phenomenally given, so that the

---

[11]   See my *Structuralist Poetics* (London: Routledge; and Ithaca: Cornell University Press, 1975), p. 67.

decision to treat certain patterns and not others as signifying patterns is an imposition of convention or meaning, not a recognition of conventionally established signs. I shall return to this shortly.

A linguistics of writing can proceed by paying attention to the forms of writing in speech, to possible relations and patterns relegated to the margins of linguistics. Acts of relegation, often curious moments where an ideology of language imposes itself willy-nilly, can make excellent points of departure for a new linguistics. One striking instance is a passage where Saussure, defending the arbitrary nature of the sign, rejects onomatopoeia.

Onomatopoeic words might be held to show that a choice of signifier is not always arbitrary. But such words are never organic elements of a linguistic system. Moreover, they are far fewer than is generally believed. Words such as *fouet* [whip] or *glas* [knell] may strike some ears as having a certain suggestive sonority. But to see that this is in no way intrinsic to the words themselves, it suffices to look at their Latin origins. *Fouet* comes from Latin *fagus* ('beech tree') and *glas* from Latin *classicum* ('trumpet call'). The suggestive quality of the modern pronunciation of these words is a fortuitous result of phonetic evolution.[12]

As Derrida notes in *Glas*, the recourse to etymology in discussing the 'intrinsic' character of a particular sign is strange in a theorist who imperiously distinguishes between synchronic facts and diachronic facts, but odder still is the exclusion of the 'fortuitous' by one who tells us that language is essentially fortuitous. In order to define the linguistic sign as *essentially* fortuitous – arbitrary – Saussure excludes fortuitous *motivation*.

These paradoxical moves, like the exclusion of writing, alert us to the possibility that what is being set aside in order to leave a pure linguistic sign or linguistic system may in fact be a significant aspect of language: fortuitous motivation might be a general mechanism of language. Even if one grants Saussure's argument that onomatopoeias are never pure, never solidly grounded in resemblance, one might nevertheless take an interest in the contamination of arbitrariness by motivation, whether this motivation is produced by the craftsmanship of poets, by the fortuitous effects of linguistic evolution, by the keen eye of readers looking for anagrams, by the errors of speakers, or by the mechanisms of the unconscious.

Although linguistic tradition and its assumptions about language that we have made our own doubtless incline us to concede Saussure's

---

[12] Ferdinand de Saussure, *Cours de linguistique générale* (Paris: Payot, 1973), pp. 101–2.

claim, that in a sense the structure of French or English is not affected by the potential suggestiveness of various signifiers, still, we could also wonder, with Derrida, whether the language one speaks or writes is not always exposed to the contamination of arbitrary signs by suggestions of imitative motivation, whether effects of motivation are not inseparable from – central to – the workings of language, whether it does not bring into the linguistic system itself questions about the subterranean dispersal of the proper name and trouble the framing gesture that seeks to separate an inside of the system from the outside of practice. 'What if', Derrida asks, 'this mimesis meant that the internal system of language does not exist, or that one never uses it, or at least that one only uses it by contaminating it, and that this contamination is inevitable and thus regular and 'normal', belongs to the system and its functioning, *en fasse partie*, that is to say, both is a part of it and also makes the system, which is the whole, part of a whole larger than itself?'[13]

The very sentence in which Saussure sets aside motivation displays effects of motivation in ways which suggest that discourse may be driven by precisely the sort of phenomena he wishes to exclude from language. '*Fouet* [whip] and *glas* [knell] may *strike* [*peuvent frapper*] some ears as having a certain suggestive sonority'. *Fouet* and *glas* both strike the ear, perhaps, because whips and bells strike: the term for what words do as they make a noise seems generated by the examples, or the choice of examples is generated by what words are said to do to the ear. This sentence, working to remotivate and thus link together supposedly arbitrary signs, displays a principle by which discourse frequently operates and suggests that arbitrary signs of the linguistic system may be part of a larger discursive system in which effects of motivation, demotivation, and remotivation are always occurring. Relations between signifiers and or between signifiers and signifieds can always produce effects, whether conscious or unconscious, and this cannot be set aside as irrelevant to language.

The lessons for a linguistics of writing drawn from Saussure's anagrams and the other examples we have considered might come more easily from writing such as *Finnegans Wake*, which poses in particularly virulent fashion the problem of echoes, patterns, motivation, forcing readers to establish relations while foregrounding the dilemma of 'reality or phantasmagoria?' that perplexed Saussure. Consider the beginning of one relatively self-contained sequence, The Mookse and the Gripes.

[13] Derrida, *Glas,* p. 109.

The Mookse and the Gripes

Gentes and laitymen, fullstoppers and semicolonials, hybreds and lubberds!

Eins within a space and a wearywide space it wast ere wohned a Mookse. The onesomeness wast alltolonely, archunsitslike, broady oval, and a Mookse he would a walking go (My hood! cries Anthony Romeo), so one grandsumer evening, after a great morning and his good supper of gammon and spittish, having flabelled his eyes, pilleoled his nostrils, vaticanated his ears and palliumed his throats, he put on his impermeable, seized his impugnable, harped on his crown and stepped out of his immobile *De Rure Albo* (socolled becauld it was chalkfull of masterplasters and had borgeously letout gardens strown with cascadas, pintacostecas, horthoducts and currycombs) and set off from Ludstown *a spasso* to see how badness was badness in the weirdest of all pensible ways.[14]

Finnegans Wake makes explicit a vision of language as sequences of letters and syllables echoing others, in ways that sometimes but by no means always form codified signs. It exposes interpretation as an abusive assimilation of sequences to other sequences: 'borgeously' is 'gorgeously' and 'Borghese'; 'horthoducts' are no doubt orthodox horticultural aqueducts; more dubiously, perhaps, 'Mookse' is moose (by phonetic propinquity), fox ('The Fox and the Grapes' resembles this fable), mock turtle ('Gripes' means Gryphon, as in Lewis Carroll's 'The Mock Turtle and the Gryphon'), and moocow (for reasons I shall come to in a minute). Most of all, the *Wake* presents what we are inclined to call 'echoes', drawing on a problematical term whose virtue is its conflation of an automatic acoustic process with a willful mimetic one. 'Eins within a space and a wearywide space it wast ere wohned a Mookse' echoes the opening of *Portrait of the Artist*: 'Once upon a time and a very good time it was there was a moocow coming down along the road'. 'A Mookse he would a walking go' recalls 'Froggy would a wooing go'. *Ere wohned* is Samuel Butler's anagram of 'nowhere' *Erewhon*, as well as the German 'he lived'. The significative status of such echoes is far from certain, and much of the energy of literary criticism is devoted to motivating them and deriving semantic consequences. Their status and the effects they induce, including the interpretive operations set in motion by them, are what a linguistics of writing particularly should address. The scope of the problem becomes clearest when the examples are tenuous: does 'the weirdest of all pensible ways' echo 'the best of all possible worlds'? Is this 'reality or phantasmagoria', as Saussure would ask? The shared elements seem minimal and the

---

14   James Joyce, *Finnegans Wake* (London: Faber, 1964), p. 152.

case for Mookse as Candide does not seem otherwise compelling. I cannot hazard a rule that would stipulate a connection yet am reluctant to abandon the relation. This, I submit, is language.

As in the case of anagrams, readers are cast simultaneously in contradictory roles: compelled to choose what possible relations to pursue, what to treat as significant, they are creators of meaning; condemned to wrack their brains for obscure words and less obscure quotations, to consult dictionaries, glossaries, and commentaries, they are inadequate recipients of a wickedly complex construction they cannot hope to grasp. The key point is that these opposites go together: the texts such as *Finnegans Wake* that most encourage readerly activity also convince one that it is the text which echoes. Readers feel that there is meaning insistent in the text: to recognize that *hybreds and lubberds* can be 'high-bred' and 'low bred', that *archunsitslike* contains the Greek *archon*, 'ruler', which explains this sort of sitting lonely, that *broady oval* may be explained as 'bloody awful', is certainly to feel one has elucidated the lines' meaning, but these are in fact only relations, echoes, whose compelling character needs to be explained by a linguistics of writing.

Such passages suggest, first, that the words of a work are rooted in other words, whose traces they bear in different ways. Though this is made obvious by portmanteau words ('tighteousness' 'famillionarily', 'chalkfull', 'borgeously') that explicitly allude to others, or by unintelligible sequences that need to be interpreted as transformations of other words ('Mookse', 'spittish'), this is also true, as Derek Attridge writes, of all linguistic sequences, which are composed of syllables from other sequences and refer obliquely to these sequences by their similarities and differences.[15] What the *Wake* enables us to conceive is that the practice of recognizing, say, *space*, as the sign 'space' is only a special case of a more general process of relating sequences to other sequences: reading *broady oval* as 'bloody awful'. The close connection between these two processes comes out clearly in cases of languages in contact, which Mary Louise Pratt argues we should take as a normal case of language, rather than relegate it to the margins while basing our account of language on the fiction of a homogeneous speech community.[16] An American listening to a Glaswegian is in much the same position as the reader of *Finnegans Wake*. In speech we are always groping to recognize the echoes of sequences we have heard before in sequences that are physically

[15] Derek Attridge, 'Unpacking the Portmanteau', in J. Culler (ed.), *On Puns: The Foundation of Letters* (Oxford: Blackwell, 1988), p. 154.
[16] Mary Louise Pratt, 'Linguistic Utopias', in *The Linguistics of Writing*, ed. D. Attridge, N. Fabb and C. MacCabe (Manchester: Manchester University Press, 1987).

distinct and interesting in their distinctness, but this impresses us more in writing, and especially in writing such as *Finnegans Wake* where we are alert for the interest of variations and unexpected combinations.

A linguistics of writing, exploiting this model, would seek to invert the usual relation between discrete, already codified signs and the material usually deemed irrelevant except as a means of manifestation. It would treat discrete signs as special cases of a generalized echoing, even, and explore whether a linguistics could be constructed on such a model and how far it could go. Above all it would need to attend to what lies outside an ordinary linguistics but furnishes much matter for literary criticism: the tantalizing prospect, that caused Saussure so much anguish in his work on anagrams, of perceiving patterns, hearing echoes, and yet being uncertain, in principle as well as in practice, about their status. The task of linguistics has been to divide the signifying from the non-signifying, excluding the latter from linguistics, but if this boundary region is central to language and its functioning – and texts like the *Wake* suggest that it is – then this geography must be revised, and the uncertainty of echoes, the problematic materiality of language which may or may not carry meaning and produce effects, must lie at the center of our concerns.

The overarching question for a linguistics of writing, then, is this: given a series of phenomena which are linguistic in a broad sense – involved with and produced by language – and which have been set aside or treated as marginal by mainstream linguistics, does one seek to *extend* linguistics to include them or should one not rather, on the assumption that there has been something at stake in the relegation of these phenomena to the periphery, take the step of attempting to reconceive the study of language with these phenomena at the center? It may not be possible to construct a linguistics on this basis – a linguistics that resembles the one we have now – but it seems a worthy experiment, from whose failure we could learn almost as much as from its success. A linguistics of writing, then, must address a textuality linked to the materiality of language, which necessarily gets misread when transformed into signs, as it must be by our semiotic drive. Such a linguistics can work on materiality of the spoken word as well as the written – the '*huuuuge* fish' that gets away from the fisherman, or such matters of tone and emphasis that are crucial to good storytelling and thus to language in its most decisive manifestations but which most of us have difficulty producing because they do not belong to a discrete code.

Index

232 *Index*

Capote, Truman, 212, 213
Carpinelli, G., 108n, 109n
catastrophe theory, 172, 177–8
Catholic Church, 75
Catholic League for Religious and
  Civil Rights, 77–8
Cervantes, Miguel de, 51
Chicago Aristotelians, 7
Chicago, University of, 12, 23, 27,
  33
chicken, 148
Christianity, 72–81
'civil religion', 50–1
close reading, 14, 111, 130
Coleridge, S.T., 51
collectables, 171–5
Columbia University, 12, 23, 33
communicative action, 185–200
comparative literature, 25–6, 51,
  79–80
composition, teaching of, 27, 37
Conrad, Joseph, 212
conservatism, xi, 25
context, ix, 60, 63, 65, 67, 92–4,
  147–9
cooperative principle, 192, 211, 213
Cornell University, 23, 107, 191
crisis narratives, 41–3, 54–5
Critical Inquiry, 23
Critical Legal Studies, 140–52
criticism: and affect, 105–6; and
  confusion, 3–4, 42–3, 53;
  deconstructive, 20, 145, 147,
  149–50; European influence on,
  15–20, 23–4; history of, vii–viii,
  3–40, 43–4, 57–9, 61–2; and
  innovation, 34–6, 52, 55; and
  interpretation, 13, 37, 130; and
  literary practice, 4, 38–40;
  Marxist, 19–20, 59; and other
  disciplines, vii–viii, 15–25, 52,
  54, 139–52; political effects of,
  14, 39, 48–53, 55–6, 58–60,
  64–8, 69–71, 77–82; and
  politics, viii–x, 21, 39, 48–53,
  57–68, 109, 149, 205–6;
  psychoanalytic, 19, 115, 139;

public, 3, 5–7, 10; redemptive,
  110–11; and religion, 71–82;
  specialization in, 26–7, 29–30,
  54–5; and theory, 15–25,
  39–40; and universities, viii,
  3–40
Crossman, Richard, 176–7
crucifixion, 73–4
culture: critique of, 49–54, 154–5,
  178–82; reproduction of, 33–5,
  37, 49, 52, 169
Curzon family, 175

Dalton, Clare, 144–8, 150–2
Dartmouth College, 38
de Beauvoir, Simone, 32
de Lisle, Leconte, 102
de Man, Hendrik, 109n
de Man, Paul, viii, x, 22, 24, 87,
  95, 105, 107–35; *Aesthetic
  Ideology*, 129–31; *Allegories of
  Reading*, 118–19, 121–7;
  Blindness and Insight, 110–12,
  113–18, 120–1; *Resistance to
  Theory*, 129–32; *Rhetoric of
  Romanticism*, 112, 127–9, 133,
  134; wartime writings, 107–8,
  131, 134
deconstruction, 20, 37, 123–5,
  139–52, 195–7, 219
defamiliarization, 39
departments: character of, 27–8;
  composition of, 31–3; role of,
  24–5, 30–1
Derrida, Jacques, 16, 19, 20, 22,
  62, 94, 115–17, 118, 140, 143,
  147, 196, 200, 223, 226–7
Descartes, 97–8
Diacritics, 23
Dial, 6
Dickens, Charles, 224
dirt, 168–70
Donoghue, Denis, 76
Douglas, Mary, 168–9, 172
Drake, William, 4, 40
Duchamps, Marcel, 179
Duke University, 27, 28